DEVELOPMENT OF EDUCATION IN MANIPUR

DEVELOPMENT OF EDUCATION IN MANIPUR

Maimom Shanti Devi

RAJESH PUBLICATIONS
NEW DELHI - 110 002

ISBN : 81-85891-29-X

Published by :
M.L. Gupta
Rajesh Publications
1, Ansari Road, Darya Ganj,
New Delhi - 110 002.
Typesetting by :
Anita Gupta
Sanjay Enterprises
New Delhi - 110 002
Printed in India at :
Graphic Print, New Delhi - 2

Ist Published in India : 2001

RAJESH PUBLICATIONS
Rs. 500.00

PREFACE

Literature on the social history of Manipur is very meagre. The prevalent indigenous system of education and features of traditional society that existed in Manipur during the pre-British rule were very much different from the present system of education and society. The development of modern education had a far reaching impact on the social environment in the state. However, there has been no proper account of the educational development and associated social changes in the state.

During the recent years, certain attempts have been made by the scholars to study the history of education and culture of Manipur. However, there has been no proper records of the educational development and its importance on the socio-cultural situation of the state except some scattered reports for administrative purposes. The present study is a humble attempt to fill up the important gap in the history of education, its problems and impact on the social development in Manipur during the period from 1872 to the present time.

The history of education in the state alongwith its problems and impacts on social development have been discussed in the present work, which presents a critical and chronological account of the growth of education and social development in Manipur since 1872.

It is a great pleasure to express my deep sense of gratitude to Professor S. N. Pandey, former Dean of Social Sciences, Manipur University for his constant supervision, valuable advice and encouragement and Professor R. P. Singh, Head, Department of Geography, Manipur University for kindly going through the manuscript of the text and giving me valuable advice, encouragement and constructive suggestions.

In the preparation of this book, I am very much obliged to

Shri N. Khelchandra Singh, Shri H. Ranbir Singh (retired Director, J.N.U. Centre, Imphal), Shri Kishun Singh (retired Principal, D.M. College of Teacher Education, Imphal) for providing me a lot of valuable information and materials. I express my sincere thanks to the authorities of the Department of Economics and Statistics and Department of Education, Government of Manipur and authorities of Manipur University for their co-operation and help in providing me required data and records, which immensely helped me in my study.

I am grateful to Dr. R. C. Singh, Head, Department of English, Oriental College and Shri L. Kamekhyakumar Singh, Head, Department of English, Imphal College for their constructive and critical suggestions.

I express my sincere thanks to Shri Chirom Shantikumar Singh of Geography Department, Manipur University for his help in the preparation of maps and graphs. Thanks are also due to Shri M.L. Gupta of Rajesh Publications, New Delhi for timely publication of this book.

The book, in its present shape, would not have come up without the valuable help, encouragement and co-operation of my husband Prof. H. Tombi Singh, Vice-Chancellor, Manipur University. I therefore, express my sincere gratitude and thanks to him.

Sagolband
Yengkhom Leirak
Imphal - 795001

M. Shanti Devi

CONTENTS

List of Maps and Diagrams

List of Tables

1

Introduction

Manipur, for its favourable climate and scenic beauty, is known as a little paradise. The state is situated in the north eastern corner of India. It has a distinctive geographical feature of beautiful ranges of hills running in its outer periphery with a tiny valley of exceptional beauty in the middle of the state. It lies between latitude 23.88°N to 25.68°N and longitude 93.03°E to 94°E with an area of 22,327 sq. kms. The valley, surrounded by the high hills, covers only 2,238 sq. kms. of area, i.e. one tenth of the state area. It is bounded by Nagaland on the north, the Chin Hills (Myanmar) on the east and south east, and Mizoram on the south, the Somrah tract and Upper Chindwin district of Myanmar on the east and the Cachar district of Assam on the west. It was an independent princely state till 1949, when it finally merged into the Indian Union. Though the state is small in its size, it has a remarkably rich and distinctive culture and social system. In the course of centuries, Manipuri society had undergone changes and the people had adjusted themselves to the new environment that progress of time has brought to them. The early Manipuri society consisted of seven *salais* or *Yeks* which ultimately merged into the Meitei community. The Meiteis, who predominantly reside in the valley of Manipur, are the largest group in the state. People of various other tribes dwell in the hills surrounding the valley. In Manipuri society *Sagei* (clan) prejudice was strictly observed, as for example, a person belonging to one *Yek* did not take food cooked by a person belonging to another *Yek*. But persons belonging to the different *Yeks* were equal in social status.[1] The caste rules in Manipur did not appear to be very rigid. Further, during the last two centuries there came two religions to Manipur. First, Hinduism was accepted in the valley by the Meiteis from the 18th century onward and next Christianity spread among the hill people in the 20th century.

With the coming of Hinduism the people of the valley of Manipur adopted two castes of high social order, i.e. the Brahmin and the Kshatriya. The majority of the Manipuris started considering themselves as Kshatriyas and wore sacred threads and also among the Kshatriyas there was a class known as Rajkumars. They were the descendants of the rulers of Manipur and enjoyed certain privileges in society during the period prior to 1891. The Brahmins being the highest caste in the Hindu Manipuri society, enjoyed considerable influence and respect among the Hindus. They acted as priests in the temples and conducted religious activities. But being more orthodox in their outlook, they observed caste distinctions more rigidly than other people. Marriage with other people was strictly prohibited among them. All of them, however, strictly observed rigidity in eating and drinking and did not take food cooked by persons belonging to other castes. On the contrary, if a girl of a Kshatriya family got married to a Brahmin, she was not allowed to eat food cooked in her parents house on the ground of losing her purity which she had acquired through the marriage. Mostly Brahmins alone had the right to read sacred Hindu Shastras and other religious scriptures. They played an important role in the social organisation of the Manipuri society. They occupied and still enjoy the highest social position in the Manipuri society.[2]

The scheduled castes (Dhobi, Loi, Namsudra, Muchi, Ravidas, Patni and Yaithibi), Christians and Muslims form the other groups of people in the state.

During earlier days, the people living in Manipur valley lived more or less in egalitarian society except for the presence of the outcaste *Loi*. After conversion to Hinduism some changes were introduced in the social customs.

But since the Meiteis were Hindus, there were fixed norms so as to specify particular ethnic groups from which food or drink could be accepted. These norms were also operative between the lineage known as high lineage and low lineage. A person belonging to a high lineage could not take food cooked in the hearth of low lineage. Taking of food or drink from other low groups was considered as polluting.[3]

In Manipuri society polygamy was practised. Widows were allowed to remarry. Sati was rarely found. However with the conversion into Hinduism, some ideals of Hindu womanhood had been inculcated. This was found in the Hindu custom of burning a woman along with her deceased husband so that she could be regarded as Sati. The first instance of Sati took place in the year 1725 A.D., when the wives of a prince named Murari volunteered to be burnt.[4] There was no system of child marriage in Manipur.

The aboriginal hill tribes who were non-Hindus, had their separate culture. The non-Hindu society was totally free from the caste system of the Hindus. No restriction on eating and drinking existed in their society. Only some extra privileges and benefits were enjoyed by the priests, chiefs and the warriors of the village. Unlike the Hindus, priesthood was not hereditary among the tribes and also not for the individual family but for the community as a whole and the village. They performed the sacrifices for the welfare of the village and community at large. Consequently the priests could not be powerful in society nor could they occupy an exalted position as we find in the Hindu social life.

In Manipur a form of class system existed. There was the nobility which formed the upper class, and being the ruling elite, could achieve supreme place in social division of the people according to status, power and dignity of the post. The distinction between the common people and the higher class was also maintained by imposing some restrictions on the use of ornaments, dress and transport, manner of sitting accomodation and the construction of types of buildings. A man of lower status was not permitted to sit in front of a person of higher class. In dress also distinctions were made from the upper strata to the common people, i.e. ordinary people were not allowed to wear certain type of dresses and ornaments. Thus in the society both class and caste system existed in the state. In the Hindu society, Brahmins being the superior caste, occupied a high status and the nobility and the royal families being the high class, not only occupied high dignity but also enjoyed certain privileges in society. All the land in Manipur belonged to the king who could give and take it at his sweet will.

Lallup was a feudal service rendered by an adult subject to the king for ten days out of every forty. The service might be in the form of military duties or development work like the construction of roads and bridges or working in the king's estate etc. and those who rendered *Lallup* service did not pay any revenue.[5] Royal families were exempted from the *Lallup* duties. Moreover, any person married in royal family was free from *Lallup*. Persons having marriage relation with the royal family were also eligible for consideration of appointment to a higher post. So in all cases of matrimonial relations with the royal families a sum of money known as *Kwagok Hanba* had to be paid by common people.

During the pre-British days Manipur had her own slave trade also. After the conquest of Manipur by the British on the 27th April 1891, slavery was abolished by Major Maxwell.

With the advent of the British rule, Manipur thus entered into a new age which had found its expression not only in her administration alone but also in her society as well. Society by and large was patrilineal in Manipur in which male dominated the family. The people belonged to different clans *(Sagei)*. The *Sagei* was divided into a number of families. And family was the smallest unit of the Meitei kinship system. It is the first major agency to introduce the child to his many social roles. Over and above, the Meitei family can be regarded as a patriarchal one in nature. Wide spread and unquestioned authority from his subordinates are enjoyed by the father. The relationship of the father and the offsprings was of respect and obedience on the part of offsprings and love and authority on the part of the father. In a joint family, the eldest member, namely, the father is the head of the family. When the father is absent due to death or otherwise the mother is the head. If parents are not alive, the eldest son of the family is also responsible to look after each individual interest while keeping in view the stability of the joint family. He is the presiding authority in all socio-religious matters of the family and also the representative of the family in all community affairs.

Women in Manipur, both in the valley and the hills, enjoyed a great deal of freedom and held a high distinctive position in social, religious and political life. Most of the household works, except the hard ones were performed by the woman. Meitei woman made crucial economic contributions and they were the mainstay of the family circle.[6] This view is shared by Capt. Dunn, Sir James Johnstone and others. Besides the household works and care for the family, Meitei women contributed much to the earning and economic welfare of the family. They helped the male in agriculture, made all the clothes required for the family and also for sale, did the work of embroidery, earned extra income by working as wage labourers and also took part in trade and marketing. Sanakeithel, a major market in the heart of the Imphal town, was the centre of activities of these women engaged in buying and selling of various goods. The whole market was managed by women. Only in July 1931, during the region of Churachand Maharaja, *Nipa Keithel* (Men's market) was established.[7] In short the courage and hard labour of Meitei women is unique. ...."The Meitei men in the past were men of courage and men of pride. Since the British came to Manipur they have lost it. But women retained their character. They remained independent and confident. Time has not changed this".[8]

Since the early days, women have been playing an active role in the political affairs of the state and they took part in administration as well. The heritage of women participation in the war continued upto the 18th century. The princess and queens occasionally led the royal army and undertook conquests of neighbouring hill tribes and thereby earned fame. There are several references to such achievements of the queens and princesses. The name of Leima Linthoingambi is still remembered for her presence of mind and courage while dealing with the Tangkhul tribes during the absence of the king.[9] To sum up, women in Manipuri traditional society equally shared with men in the affairs of the state politics.

In Manipuri society, every village or *Leikai* is organised on the basis of mutual help and co-operation. When a member of the society is dead other members are present at his house day and night.[10] Moreover, the group division in society indicates the different professional castes of men in the society of the valley.[11] Different groups were assigned different works by the king and the royal family.[12]

In Manipur every household possessed some amount of land which was the main source of its subsistence. The essential necessities of Manipuris regarding food and cloth were produced in their own land. Agriculture and cottage industry were the two important means of their livelihood. Weaving was done in every house. The qualification of a bride was assessed by the quality of cloth she could weave. Handloom weaving was the most important craft of the state practised by almost every housewife. Every girl knew how to weave and was given a loom as a part of her dowry. Nearly every housewife was capable of weaving all the clothes needed by her family.[13]

Marriage system of the Meiteis was varied and elaborate. In the early days the system of both polygamy and polyandry was there. But with the introduction of patrilineal society, the system of polyandry discontinued but polygamy continued to exist. Inspite of all these there was still heritage of polyandry in the Meitei society.[14] Again there were many different forms of nuptial relations among men and women besides licensed marriages. Among the Meiteis, marriages are settled by the guardians but very often an understanding is reached between a boy and a girl before the formal consent of the guardian.[15] To become a husband and a wife, the proper ritual which solemnises the tie is known as *Luhongba* (marriage).[16] Divorce between a wife and a husband and marriage of widows were freely allowed in society. In the traditional Meitei society there were different styles of becoming a husband and a wife. They were, (i) *Haina-shingnaba* (go between), (ii) *Chenba* (elopment), (iii) *Chingba* (kidnapping), (iv) *Keina katpa*, (v) *Nambo Thaba.*

The Meiteis of Manipur are religious minded people. As a traditional aspect of religiosity various ceremonies connected with the life cycle are performed. Important occasion of such religious feasts are *chaumba* (*anna prasan*), *Nahutpa* (*karnabedh*), *Lugun thangba* (*upanayana*), *Luhongba* (Marriage ceremony), *Shradha* ceremony, *Phiroi* (death anniversary), *Tarpon chak pijaba* (feast dedicated to the spirits of the dead forefathers) etc.

Though the people of Manipur were under the direct colonial rule, they were acutely conscious of their own customs, tradition and culture. So the British were not allowed even to enter any of the Meitei houses. The particular house was considered polluted in case any outsider entered it. That house was either demolished or renovated. There is a reference to such an incident in Cheitharol Kumbaba. Some British officials entered the Govindaji Mandop on the 1st May 1892, to witness *Khubak Esei*. The Meitei people felt that Mandop was polluted. So the Govindaji Mandop was renovated on the 29th May, of the same year.[17]

The Manipuris are a fine race of people. They are endowed with artistic qualities of high order. They have very fine artistic instincts and are lovers of art and nature. They have made a distinct contribution to the Hindu art of dancing and singing. The art of drama and poetry is very well developed among the Manipuris. Their textile and metal works carving are as good as can be found anywhere else in India. They have their own indigeneous games and sports. Another important contribution that Manipur has made to the outdoor game is her polo.[18]

The people of Manipur find enough leisure to sing and dance, to play games and enjoy festivals throughout the year. It is a place where festivals and festivities can be observed throughout the year around.

Being a martial race the education of warfare and military activities was very important to the Manipuris.[19] Martial arts, wrestling, fighting in combat, riding a horse, excellence in sword and spear, hunting, polo, race etc. were some of the military games. There are references to the military skills of the people of early Manipur. Might as a power motif continued to determine the political prowess.

Every member of the society particularly the male members possessed military skill. Utmost priority was given more to military education than the pursuit of excellence of the mind. The people and the rulers both were concerned more with military activities than that of the formal education. In the past the people were highly patriotic and noted for chivalrous activities and gallantry.[20]

But there was no public military school. Even the royal members learned this military skill from skilled persons, probably the common people took this education from their elders. Their homes were the institutions of their education. After receiving the preliminary knowledge from the father or brother at home, one was expected to live under the guidance of an expert teacher. In 1704 A.D. king Loyumba established the man building clubs to train people in many physical activities. The females had to learn singing and dancing.[21]

The king controlled the male populace. He encouraged and patronised men of courage and of athletic ability to join various state affairs and athletic competitions which demanded high standard of martial skills, e.g. Polo, Horse racing, *Thang Ta* (A war game of sword and spear), Boat race, *Mukna* (wrestling) etc. Men showing merit in any of these skills were rewarded with high posts in administration and were married to daughters of the royal family.[22] It was compulsory for every able bodied male above sixteen years of age irrespective of caste and creed to attend *lallup*, the war association. But inspite of their constant occupation with military activities, the Meitei kings patronised learning and learned men.

In Manipur, the *Maichous*, the priest scholars imparted learning to the royal princes, to nobility and to selected commoners in their respective residences. For example prince Naothingkhong (663-763 A.D.) was sent to the house of Luwang Ningthou Punshiba to learn the art of royalty and administration as well to receive education in different arts.[23] Same was the case with the commoners also. Aspirant pupils gathered in the home of Gurus receiving philosophical instructions during daily work periods. They worked for their own living and that of their Guru.

In short, before 1885 formal schooling on western model was unknown in Manipur. Only indigeneous education consisting of literacy, physical education, health and hygiene, games and indigeneous medicines etc. was conducted by *Maichous* and Pandits. Report of Education in Manipur prepared by N.C.E.R.T. team in 1972-73 observes : "Inspite of their constant preoccupations with military exploits, Manipuri kings were great patrons of art and learning as is evinced by the ancient literature. Learning of Sanskrit was popular in earlier ages and was imparted through the indigeneous schools called Tols".[24] There was no evidence of any organised system of education during pre-British period. Regarding the system of education more emphasis was given to practical education than that of the theoretical knowledge.

Since long before the arrival of the British in Manipur, the Meiteis (Manipuris) had their own system of education. Books were written by hand on leaves and for preservation of books of higher learning indigeneously made ink was used.[25] Writing was done on *agarpat* (Also, Agalocha) and palm leaves were also used for the purpose of writing. The original Manipuri script itself appears to be of great antiquity and quite unique in character.

In the hills among the tribal people, the traditional education was imparted through the village *Morungs* or the dormitories in the form of training in martial arts and warfare, handicrafts, creative arts, custom and traditions, morality and discipline.[26] The objective of the traditional tribal education was to produce an all round individual, a tribal warrior, a committed member of the village community with full knowledge of the creative arts, dance and music, well versed in the tradition and folklore of his tribe, clan and village. In other words, education was a life long continuous process in the tribal society. Thus in the traditional society, despite the absence of literacy, the social and moral fibre of the people sustained the society.[27]

Physical Education

In a state like Manipur where warfare was the way of life of the people every individual had to maintain physical fitness. As soon as boys attained the age of maturity they used to learn *mukna* (wrestling), *kangjei* (hockey), *mangjong, chenjong, khongyai, khubei, lamjen, nunghunba, tahunba* and *taokpa*.[28] Education primarily consisted of the male's learning military techniques, physical exercises, use of *arambai* (dart), sword, spear, and riding of ponies. The duty of a male was to engaged in war and to catch the wild animals.[29] But in the absence of the formal schools for learning these arts, young boys depended on their eleders. It took a number of years to become proficient in these arts. So by maintaining strict canon of discipline, students used to stay in the house of the teachers. The polo, the national game of Manipur was played by the young and old alike. The yearly propitiation of *Umanglai* (sylvan deities) gave an opportunity to show the skills of these indigenous games and sports to the young men. Thus games and sports not only improved physical ability but also taught skills of hunting and warfare.

Education Through Art Form

There are various forms of art that help in promoting the growth of education among the people. Family also plays a very important role in imparting education. The advancement of a nation is mirrored in the conditions of its homes or families.[30] The family is the organic starting point of education. It is so to say the ideal school of life. The relation between the child and the home is like that which exists between a bird and its nests.[31] The mother, the most outstanding personality in the family, is the guiding star of the child. She is the first and the best teacher of her child and the education and training she imparts may be of a far reaching character. In Manipur children used to learn the preliminary art of dancing (*Tadhing*) from their mothers and other members of their family. The most important form of art among Manipuris is *Jagoi* (dance). This composite term *Jagoi* is of various types. The most important of which is *Rasa dance*, depicting the Hindu mythological story of love between Radha and Krishna. The origin of *Rasa dance* is traced to the original pre-Hindu form of dance *Lai Haraoba*. The nucleus of Rasa developed from the form and the name of the *Lai Haraoba*. It is connected with the worship of *Umang-lais* (sylvan deities) of the whole state. *Lal Haraoba* represents the Meitei concept of creation of the world and the making of the human body. The entire village participates in the festival. It comprises of, besides ritual dances, sports like polo, boat race, horse riding, sword fighting, wrestling and racing.

It is believed that Rajshri Bhagyachandra Maharaja (1767-1798 A. D.) by taking the principle and technique from Lai Haraoba dance conceived the Rasa Dance. Lai Haraoba is the basis of the modern Manipuri school of dancing. The Rasa dance of Manipur has four categories, (i) Kunja Ras, (ii) Maharas, (iii) Vasanta Ras, and (iv) Nitya Ras. Different seasons are alloted for different types of Rasa dance and dance forms are also different accordingly.

Other categories of dances are *Sansenba* (*Goshta*), *Diva* Ras, *Holi Nritya*, *Khubak Esei* (during Ratha Jatra festival), *Nupi palla* (during Jhoolon) and *Thabal chongba*, dancing in the moon light during the Holi festival, etc.

The establishment of *Pala Loisang* which means a group of dancers and musicians is a major contribution to the artistic development of the country. Evidence shows that it was established in 1776 A.D. by King Bhagyachandra and was improved by his successors. Here they are taught music and dance of Hindu tradition. New innovations have also been made in course of these centuries.[32]

To encourage both traditional and classical dance and music many formal cultural institutions also have sprung up with state subsidies. Nowadays dance teachers are appointed to impart dance instructions and are attached to many educational institutions and a Dance Academy separately run by the Government of India, has also been established to cater to the needs of the pupils desirous of undergoing advance training in Manipuri dance.

Other agencies which impart informal education through art forms to adults are *Wari Taba* and *Lairik Taba*. These agencies have contributed in their own ways knowledge of the sacred lores. It not only imparts the idea of religeosity but moral lessons of the triumph of good over evil are also part and parcel of it. People in their old age indulge in such activities in a cherished manner. It not only gives them recreation but also good moral education. In Manipur, although there was no technical school in the pre-British period in the modern sense of the term, the youths got practical training in many arts and crafts. The traditional blacksmith, potter, the goldsmith, the oil pressurer, the bell metal worker and others manufactured different articles required by the people and the youths got training in those crafts in their own family.

Likewise there was no school for medical studies and it was also confined within the families who practised the art of curing of the diseases by applying various herbal medicines.

Training in Weaving

In Manipur weaving is done in every house. In other parts of India weaving was a profession but in Manipur it was a domestic activity. Each and every family, high or low, rich or poor, has, at least, one loom and the female weave cloth for the members of the family.[33]

Girls in their pre-adolescence period generally help their mothers in their weaving routines. At first the girl is introduced to the art of reeling thread and then to weaving itself. She learns the whole operation from the beginning to the end by observation and participation.[34] She becomes an expert weaver and inherits whatever art of weaving is known to her mother. This art itself is an essential qualification for a good bride. In early days in selecting a bride, knowledge of weaving of the girl was asked and the weaving equipments were regarded as an essential item of a bride's wealth. Hence the qualifications of a bride included the quality of clothes she could weave.

Training in Dancing and Singing

Though the definite institutions for teaching, dancing and singing to the young aspirants were not there, yet they used to learn mostly through observation and practice. In the traditional system of education, the females had to learn singing and dancing. There were in each village some old men and women who trained the youngsters in music and dancing and to them, children used to go for training. They taught them at their leisure and the pupils regarded their tutor with respect and offered suitable gifts.[35] In olden days, the study of dancing and music was regarded as a part of educational training.

There were occasions when the whole village indulged in dancing and singing. The yearly worship of *Umanglai* (sylvan deity) and *yaosang* (Holi festival) were the important occasions. In such festivals dance and music formed the main items of the programmes. Even the young children of five and six years of age were allowed to participate in it. And they tried to imitate their elders.

Thus the reinforcing influence of family and community, backed by the weight of custom and religious beliefs placed children within a unified learning situation. Every child was exposed to similar influences and learnt the whole range of behaviour and belief of community. In conclusion it can be argued that an ancient system of Education was already existing long before the introduction of the British oriented modern education system in Manipur.

References :

1. **L. Ibungohal Singh :** *Introduction to Manipur* (1963), p.18.

2. **N.C.E.R.T. :** *Survey Report* (1972-73), p.6.

3. **S. Gyaneswar Singh :** *Impact of Modern Education in Manipur*, Unpublished Ph.D. Thesis, Gauhati University (1979) p.399.

4. **L.Ibungohal Singh & N.Khelchandra Singh (ed.) :** *Cheitharol Kumbaba* (1967), p.74.

5. **Gangmumei Kabui :** *Social and Religious Reform Movements in 19th and 20th Centuries*, Ed. by S.P. Sen (1979), p. 413.

6. **Manjusri Chaki Sircar :** *Feminism in a Traditional Society* (1984), p. 224.

7. **L. Ibungohal Singh and N. Khelchandra Singh (ed.)**, *op.cit.*, p. 606.
8. **Manjusri Chaki Sircar :** *op.cit.*, p. 34.
9. **N.Khelchandra Singh :** *Thangmeiron*, unpublished, p.7.
10. **L. Ibungohal Singh :** *op.cit.*, p.22.
11. **R.Brown :** *Statistical Account of Manipur* (1974), p.12.
12. Brahman, Kshatriya, Ganak, Baisya, Kyastha, Kamoo, Gugi, Dhobi, Goldsmith, Napit, Teli, Fisherman.
13. **T.C. Hodson :** *The Meitheis* (1908), p.27.
14. **N. Birachandra Singh :** *Socio-Religious life of the Meitheis in 18th Century A.D.*, Unpublished Ph.D. Thesis, Manipur University (1987), p.108.
15. **J. Roy :** *History of Manipur* (1973), p. 17.
16. **N. Birachandra Singh :** *op.cit.*, p. 118.
17. **L. Ibungohal Singh and N. Khelchandra Singh (ed.) :** *op.cit.*, p. 500-501.
18. **B. K. Ahluwalia and Shashi Ahluwalia :** *Social Change in Manipur* (1984), p. 57.
19. **Th. Mangoljao Singh :** *Western Education in Manipur*, Vol. I. (1967), p. 2.
20. **N. Khelchandra Singh :** *Chainarol* (1968), p.1.
21. **L. Ibungohal Singh :** *op.cit.*, pp. 71-74. **M. Kirti Singh**, *Religious Developments in Manipur in the 18th and 19th Centuries* (1982), p. 181.
22. **Manjusri Chaki Sircar :** *op.cit.*, p. 33.
23. **N. Khelchandra Singh :** *Naothingkhong Phambal Kaba* (Coronation of Naothingkhong) (1967), p.1.
24. **N.C.E.R.T. :** *Survey Report*, 1972-73, p.8.
25. **M. Kirti Singh :** *op.cit.*, p. 182.
26. **J. P. Mills :** *Rongma Nagas* (1980), pp. 47-51.

27. **Gangmumei Kabui :** *Education in North East India, Problems of Democratisation* in the Seminar, Democratisation of Education in North Eastern Region held in Manipur University (1988).

28. **S. Gyaneswar Singh :** *op.cit.*, p. 132.

29. **L. Ibungohal Singh :** *op.cit.*, pp. 71-74.

30. **Lakshahira Das :** *A text book of Education* (1976), p. 36.

31. **K.K. Mukherjee :** *New Education and its Aspects* (1953), p. 192.

32. **M. Kirti Singh :** *op.cit.*, p. 194.

33. It is learnt from '*Loyumba Sinyen*' that there were not less than 35 varieties of the designs of clothes prepared by the people of Manipur in 11th and 12th centuries. **N. Khelchandra Singh,** *Ariba Manipuri Sahityagi Etihas*(1969), p. 85.

34. **S. Gyaneswar Singh :** *op.cit.*, p. 140.

35. **Footlight Louise :** *Dance Rituals of Manipur*, India (1958), p. 43.

2

Primary Education

The welfare and progress of a nation depends on the quality of education prevailing in that country. In a democratic set up, the role of education becomes particularly important since democracy can function effectively only if there is an intelligent and active participation by the people in the solution of the problems of the country and this participation comes only through education.[1]

Education has a tremenduous role to play in the life of every child of a nation. On the other hand, primary education is the backbone of educational pattern of a country. Any system of education can never be successful so long as it does not have a sound primary education system. Primary education lays the deep foundation of the educational system of a country. It starts with a special scheme for the development of the child commensurate with his growing age. It is during primary education that the child learns to adjust himself with the school-life, and the education in the school life prepares the child for higher education. It is a potent factor for the development of a child's personality.

At this stage the child starts interacting with the environment around him that helps him to attain a complete living in his future life.[2] It is, therefore, with this view that our national leaders have always been making constant efforts for mass education in our country.

The Education Commission (1964-66) clearly pointed out that 'destiny of India is being shaped in her classrooms'. This indeed projects that education is a force which is very much necessary for the coming generations so that the new generation may be fully equipped with the talent and skills to match the demands of the changing society and the world at large.

With the dawn of freedom in India, Manipur also became a part of India. With the merger to the Indian Union in 1949, all the constitutional clauses of the country became automatically applicable to Manipur also. Earlier the state was backward in her educational set up and lacked educational facilities even in the most developed areas like Imphal town. At the time of its merger only 11.4 p.c. of the population of the whole state was literate. The percentage of literacy increased as the state took up the various programmes of a welfare state, like the other states of the Indian Union. It is obvious that great emphasis was laid on the expansion of primary education during the period after merger.

Development of Primary Education in Manipur :

The origin, rise and progress of education in India and its gradual development into an important branch of administration of the state, constitute one of the most significant episodes not only in India, but in the history of the civilised world also. A number of acts, rules and codes for the purpose of administering education in their jurisdiction have been introduced by the respective governments in most states of India, particularly those which have been in existence for a long time. These legislations or executive orders concern the area of operation of education department of the state government as well as the bodies and institutions under that department. They lay down procedures, conditions and other requirements for performing specified educational activities. They, therefore, constitute legal foundations of the edifice of education and its administration in that particular state.

To fulfill the provision of Article 45 of the Constitution of India for free and compulsory education for all children until they complete the age of 14 years, most of the state governments and Union Territory administrations have enacted legislations relating to compulsory primary education. The acts empower the concerned governments and administrations to introduce compulsory education in particular area and establish a machinery for the enforcement of relevant provisions of the act in this area. These acts also provide for specified penalties on the defaulting guardians. It has however been observed that in most cases the penal clause of the Acts have been enforced mainly because of the various social and economic difficulties including the poverty of the concerned parents. Hence, the programmes of bringing more and more school going children to the educational institutions are being implemented through persuasion and incentives. Several states have also introduced acts relating to local body governments. These legislations spell out the responsibilities and functions of such local bodies in various fields including education. They also lay down compositions of the authorities concerned with planning, organising and implementing relevant educational programmes. The possible sources of income of the local body governments and the sharing of educational expenditure particularly with their state goverments in regard to discharge of the prescribed educational and other responsibilities is also indicated in such legislations. Manipur does not have such a legislation because there are no local bodies in the state. In some states an enactment has been introduced with respect to teachers working in the aided educational institutions. These acts cover activities like recruitments, discipline and payment of salaries to the teachers.

The state of Manipur has not yet made any enactment or introduced any code or manual but for the Manipur Secondary Education Act 1973 which was enacted for constituting the Board of Secondary Education, Manipur. However, an educational code is reported to be under preparation. For all practical purposes the rules and codes which were in vogue in the states of Assam are followed, naturally, with modifications, or amendments warranted by the special circumstances prevailing in the state.

The grant-in-aid system of the state functions in accordance with the provisions of the rules issued by the Ministry of Education, Government of India.

Primary Education :

The Constitution of India (Indian Constitution, 1950) under Article 45 lays down as follows :- "The state shall endeavour to provide within a period of 10 years from the commencement of this constitution for free and compulsory education for all children until they complete the age of 14 years".

It is clear from this article that the makers of Indian Constitution desired that by 1960 there should be free and compulsory education upto the age of 14 throughout India. But this target has not been achieved uniformly in all states of India. The Government of India has resolved through their New Educational policy to achieve this goal as soon as possible. Thus, there is more thrust in universalisation of primary education. This could have been achieved by 1960 but in view of immense difficulties involved such as lack of adequate resources, tremendous increase in population, resistance of the education of girls, large number of children in the backward classes, general poverty of the people and the illiteracy of the parents; it was not possible to make adequate progress in the primary education. Therefore the constitutional directives have remained unfulfilled.[3]

The Beginning of Modern Education in Manipur :

Schools on the modern lines were first introduced by the officers of the British Political Agency in Manipur in order to impart instructions to their own children. In 1872, a vernacular school was established in Manipur on the suggestion of the then Political Agent, Major General W.F. Nuthall and the Government of bengal presented books, maps etc. to the value of four to five hundred rupees but for want of encouragement on the part of the authorities it was nearly closed.[4]

Earlier a primary school had been established by Captain Gordon but it soon died out.[5] In 1885 a Middle English School was opened by the then Political Agent, Sir James Johnstone with the permission of Maharaja Sir Chandra Kirti Singh, K.C.S.I., who was a great patron of learning. Since then education has been making gradual progress in Manipur.[6]

But Sir James Johnstone in his book `My Experience in Manipur and Naga Hills' mentioned that he established one Middle School in 1885-86. By taking his name the school was named as Johnstone Middle English School and the same has developed now into a Higher Secondary School in Imphal.

After the Manipur War of 1891, the Middle English School established by Johnstone was re-opened on Ist June 1892 in a temporary building as the former had been destroyed. The number of the students was 113 on 31st March 1893 and the daily attendance of the students was only 57%. The total expenditure on the school was Rs. 916, towards which the State Government contributed Rs. 360 and from the Imperial Fund another Rs. 360. Altogether they received Rs. 720 as grants for the school.[7]

In the year 1892-93 a Lower Primary School was established at Sekmai and subsequent efforts were made by the then Government to open more schools in the suitable villages in the valley and at Mao Thana on the Naga Hills frontier. In the year 1893-94, a school at Thoubal in the valley was opened, but was closed down again for lack of support. The reasons for the lack of support on the part of the people towards modern education were numerous. As Manipur had been conquered by the British in 1891, the people were suspicious towards the intentions of the alien rulers and, therefore, discouraged their efforts. Secondly, they had their own system of indigenous education, through the medium of Meitei Mayek (Manipuri script) as old Manipuri character was still in use in parts of the valley and that the Bengali character had not yet entirely ousted it.[8] In fact the rulers of the day undermined the potentiality and effectiveness of indigenous system of instructions due to their lack of sound educational principles and philosophy. Thirdly, there was general apathy towards the English education. Manipuris considered it as unclean and polluting.

Gradually primary schools were established at Sekmai, Phoijing, Tera, Thangmeiband and Moirang in the valley area of Manipur in 1895-96.[9] Table 1 brings a complete list of schools established during the period 1885-1900.

In the year 1885-86, there were 8 schools, one was Middle School and the other 7 were Primary Schools. In 1900, the number of Primary Schools rose to 14 and there was only one Middle School. It means that two schools per year were opened. In the year 1892, the number of students was 113 which increased to 1220 by 1900. With the increase in the number of students the average attendance of the students also increased from 50% in 1892 to 67.3% in 1900 indicating a significant improvement in the average attendance. In the year 1892, Rs. 916 was spent for the running of each school, while in the year 1900, Rs. 15,437 was spent on 15 schools. The average expenditure per school was Rs.

1029. It shows an enhanced expenditure per school during this period.

Table 2.1
Schools Established in Manipur during 1885-1900

S.No.	Name of the School	Type of the Institutions	Year of establishment
1.	Johnstone	Middle English School	1885-86
2.	Sekmai	L.P. School	1892-93
3.	Mao Thana	"	1893-94
4.	Pettigrew	"	1894-95
5.	Tera	"	1894-95
6.	Phoijing	"	1894-95
7.	Thangmeiband	"	1895-96
8.	Moirang	"	1895-96
9.	Ukhrul	"	1896-97
10.	Regiment, 4th Assam Rifles	"	1897-98
11.	Thoubal	"	1897-98
12.	Ningthoukhong	"	1898-99
13.	Thanga	"	1898-99
14.	Moirangkhom	" (Girl's)	1899-1900

Source : Th. Mangoljao Singh, Western Education in Manipur, Vol.-I & II, 1989, pp. 11, 14, 16 & 18.

The first girls school in Manipur with 22 pupils was opened in December 1899. The number of girl students rose to 53 at the end of the next year.[10] Female education in Manipur was mostly limited to the primary stage in the beginning. The education of girls was not carried beyond the primary stage in any district except Imphal. Girls were taught in separate girls' school as well as in boys' schools. The various causes for the slow progress of female education in Manipur were -

(i) Social conditions such as (a) Conservatism of the parents, (b) Early marriages of the girls in the backward classes of society, (c) Poverty of the parents, (d) Utility of girls at home for helping their mothers in their household work.

(ii) Economic backwardness of the rural community.

(iii) Lack of educational facilities in rural areas.

(iv) Absence of the subjects in the school curricula helpful to girls for their professional preparation.

(v) Lack of adequate aid from the state and other public funds.

By the end of 1900-1901 there were 16 schools, out of which one was a middle school and 15 were primary schools in the whole of Manipur state (13 in the valley and 2 in the hills). There were 1176 students in the primary schools and the daily average attendance was 775 at the primary level. At the middle school level the average daily attendance was 18 out of 50 students in the previous year. The expenditure on education was Rs. 15,435/-. In 1910-11 there were 66 primary schools and 2 middle schools indicating 4.13 times increase in a decade. The first Naga School was set up by the Missionary, Mr. Pettigrew, in the year 1909-10 at Ukhrul. The total number of students enrolled in the middle school increased from 50 in 1900-01 to 164 in 1910-11. At the primary level number of students was 4086 in the year 1910-11 against 1176 in the year 1900-01. The total daily average attendance increased from 793 to 2315 in a decade.

In education, the expenses incurred were Rs. 17,784 in 1909-10, as against Rs. 15,437 in 1900-01. This was not adequate for the proper expansion of education as it represents only 1.14 time increase in the expenditure in course of a decade. The progress of education in Manipur can be visualised from Table 2.2 which shows the number of schools and pupils since 1872 till pre-independence period.

In the year 1907 Maharaja Churachand Singh came back to Imphal after completing his education from the Mayo College, Ajmer. It was a great fortune on the part of the Manipuris as the Maharaja came back with the knowledge of western education and culture. He took keen interest in imparting western education to his subjects, and new developments in the field of education in Manipur followed.

During 1910-11, the number of primary schools was 66 and there were 2 middle schools. By the end of 1920-21 the number of primary schools further increased to 83 and of middle schools to

3. In a decade 35 more schools were opened at the primary level while at the middle school level 1 (one) school was closed due to want of students. The increase in number of schools from 1920-21 was 1.41 times to 1930-31.

Table 2.2
Primary and Middle Schools and Pupils
(Pre-Independence Period)

	L.P./Primary		Middle Schools (ME & MV)	
Year	No. of Schools	Pupils	No. of Schools	Pupils
1872-92	Nil	Nil	1	N.A.
1892-93	1	N.A.	1	113
1895-96	7	487	1	53
1900-01	15	1176	1	50
1905-06	41	2248	1	116
1910-11	66	4086	2	164
1915-16	67	3713	3	157
1920-21	83	5667	3	207
1925-26	99	6435	4	N.A.
1930-31	118	6615	3	N.A.
1935-36	217	N.A.	6	N.A.
1940-41	N.A.	N.A.	N.A.	N.A.
1945-46	N.A.	N.A.	N.A.	N.A.

Source : 1. Administrative Reports of the Manipur Political Agency (1872-1907).

2. Th. Mangoljao Singh, *Western Education in Manipur*, vol. I & II, 1989, pp. 42, 43-44, 75 & 76.

The total number of students at primary and middle school level was 4,250 in the beginning of the 1910-11 while during the 1920-21, the number of students at primary and middle school levels was 5874. It shows an increase in the number of students by 1624 indicating 1.38 times or 38.21% increase over a decade.

The expenditure in the beginning of the year 1910-11 was Rs. 27,890 and by 1920-21 it increased to Rs. 49952 indicating 1.79 times or 79.10% increase in the expenditure to keep pace with the growth in number of students by 1.35 times. The expenditure on education was further increased to Rs. 54,994 during 1930-31.

Table 2.3
Expenditure Incurred on Education in Manipur

Year	Total expenditure (Rs.)
1892-93	916
1895-96	4,581
1900-01	15,437
1905-06	36,554
1910-11	27,890
1915-16	36,589
1920-21	49,952
1925-26	48,844
1930-31	54,994
1935-36	N.A.
1940-41	N.A.
1945-46	N.A.
1950-51	1,244,000
1955-56	2,065,000
1960-61	7,342,000
1965-66	15,545,000
1970-71	41,573,000
1975-76	69,858,000
1980-81	1,85,173,000
1985-86	4,06,229,000
1990-91	6,68,202,782
1995-96	16,51,074,533

Source **:** 1. Administrative Reports of the Political Agency of Manipur (1892-1903).

2. Th. Mangoljao Singh - *Western Education in Manipur*, Vol. I & II (1989), pp. 25, 60, 61.

3. Statistical Handbook of Manipur, 1992, p. 55.

In 1920-21, the total number of institutions was 93, out of which 90 were primary schools and 3 were middle schools. After a decade i.e. in 1930-31 the number of institutions increased to 130 with 127 primary schools and 3 middle schools indicating an increase of 1.40 times during the decade.

The total number of students was 5850 at the primary and middle school levels during the year 1920-21. But in 1925-26 and

Table 2.4
Development of Primary Education in Manipur (Pre Independence Period)

Year	No. of Primary Schools	No. of Middle Schools	Total Schools (Primary & middle)	Growth in % of the base year	Total No. of Students enrolled					Expenditure (state) incurred in (Rs.)
					Female		Primary	Middle	Total Students	
					Primary	Middle				
1872-92	-	1	1	-	-	-	N.A.	N.A.	N.A.	N.A.
1892-93	1	1	2	100	0	0	N.A.	113	N.A.	360
1895-96	7	1	8	300	-	-	487	53	540	5,122
1900-01	15	1	16	100	22	40	1,176	50	1,226	16,105
1905-06	41	1	42	162.5	N.A.	-	2,248	116	2,364	36,554
1910-11	70	2	72	71.43	22	18	4,064	164	4,228	27,890
1915-16	71	3	74	2.78	45	32	3,668	157	3,825	36,589
1920-21	90	3	93	25.68	24	15	5,643	207	5,850	49,952
1925-26	108	4	112	20.43	22	N.A.	6,435	766	7,201	48.844
1930-31	127	3	130	16.07	56	N.A.	6,615	N.A.	N.A.	54,994
1935-36	217	6	223	71.54	N.A.	N.A.	N.A.	N.A.	N.A.	N.A.
1940-41	N.A.	N.A.	157	-29.60	N.A.	N.A.	N.A.	N.A.	N.A.	N.A.
1945-46	N.A.	N.A.	N.A.	-	N.A.	N.A.	N.A.	N.A.	N.A.	N.A.

Source : 1. Administrative Reports of manipur Political Agency (1903-1920).
2. Th. Mangoljao Singh, Western Education in Manipur.

1929-30 the total number of students increased to 7,201 and 8,650 respectively. In 1936-37, no doubt the number of schools was 264 but due to want of students many schools were closed and finally at the end of the 1940 the number was only 213. The number of students at the primary stage was 6,455 showing a decline in the number of the students but improvement in daily average attendance from 64.3% to 83.3% at the end of the decade. In 1943-44, the number of institutions declined to 192 out of which 182 were primary and 10 were middle schools. But in 1947-48 the total number of schools increased to 291 again with 278 primary schools and 13 middle schools.

In 1943-44 the number of students was 5,693. which increased to 15.496 students in 1946-47. It shows a rising trend in the number of students. The expenditure on education increased by six-fold in 1960-61 (7,342,000), from 1951 ; nearly six-fold in 1970-71 ; nearly five-fold in 1980-81 ; four-fold in 1990-91 and again nearly three-fold during the 5 year period till 1995-96 with a total amount of Rs. 16,51,074,533.

Educational Administration

Educational administration in Manipur during the Maharaja's rule was the direct responsibility of the Manipur State Darbar. In the State Durbar there was a member in charge of Education. He was responsible for the schools in the valley of Manipur. There was no separate department of Education. The work of inspection and supervision was done by the British Officials and most particularly by the Political Agent himself during the tour. In 1897-98, Rev. Pettigrew, an American Baptisht Missionary acted as honorary Inspector of Schools. As advised by the Rev. Pettigrew, an Inspecting Pandit was appointed in order to visit and inspect all the primary schools in the valley and in 1899-1900 one more Inspecting Pandit was appointed. This was the beginning of Education Department in the State. The Education Department came into existence in 1910 with a Deputy Inspector of Schools and two Inspecting Pandits.[11] The administrative machinery of education department was divided into two parts - one for the hills and other for the valley. All the schools in the hills of Manipur were under the control of the Vice-President of the Manipur State Durbar. The administrative machinery of education in Manipur valley was organised as a seperate system. The administrative set up of Education department during the early part of the 20th century can be described as follows.

The Maharaja
↓
Durbar
↓
Member of the Durbar incharge of Education
↓
Deputy Inspector of Schools
↓
Inspecting Pandits (later Sub-Inspector of Schools)[12]

Medium of Instruction

Since the inception of modern education in Manipur, the media of instruction were through English and Bengali. As far back 1902-03, efforts were made for the introduction of Manipuri (Meitei) as a medium of instruction. In 1907, His Highness Maharaja Churachand Singh, being the President of the Durbar passed a resolution for the introduction of mother tongue in the lower primary stage of education. There was a decline in the number of boys attending schools. According to the Administrative Report of the Manipur Political Agency, 1902-03, - "Mr. Pettigrew, Honorary Inspector of Schools attributed the decrease principally by having done away with Bengali in the Pathsalas and also insisting on a better average of attendance at schools. Bengali has been since re-introduced as it is no doubt the wish of the people to have their children taught that language".[13] Since then, translation of Bengali literature into Manipuri started. On 15th May, 1907 Sir Churachand Singh took the responsibility of Durbar as a Chairman. In the Durbar they took resolution to teach mother tongue as the medium of instruction in the lower primary schools. The act of the Durbar was a stepping stone for the gradual development of Modern Literature in Manipur. Since then translation of Bengali literature into Manipuri started. The first Manipuri primers of Sri Makar Singh and Sri Munal Singh were published. In 1924, Manipuri as a vernacular language was recognised by the Calcutta University for the schools.

To meet the question of instruction, as well as to solve many other problems in connection with the instruction of Manipuri, the Durbar sanctioned the formation of the Standing Committee on educational matters with the Education Member as the Chairman. In 1924-25 a Spelling Committee was formed. The Committee submitted a framed spelling rules on 30th May 1925, and this rule remained in vogue.[14]

Examination and Innovation

In Manipur there were four types of public examinations. Three of them were conducted by the State Government and one was conducted by the Board. The lower primary and upper primary merit examinations were conducted by the Education Department. On the other hand it was also the promotion examination. Those students who had not passed the lower primary examination were not allowed admission in the upper primary schools. Over and above, those students who could not pass the upper primary examination were not allowed admission in the Middle English Schools. In the hill areas one merit examination was conducted by the P.M.S.D. and S.D.O. in the second year of the L.P. stage. According to the result of the examination they were granted scholarship of 2 Rupees per month for two years. But it was not compulsory and only for some selected candidates this examination was conducted in the form of public examination in order to give scholarship. All the Sanskrit examinations were conducted by the Assam Sanskrit Board.

For every stage of primary education there was the promotion examinations. And for every school there was the test examination. This test examination was held in order to select students for public examination.

Innovation

The Survey Report (1972-73) felt that Educational innovations are yet to be introduced in the State. The first educational innovation at the primary school level introduced in the State was the introduction of a new syllabus from Class I to Class VIII prepared by the State Institute of Education from the Session 1981-82. Despite a number of criticism of the syllabus it has certain good features worth mentioning. Firstly, the syllabus introduced socially useful productive work in all classes of primary education in an integrated manner. Secondly, it makes provision for teaching and learning Manipuri as a second language in the schools of hill areas and also for the non Manipuri speaking children. An orientation programme on socially useful productive work for the key persons of the N.E. Region was held at Imphal in December, 1981 for preparing the teachers to implement it in the school properly.

Primary Education Since Independence

With the Independence of India in 1947, some political changes took place in Manipur. A popular ministry was formed in 1948, but the Legislative Assembly and the Government were, however, dissolved on the integration of the State with the Indian Union on the 15th of October, 1949 and Manipur became a part "C" State when the Constitution of 1950 came into force. The progress of education since the attainment of Independence and the setting up of a popular Government made liberal provisions for the development of education within a short span of its life. Primary education progressed rapidly after 1947-48 in Manipur. The development of primary education is presented in Table 2.5 which shows the number of primary schools in the state since 1892-93.

Table 2.5
Growth of Primary Schools* in Manipur (1892-93 to 1996-97)

Year	No. of Boys Schools (including co-education Schools)	No. of Girls Schools	Total No. of Schools
1892-93	1	Nil	1
1896-97	8	Nil	8
1900-01	16	1	17
1905-06	-	-	42
1910-11	-	-	72
1915-16	-	-	74
1920-21	-	-	93
1925-26	-	-	112
1930-31	-	-	130
1935-36	-	-	223
1940-41	NA	NA	157
1945-46	NA	NA	NA
1950-51	430	25	455
1955-56	839	38	877

1960-61	1493	167	1660
1965-66	1849	288	2137
1970-71	2160	312	2472
1975-76	3178	287	3466
1980-81	2637	223	2860
1985-86	2477	201	2678
1990-91	2986	204	3190
1995-96	3000	83	3083
1996-97	2366	167	2533

* Pre-Primary/Junior basic/Upper Junior Basic Schools.
Source : 1. Th. Mangoljao Singh, *Western Education in Manipur,* Vol. I & II, pp. 6, 13, 20, 24, 42, 43 & 67.
2. Statistical Handbook of Manipur, 1992, p. 44 & 45.
3. Directorate of Education.

From one school in 1892-93, educational institutions in Manipur increased to 157 during 1940-41. In 1950-51 there were only 455 primary schools in the state, out of which 430 were for boys and 25 for girls. But in a ten year period, i.e. by 1960-61 boys' schools rose to 1493 whereas the number of girls' schools were only 167. This shows that in a year about 120 more schools were opened. Fig. 2.1 further shows a gradual increase of primary schools in the state till 1975-76. During this period more boys' schools were opened than the girls' schools. As shown in the table, the state in 1975-76 has as many as 3466 primary schools out of which 287 were girls school (8.28%). This shows backwardness of the state in field of girls' education. Thus, there was a phenomenal rise in the number of primary schools. But the number of girls' schools declined to 167 in 1996-97. This may be due to the fact that some of the girls' schools might have been converted to co-educational institution or might have been closed down due to poor response from the locality.

Enrolment of Students

From Table No. 2.6 it is clear that enrolment of students specially at primary stage during the period from 1892-93 to 1996-97 has increased gradually. One may wonder that in the year 1950-51 only 35,318 students (29,977 boys and 5,341 girls) were enrolled in the primary schools. By 1960-61 enrolment at this stage increased considerably. Among the boys, enrolment was almost trebled

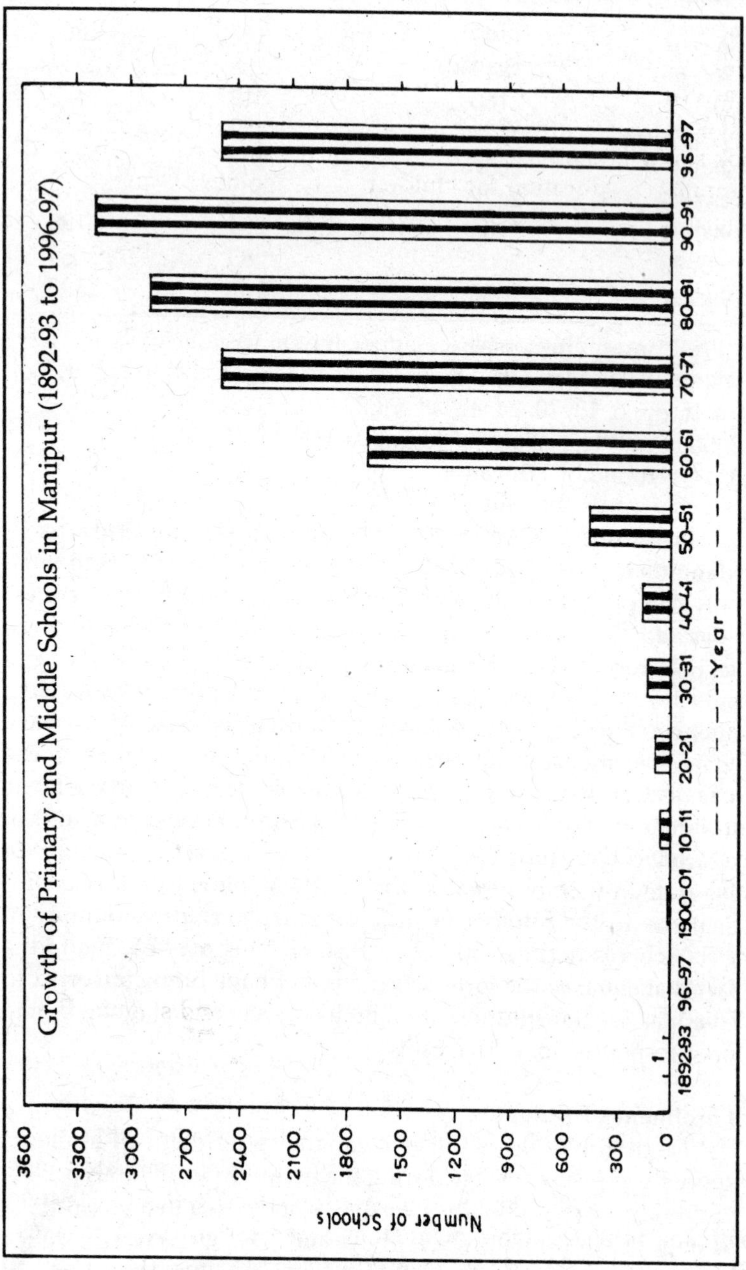
Growth of Primary and Middle Schools in Manipur (1892-93 to 1996-97)
Number of Schools
3600
3300
3000
2700
2400
2100
1800
1500
1200
900
600
300
0
1
1892-93
96-97
1900-01
10-11
20-21
30-31
40-41
50-51
60-61
70-71
80-81
90-91
96-97
Year

Fig. 2.1

whereas among the girls it was almost eight times showing the total number of enrolment as 13,1938. By the end of Second Five Year Plan the enrolment rose to 1,19,765 consisting of 72,957 boys and 46,808 girls. This is due to the fact that the State Government took special attention for enrolment to fulfill the goal of free and compulsory education for children upto age of 14 years. In this regard it may be recalled that in 1955-56, there were only 877 primary schools (839 for boys and 38 for girls), which increased to 1660 in the year 1960-61. One of the interesting phenomenon during this period is that the number of girls' schools increased from 38 in 1955 to 167 whereas the boys' schools increased from 839 to 1493 in 1960-61. From this it may be concluded that the State Government took more interest for the girls education during this period.

Table 2.6 further shows that by 1970-71 enrolment of girls in the schools was tremendous considering the enrolment in 1960-61. The number of students enrolled during 1970-71 was 201,535 of which 122,179 were boys and 79,356 were girls. Again in 1975-76 enrolment of girls rose to 1,03,654 and boys to 1,50,509 with a total enrolment of 2,54,163, indicating the highest enrolment during 1975-76. Inspite of all this rise, the target of 100% enrolment of children for the age group of 6-14 could not be achieved so far due to slow progress of enrolment mainly in the rural and tribal areas and also in the enrolment of girls. During 1980-81, the enrolment of students in primary and middle schools were reduced by about 42,000 from 1970-71 data. (see fig.) Inspite of that, the following years shows increasing trend of enrolment and by 1996-97, almost 2,78,590 students were enrolled in primary and middle schools of which 1,31,473 were girls accounting for 47.19% of the total students. The decreasing trend of enrolment during the period 1970-71 to 1980-81 was mainly due to wastage and stagnation.

According to the Survey Report of N.C.E.R.T. (1972-73), 529 village out of the total 1,993 villages of Manipur were without any schooling facilities and as many as 1,845 villages either have no educational facilities or have some kind of educational facilities upto Class VI. Only 988 villages have facilities upto Class II only. Of these 28 have a population of more than two thousand. Facilities upto Class V were available in 95 schools, upto Class VI in 232 schools and beyond Class VI in 104 schools. There were

2,658 schools in the rural areas and tribal areas as against 203 urban schools. L.P. and U.J.B. schools were run by Government and private agencies through Governments' aid. Enrolment percentage for 6-11 age group was more than 94% and for the 11-14 age group was about 47.47% only. The percentage of enrolled scheduled tribe students with reference to the total enrolment at the stage of I-V was 27.81%.[15]

The declining enrolment in the age group of 6-14 years may be attributed to many factors. One reason may be that by the time when Manipur attained statehood, literacy rate of the state rose even at par with the national average. But employment facilities were so meagre that there were many unemployed youths who could not get benefit of their education. Thus, some of the parents having undergone such lamentable experience stopped sending their wards to the schools. This may even be true in case of rural areas. Another factor which may be treated as the main cause was that the parents would like to send their children to the English medium schools. Since late 1970's a good number of Mission or English medium schools were started in different parts of the state. In the establishment of these schools, only voluntary organisations and private bodies took keen interest. These schools were not given any grant, nor were they recognised by the State Government. Therefore, a sizeable number of students enrolled in such schools or Balwadis or Mission schools were not counted by the State Education Department. Due to these reasons, enrolment at this stage after 1975-76 declined. However, if the enrolment at this stage in such schools were counted, then the enrolment after 1975-76 may have the same trend of gradual increase.

The percentage of wastage is 64% in the lower classes of primary schools in the case of the girls and children coming from the weaker sections of the society both in the rural and tribal areas.

Since the state has a total literate population of 9,16,692 persons out of the total population of 18,37,149 persons as per 1991 census, the literacy rate of the state during the period was recorded as 59.89 percent of the total nine districts, Imphal West, Imphal East and Ukhrul districts have literacy rate well above the state average (Fig. 2.2) where literacy of Imphal West district is the highest being

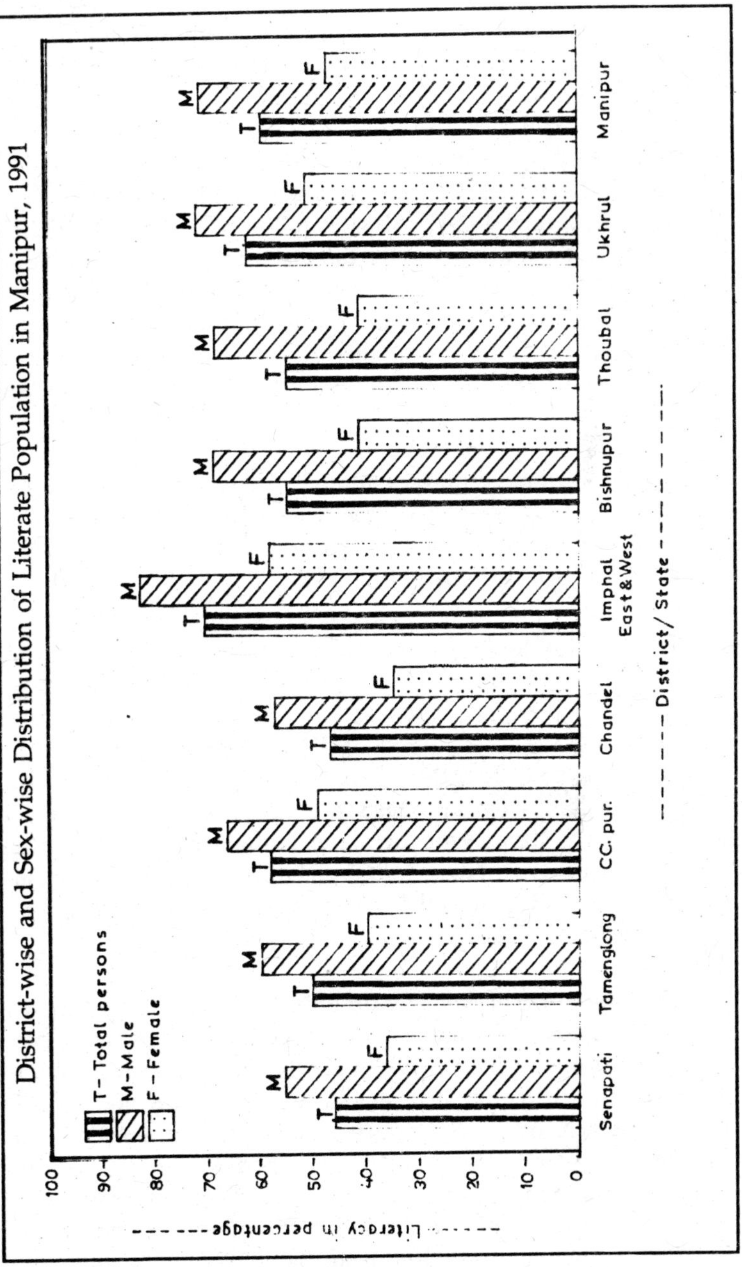
District-wise and Sex-wise Distribution of Literate Population in Manipur, 1991
T- Total persons
M-Male
F-Female
Literacy in percentage
100
90
80
70
60
50
40
30
20
10
0
Senapati
Tamenglong
CC. pur.
Chandel
Imphal East & West
Bishnupur
Thoubal
Ukhrul
Manipur
District / State

Fig. 2.2

73.01%. Greater literary in Imphal West and Imphal East districts may be due to positive response of the people inhabiting the districts towards education and greater educational facilities available in the districts and in Imphal City in particular. However, all the remaining six districts have literacy rate below the state average. As illustrated in the table, Senapati district has the lowest literacy rate of only 46.04% which is followed by Chandel District with 46.68% lower literacy in the hill districts and remaining valley districts of Thoubal and Bishnupur may be attributed to their poor economy, lesser awareness about importance of education, greater emphasis on agricultural activities rather than educating children, and above all lack of sufficient educational facilites and infrastructure.

In case of female literacy too, Imphal West has the highest rate of 61.12% followed by Imphal East (54.99%) and (51.57%), Chandel on the other hand has the lowest female literacy (34.80%), followed by Senapati District (36.13%).

The trend of literacy is increasing continously except in 1931. However, growth-trend of literacy before independence was very slow where the literacy rate have increased to only 5.06% during 1941 from 0.93% in 1901 making a growth rate of only 1.03% per decade. With the attainment of India's independence, greater emphasis was given on education and as an impact, the literacy of the state was fast increasing making 11.41% during 1951. Now, Manipur has become one of the state having highest literacy in the whole country where literacy rate in 1991 was 59.89% (Table 2.8).

The first cause of the slow progress of primary education was the grinding poverty of the majority of population which prevented them from sending their children to schools or to keep them there for more than a couple of years since child labour and valuable economically productive oppurtunities both in domestic Chores and outside work were profitable.[16] The distance of the schools from most of the villages is one of the causes of hinderance to the expansion of primary education. On the other hand the parents used to remove their children from the schools from where they derived no benefit. This fact affected the progress of primary

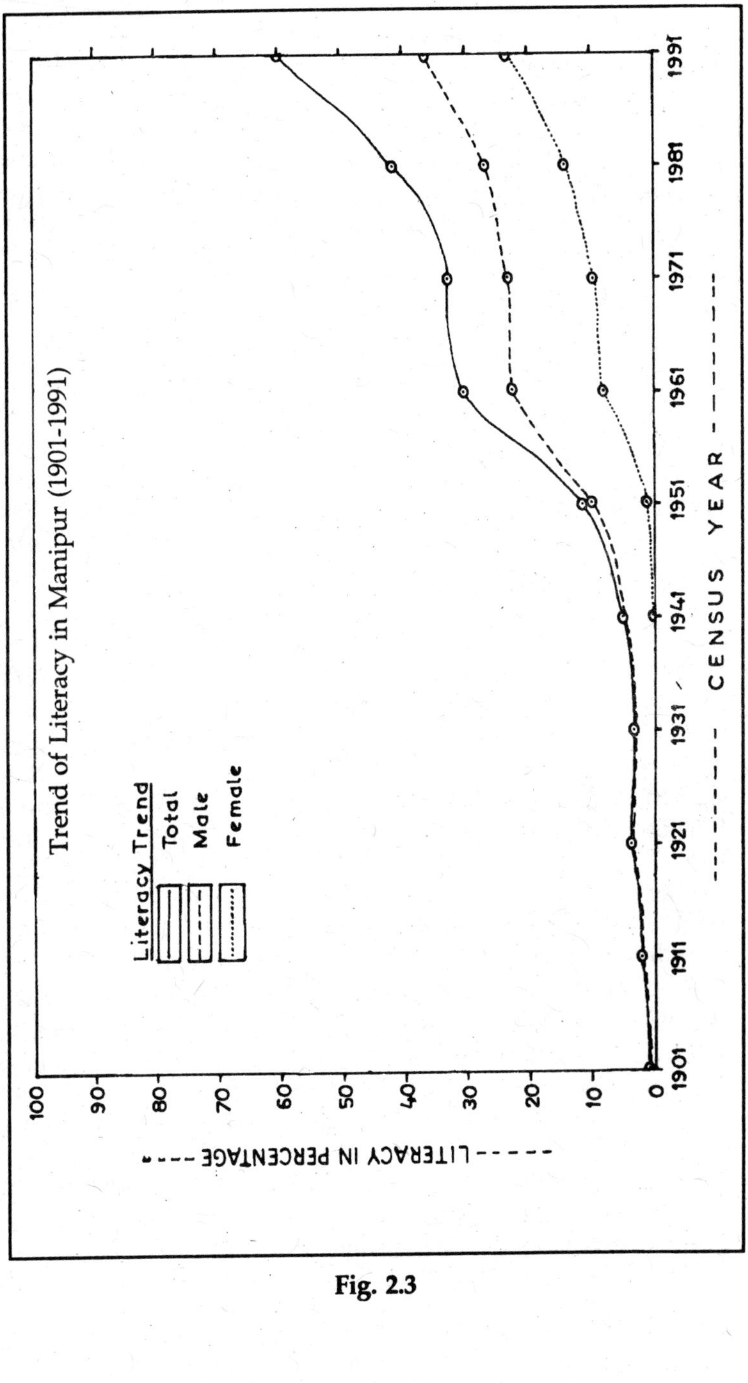
Trend of Literacy in Manipur (1901-1991)
Literacy Trend
Total
Male
Female
CENSUS YEAR
1901
1911
1921
1931
1941
1951
1961
1971
1981
1991
0
10
20
30
40
50
60
70
80
90
100

Fig. 2.3

education. Over and above, in some areas the government could not provide financial of assistance for the establishment and development of primary education. These are some of the causes of slow progress of primary education in Manipur.

Table 2.6
Enrolment Trends of Students in Primary & Middle Schools 1892-93 to 1996-97

Year	Boys		Girls		Total
	Numbers	% of Total	Numbers	% of Total	
1892-93	113	100	-	-	113
1895-96	540	100	-	-	540
1900-01	1164	94.94	62	5.06	1226
1905-06	N.A.	-	N.A.	-	2364
1910-11	4188	99.05	40	0.95	4228
1915-16	3748	97.99	77	2.01	3825
1920-21	5811	99.33	39	0.67	5850
1925-26	N.A.	-	N.A.	-	7201
1930-31	-	-	-	-	N.A.
1935-36	-	-	-	-	N.A.
1940-41	-	-	-	-	N.A.
1945-46	-	-	-	-	N.A.
1950-51	29,977	84.88	5,341	15.12	35,318
1955-56	56,716	74.94	18,963	25.06	75,679
1960-61	88,092	66.77	43,846	33.23	131,938
1965-66	1,02,111	61.28	64,524	38.72	166,635
1970-71	1,22,179	60.62	79,356	39.38	201,535
1975-76	1,50,509	59.22	1,03,654	40.78	254,163
1980-81	1,20,212	56.68	91,880	43.32	212,092
1985-86	1,36,513	56.69	1,04,283	43.31	240,796
1990-91	1,44,014	54.46	1,20,424	45.54	264,438
1995-96	1,47,980	53.24	1,29,985	46.76	277,965
1996-97	1,47,117	52.81	1,31,473	47.19	278,590

Source : 1. Th. Mangoljao Singh, *Western Education in Manipur*, Vol. I & II, 1989, pp. 45, 53 & 54.
2. Statistical Handbook of Manipur, 1992.
3. Directorate of Education (s).

Table 2.7
District-wise Distribution of Literate Population, 1991

State/Dist.	Area in Sq. km.	Total Population			Literate person			Literacy in percentage (excluding 0-6 pop.)		
		P	M	F	P	M	F	P	M	F
Senapati	3,271	2,08,406	1,07,310	1,01,096	81,047	50,404	30,643	46.04	55.26	36.13
Tamenglong	4,391	86,278	44,593	41,685	36,039	22,289	13,750	50.16	59.92	39.68
Churachandpur	4,570	1,76,184	91,218	84,966	85,355	50,597	34,758	58.17	66.38	49.30
Chandel	3,313	71,014	37,118	33,896	27,711	17,920	9,791	46.68	57.39	34.80
Imphal East	673	3,30,460	1,68,125	1,62,335	1,85,776	1,12,068	73,708	68.05	80.65	54.99
Imphal West	555	3,80,801	1,92,441	1,88,360	2,35,949	1,38,300	97,649	73.01	84.63	61.12
Bishnupur	496	1,80,773	91,125	89,648	82,063	51,525	30,538	54.94	68.59	41.13
Thoubal	514	2,93,958	1,48,432	1,45,526	1,26,361	83,057	43,304	52.47	68.33	36.31
Ukhrul	4,544	1,09,275	57,997	51,278	56,391	34,724	21,667	62.54	72.11	51.57
Manipur	22,327	18,37,149	9,38,359	8,98,790	9,16,692	5,60,184	3,55,808	59.89	71.63	47.60

Source : 1. Statistical Abstract of Manipur, 1992, Directorate of Economics and Statistics, Govt. of Manipur, pp. 1 & 6.
2. Statistical Handbook of Manipur, 1992, p. 14 & 15.

Table 2.8
Literacy Trend in Manipur, 1901 - 1991

	Total Population				Literate			
	Males	Females	Total	Decennial gowth in %	Males	Females	Total	Literacy in %
1901	1,39,632	1,44,833	2,84,465	-	2,596	62	2,658	0.93
1911	1,70,666	1,75,556	3,46,222	21.71	6,889	217	7,106	2.95
1921	1,88,119	1,95,897	3,84,016	10.92	14,396	291	14,687	3.83
1931	2,15,815	2,29,791	4,45,606	16.04	13,806	689	14,495	3.25
1941	2,49,183	2,62,886	5,12,069	14.92	24,339	1,594	25,933	5.06
1951	2,83,685	2,93,950	5,77,635	12.80	58.933	6,962	65,895	11.41
1961	3,87,058	3,92,979	7,80,037	35.04	1,74,656	62,620	2,37,276	30.42
1971	5,41,675	5,31,078	10,72,753	37.53	2,49,383	1,03,707	3,53,090	32.91
1981	7,21,006	6,99,947	14,20,953	32.46	3,84,231	2,03,387	5,87,618	41.35
1991	9,38,359	8,98,790	18,37,149	24.29	5,60,884*	3,55,808*	9,16,692*	59.89

*Excludes population below 6 years of age.

Source : Statistical Handbook of Manipur, 1992., Directorate of Economics and Statistics, Govt. of Manipur, pp. 18-19.

Teachers in the Primary Schools

The growth of teachers in the primary schools during the period from 1950-51 to 1996-97 presented in Table 2.9 shows that in 1950-51 there were only 1,233 teachers in the state. At this time the number of schools were 455 having 35,318 students. This indicates the average of less than 3 teachers for one school whereas the teacher - pupil ratio was 1:29 and enrolment per school was 78 approximately.

During 1955-56 there had been sizeable growth in all these aspects. The number of schools was 877, having enrolment of 75,679 pupils and the number of teachers employed was 2,444. The teacher - pupil ratio was 1:31, teachers per school were 2.8 only. In terms of the teacher - pupil ratio during 1950-51 to 1955-56, it was found to have slightly increased, whereas enrolment of pupils per school increased from 78 to 87 while teachers working per school recorded slight increase. Again by 1960-61 the total number of teachers was 5,594 which marked two fold increase from 1955-56. The number of students was 1,31,938 in 1,660 schools indicating about 79 students per school.

In the year 1970-71 total enrolment was 201,535 of which 122,179 were boys and 79,356 were girls. The girls enrolment almost doubled in the decade whereas there has been only slight increase in male enrolment. The growth of teachers in both the cases as well as institutions were found to have sudden increase during the period 1975-76. Whereas employment of male teachers rose to 11,570 and female to 1230. However, in 1980-81, the total number of teachers employed in primary and middle schools were slightly reduced by about 442 from 1975-76 level and their total number became 12,358. The fluctuation in the number of teachers was mainly due to the fact that the state government converted the primary schools to the middle schools and again middle schools to High School level. It is because of this reason that many teachers serving in the primary schools were absorbed as teachers of Middle schools. In addition to these, some private schools were closed down due to financial hardship.

As per Vth All India Educational Survey, 1986-87, 18.50% of the total primary schools (510) were single teacher schools (490 in rural areas and 20 in urban areas) and 820 primary schools (29.74%

of the total 2757 were two-teacher schools (779 in rural areas & 41 in urban areas) of the total 2614 rural habitats, the survey also identified 418 schoolless villages accounting for about 15.99% of the total rural settlements.[17]

Table 2.9
Teachers in Primary and Middle Schools, 1950-51 to 1996-97

Year	Teachers							
	Nursery School		Primary School		Middle School		Total (P+N+M)	
	Male	Female	Male	Female	Male	Female	Male	Female
1	2	3	4	5	6	7	8	9
1950-51	-	-	928	34	264	7	1,192	41
1955-56	-	-	1,992	50	393	9	2,385	59
1960-61	-	2	4,110	195	1,224	63	5,334	260
1965-66	-	2	5,894	424	1,427	81	7,321	507
1970-71	-	3	6,534	553	1,916	139	8,450	695
1975-76	-	4	9,373	901	2,197	325	11,570	1,230
1980-81	-	4	8,097	1,098	2,714	445	10,811	1,547
1985-86	-	4	7,284	1,653	3,086	795	10,370	2,452
1990-91	-	5	8,431	2,575	4,978	1,745	13,409	4,325
1995-96	-	4	6,372	2,943	3,994	2,038	10,366	4,985
1996-97	-	-	6,072	3,016	4,023	2,093	10,095	5,109

Source : 1. Th. Mangoljao Singh, *Western Education in Manipur*, Vol. I & II, 1989, p. 116.
2. Statistical Handbook of Manipur, 1992, pp. 52-53.
3. Statistics of Education in States Ministry of Human Resource Development, Dept. of Education ., Govt. of India.

By 1990-91, teachers employed in primary and middle schools reached 17,734 for 2,64,438 students enrolled in 3190 primary and middle schools where the teacher-pupil ratio works to be 1:15. Though enrolment of students in primary and middle schools were increased substantially, the number of teachers employed and number of schools declined to some extent because of the upgradation of primary schools to middle and middle to high schools level. Thus, primary and middle schools numbered 3071 employing 15,204 teachers, with the average number of teacher serving per schools came to about 5 during 1996-97. With a total enrolment of 2,78,590 students, teacher-pupil ratio in primary and middle schools during 1996-97 was 1:18.

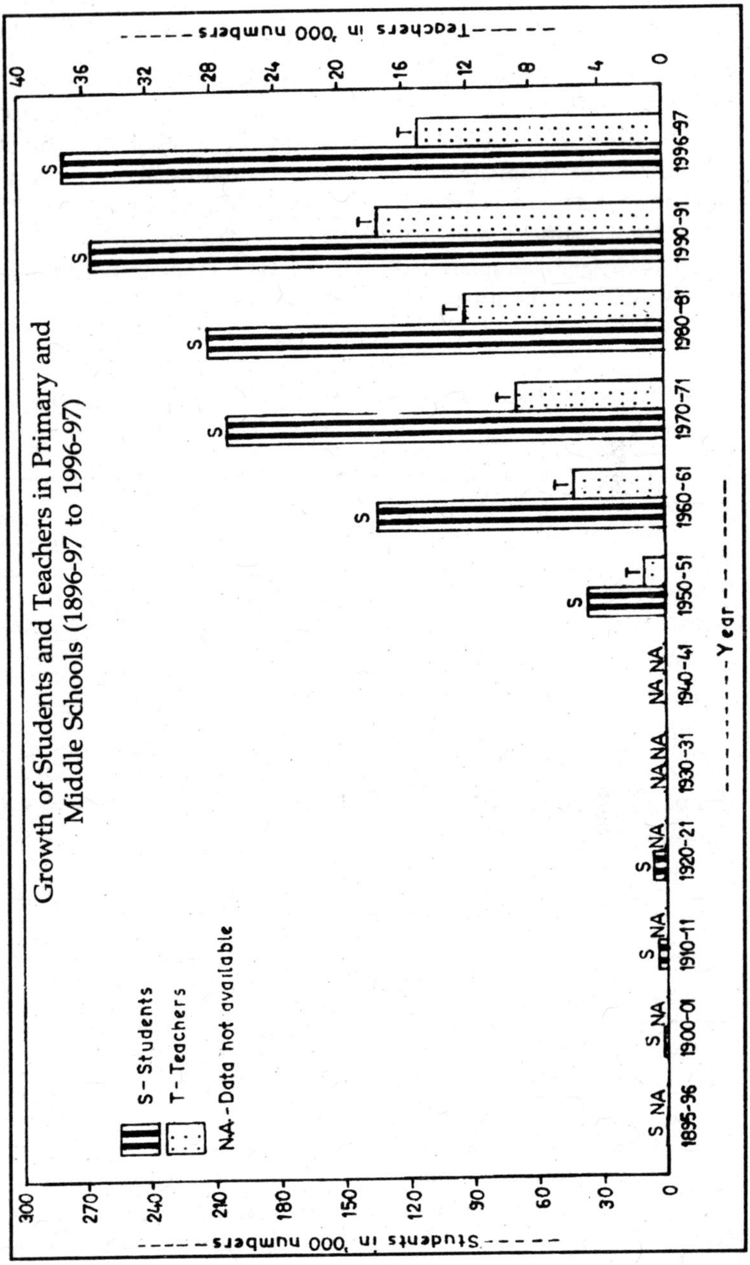
Growth of Students and Teachers in Primary and Middle Schools (1896-97 to 1996-97)
S-Students
T-Teachers
NA-Data not available
Students in '000 numbers
Teachers in '000 numbers
Year
1895-96
1900-01
1910-11
1920-21
1930-31
1940-41
1950-51
1960-61
1970-71
1980-81
1990-91
1996-97
0
30
60
90
120
150
180
210
240
270
300
4
8
12
16
20
24
28
32
36
40
S
T
NA

Fig. 2.4

Table 2.10 portrays the district-wise distribution of primary and middle schools in the state. Imphal West and East Districts (including Jiribam sub-division) have together more than 29% of the total primary and middle schools though these districts share only 5.5% of the total area of the state. Accounting about 2.3% of the state area, Thoubal District ranks third by sharing about 12.57% of the total primary and middle schools. On the other hand, Senapati District, comprising 14.65% of the total state area has a meagre 4.82% of the total primary and middle schools. (Fig. 2.5)

Table 2.10
District-wise Distribution of Primary and Middle Schools
1996-97

District	Total Schools Primary	Middle/ Junior H/S.	Total	In % of total (Primary + Middle)
Imphal West	349	99	448	14.59
Imphal East	358	88	446	14.52
(Jiribam)	(70)	(9)	(79)	(2.57)
Thoubal Dist.	319	67	386	12.57
Bishnupur Dist.	218	46	264	8.60
Ukhrul Dist.	222	46	268	8.73
Senapati Dist.	115	33	148	4.82
Kangpokpi Dist.	246	42	288	9.38
Tamenglong Dist.	213	40	253	8.24
Churachandpur Dist.	256	77	333	10.84
Chandel Dist.	218	19	237	7.71
Manipur	2514	557	3071	100.00

Source : List of Institutions for Schools (General Education), 1996-97, Planning and Statistics Section, Directorate of Education (s).

Since the IIIrd All India Educational Survey observed the need for introduction of Educational Innovation in Manipur particularly at the Primary school level, the state Institute of Education (Now SCERT) have introduced a new syllabus from class I to III from 1981-82 onwards as a first step for introduction and implementation of educational innovations.

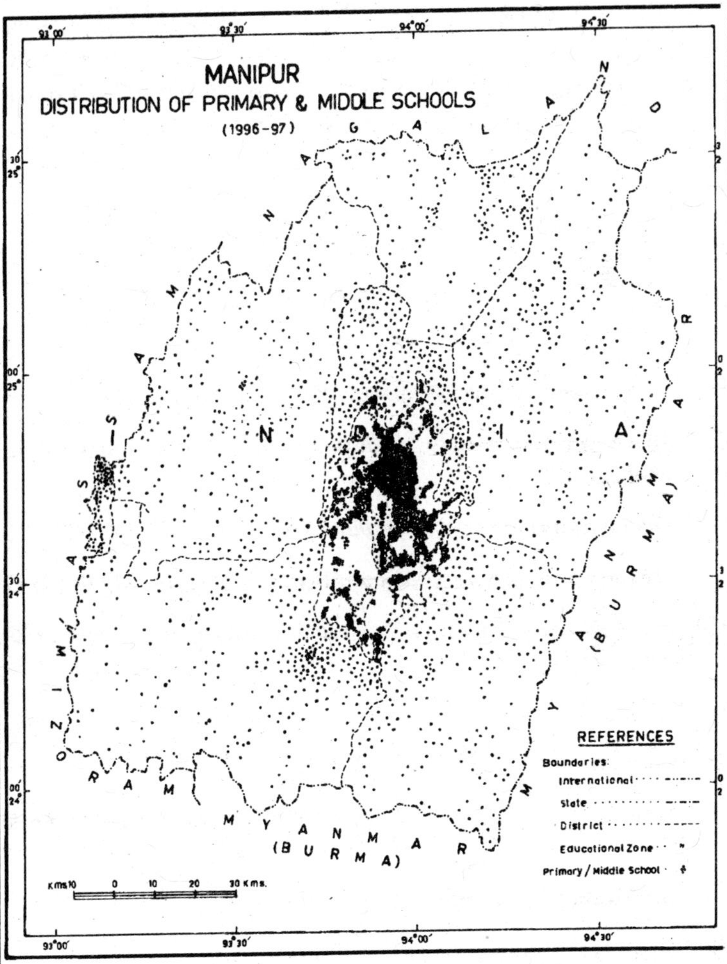
MANIPUR
DISTRIBUTION OF PRIMARY & MIDDLE SCHOOLS
(1996-97)
NAGALAND
ASSAM
MIZORAM
MYANMAR (BURMA)
INDIA
REFERENCES
Boundaries:
International
State
District
Educational Zone
Primary / Middle School
Kms 10 0 10 20 30 Kms.
93°00′
93°30′
94°00′
94°30′

Fig. 2.5

Now, Manipur in progressing well in providing primary education as part of the universalization of free and cumpolsory primary education.

References :

1. **Singh and Singh** : *Current problems of Indian Education* (1966), p.75.

2. **S. Devi and S. N. Pandey** : *Universalisation of Primary Education in Manipur*. Proceedings of the 75th session of I.S.C.A. Pune, Sec. Psychology and Educational Sciences (1988).

3. *Education Commission Report*, 1964-66, p. 151.

4. **R. Brown** : *Statistical Account of Manipur* (1974), p.93.

5. **N.C.E.R.T.** : *Survey Report* (1972-73), p. 8.

6. *The Imperial Gazetteer of India*, Vol. XVII, (1908), p. 195.

7. **Th. Mangoljao Singh** : *Western Education in Manipur*, Vol. I (1967), p. 7.

8. *Administrative Report of Manipur Political Agency* (1893-94), p.13.

9. *Administrative Report of Manipur Political Agency* (1895-96), p.12.

10. *Administrative Report of Manipur Political Agency* (1899-1900), p.20.

11. **N.C.E.R.T.** : *The Indian Year Book of Education* (1961), p. 166.

12. **S. Gyaneswar Singh** : *op.cit.*, p. 154.

13. *Administrative Report of Manipur Political Agency* (1902-1903), p.7.

14. **Th. Mangoljao Singh** : *op. cit.*, p.60.

15. **N.C.E.R.T.** : *Survey Report* (1972-73), p. 27.

16. **Y.B. Singh** (ed.) : *The Economic History of India* (1857-1956), pp. 735-36.

17. **N.C.E.R.T.,** : *Vth All India Educational Survey*, (1986-87).

3

Secondary Education

The three important stages of education in modern times have been primary, secondary and higher education. Modern India also recognises these three stages of education and has divided her educational system into these three parts. The primary stage of education is the means of educating masses, whereas the secondary education is the gateway to higher education.

Secondary education, as it is understood at present in India, is half way between primary education and university education. On the one hand, it is a link with elementary education, on the other it leads up to university education.[1]

The genuine importance of secondary education cannot be overemphasised in the context of the present day situation. Unless secondary education is improved radically, it will not be possible to improve the academic standards in schools, colleges and universities and it will not be able to produce citizens of good qualities. Secondary education feeds the requirements of the university education from where the intellectuals, scholars and leaders in various fields come out and it also prepares good and matured citizens for the future. The Education Commision (1964-66) headed by Dr. D.S. Kothari has rightly pointed out that "The destiny of India is being shaped in her classrooms".[2] This means that education is a force which is very much essential for raising a generation and the nation so that the new generation may be fully equipped with all the required traits to meet the challenges of the modern world.

Secondary education in Manipur can be said to have begun when, in 1909-10, Johnstone Middle English School was upgraded and teaching was started upto high school standard. In 1921-22 the Johnstone High School was formally recognised by the Calcutta University for presenting pupils to appear in the Matriculation examination. Uptil 1930-31, the Johnstone School remained as the lone high school in Manipur.

Given proper impetus by His Highness Maharaja Sir Churachand Singh in the sphere of education of his people, some enlightened Meiteis started establishing private high schools at Imphal. They had a keen desire to acquire a superior education with a view to obtaining employment as state servants.[3] In 1930-31, Manipur Institution was established at Imphal through public initiative to cater to the increasing demand of English education in the capital town. The school got provisional recognition from the Calcutta University in 1931-32.

Table 3.1
Result of Matriculation Examination

Year	No. of candidates appeared	Number of students passed			Total
		1st Divn.	2nd Divn.	3rd Divn.	
1922-23	9	4	2	-	6
1923-24	13	10	1	1	12
1925-26	17	11	5	-	16
1926-27	16	Figure Not Available			
1927-28	19	12	2	-	14
1928-29	27	17	6	-	23
1929-30	27	16	7	-	23
1930-31	29	10	11	1	22
1931-32	37	19	10	3	32
1932-33	33	15	14	2	31
1933-34	39	11	15	2	28
1934-35	34	13	9	1	23

Source : Administrative Reports of Manipur Political Agency from 1922-23 to 1936-37.

This school also sent up students to appear at the Matriculation examination. Later on, the school was renamed after Maharaja Churachand Singh who had donated land and granted financial assistance for constructing a school building. Another High School was established at Uripok (Imphal) by the public initiative in 1932-33. In 1936-37 the school was named after Maharajkumari Tombisana Devi, daughter of His Highness Sir Churachand Singh and the building of the school was constructed from the fund donated by the Majarajkumari. In 1934-35, the Bengali School was upgraded to the level of high school. This was the fourth high school in the state.[4]

The Manipur Girls' High School was established in 1934-35. Another private girls high school was also established in May 1935 which was named after Maharajkumari Tamphasana Devi. With the development of the later girls' high school, the former was abolished gradually. Between 1931-41 there were five high schools in Imphal. Out of which four schools - Johnstone High School, Churachand High School, Tombisana High School and Bengali High School were for boys and Tamphasana High School for girls.

Table 3.2
Number of Meitei Students in Relation to other Communities

Year	Total strength of students*	Meiteis	Muslim	Tribal	British Subjects & others
1909-10	259	245	11	2	1
1914-15	260	252	3	-	5
1919-20	147	143	3	-	1
1924-25	260	234	1	6	19
1929-30	307	266	6	24	11

Source : Administrative Reports of the Manipur Political Agency from 1909-10 to 1940-41.

* The figures indicate number of students of only Johnstone Middle English School, Imphal. The reduction in number is due to the separation of the lower classes into a new upper primary school and lower primary school.

This decade (1931-1941) can be regarded as the decade of private enterprise in the history of modern education in Manipur. By this period, people have fully realised the importance and benefit of modern education. The state authority also encouraged such public enterprise, by giving material and financial assistance.

The progress and development of secondary education in Manipur from the year 1922-23 to 1934-35 is presented in Table 3.1 below.

In the gradual progress of educational development in Manipur, it would be convenient to see the extent of participation by different communities in Manipur- the Meiteis, the hill people, the Muslims and others since the beginning of this century. Table 3.2 presents a picture of the extent of Meitei participation in education in relation to other communities.

Progress Since Independence

When India became independent on the 15th August 1947, Manipur also had her own share of administration. The administration of the state was handed over by the British Government to Maharajkumar Priyobarta Singh, the erstwhile member, Manipur State Durbar on behalf of His Highness, Maharaja Bodhchandra Singh. Shri Priyobarta Singh had been a Durbar member in charge of Education for a long period during the British regime. He and other ministers of the state were interested in the spread of education and the general public also had already learnt the benefits of education during the outbreak of the Second World War. Hence, the Government and the general public were hand in hand in taking up educational development programmes in the state. Moreover, during the war, a number of citizens had also grown rich. Sufficient public contributions from these people towards educational propagation was available in the state.[5]

With the dawn of freedom in India, Manipur also became a free state. Under the policy of Sardar Patel's integration of independent princely states, Manipur also merged into the Indian Union on 15th Oct, 1949 and since then all the clauses of the Indian Constitution have been applicable to this state. Before that, the educational set up, that prevailed in the state, was backward and even in the capital town Imphal, the situation was not praiseworthy. The condition was even worse in the hill areas in terms of educational infrastructures and facilities available. After 1949, there have been major changes both in the valley and in the hills in the educational set up. The popular government made liberal provisions for the development of education within a short span of its life.

Expansion of secondary education was tremendous after 1947. By 1947, the number of high schools was six.[6] Since its merger into India, there had been a growing demand for education in the state. At the time of merger there were only 8 high schools. After the merger the facilities for secondary education were expanded for both the sexes. Though the state government took keen interest in this field, the demand from the public could not be met. Therefore some voluntary organisations also started opening private schools. The people were so enthusiastic that instead of waiting for government help, they took initiative to start schools in their localities and thus within a short period a number of schools began to grow up entirely at the public cost.

Table 3.3
Growth of Secondary Schools in Manipur 1921-22 to 1996-97

Year	No. of Boys Schools (including Co-education Schools)	No. of Girls Schools	Total No of Schools
1921-22	1	-	1
1925-26	1	-	1
1930-31	2	-	2
1935-36	4	1	5
1940-41	4	1	5
1945-46	4	1	5
1950-51	10	1	11
1955-56	22	1	23
1960-61	52	5	57
1965-66	104	14	118
1970-71	104	19	123
1975-76	187	25	212
1980-81	258	32	290
1985-86	313	45	358
1990-91	375	55	430
1995-96	488	51	539
1996-97	503	53	556

Source : 1. Th. Mangoljao Singh, *Western Education in Manipur*, Vol. I & II, 1989.
2. *Statistical Handbook of Manipur*, 1992 Directorate of Economics and Statistics, Government of Manipur.

The beginning of appointments of government employees in the offices according to academic qualifications instead of position on the basis of caste or birth, drew the interest of the people to educate their children and raise the demand for the establishement of schools in their own locality. But, lack of good communication system and poverty made it impossible for the people of remote areas to send their children to the schools far away from their home.

To meet the growing demands of the people, many private individuals tried to establish schools as far as practicable. Table 3.3 presents the growth of schools at the secondary stage during the period 1921-22 to 1996-97 (Fig. 3.1)

The expansion of secondary education was very slow before Independence. The total no. of schools increased to only 5 by 1945-46 from only 1 in 1921-22 indicates a total increase of only 4 secondary schools during the long 24 years period. There were only 8 secondary schools at the time of merger (1949) which increased to 11 in 1950-51. But there were 23 secondary schools in the state during 1955-56. Among them 22 were for boys and only one for girls. In this connection, one may rightly point out that girls education remained much neglected. The number of schools increased from 57 in 1960-61 to 123 in 1970-71 and in the next 10 years it further increased by two and half times.

During the period 1960-61 to 1970-71 and 1970-71 to 1980-81, the growth trend of boys schools were two times and two and half-times respectively, whereas, in case of the Girl's schools, the growth trend for the same period were almost four times and one and half-times respectively. The table also shows the maximum growth of girl's schools during 1990-91 after which a negative growth trend followed, as the number of girl's secondary schools was reduced to 53 by 1996-97. The boys' secondary schools maintained a continous growth trend during the same period, from 258 to 503, accounting for 94.96% growth. From this table, it is clear that inspite of its slow-increase in absolute numbers, the share of girls' schools has declined. Whereas girls' schools shared almost 25% during pre-independence period and about 18% in 1970-71, their share remained only 4.53% of the total Secondary by 1996-97. However, the reduction in share of girls' secondary schools

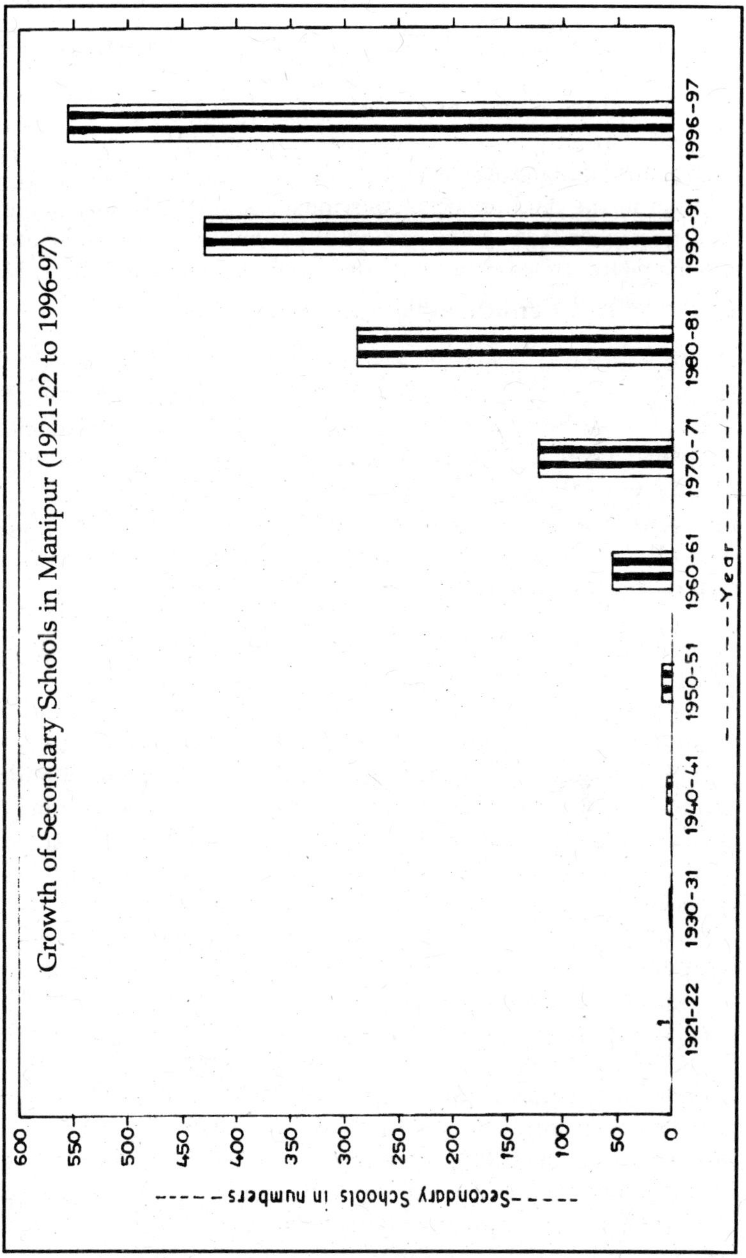
Growth of Secondary Schools in Manipur (1921-22 to 1996-97)
Secondary Schools in numbers
0
50
100
150
200
250
300
350
400
450
500
550
600
Year
1921-22
1930-31
1940-41
1950-51
1960-61
1970-71
1980-81
1990-91
1996-97
1

Fig. 3.1

may be related their conversion into co-educational schools.

The advancement of modern science and technology has helped in removing orthodox ideas, unscientific beliefs and superstition among the general public. It brought a major break-through in the field of social consciousness. It has enabled more and more girls from every section of society to join schools. For enhancing this process, the government should also put some extra efforts than what is prevailing at present.

To conclude, secondary education, though it was neglected before the merger or during the British rule, its expansion took place slowly after integration with the Indian Union and there had been rapid progress after achieving statehood in 1972 by Manipur through the efforts of the state government and the generous help from the central government providing all possible facilities to the state aiming at achieving the national goal of free and compulsory education upto the age of 14.

From Table 3.3 it is clear that there have been rapid progress in secondary education during the last 77 years in Manipur. It can be regarded as qualitative expansion of education. About other facilities, Report on Higher Education records that the facilities in schools were not satisfactory. Many schools were without proper furniture and properly trained staff. In government schools much wastage and stagnation was noted than in aided and public schools. It may be on account of feeling that these government institutions and the men who are employed there have the feeling as if they have nothing to do for the promotion of education. Most of them are interested only with salary and are the least concerned with regular teaching. They have joined the teaching profession as a means of earning, not from the point of view of missionary zeal. Because of this, quality of education suffered and required great improvement. Though the number of schools rose from 11 in 1950-51-50 to 556 in 1996-97, there is still the need for establishing more schools to meet the needs of the growing population. The rapid growth came only after achieving statehood, that too again in a random and in a very hurried manner. Because of these factors some of the aided schools and even government schools are not having proper facilities and infrastructures which they are supposed to have. For example, adequate class-rooms, library facilities, teaching aids, playgrounds co-curricular activities etc. are not available in many schools. The condition is worse in the hill areas.

Another fast growing ailment is the deterioration of the quality of education in the government and aided schools. But the private institutions are gaining upper hand at the cost of the government and aided schools. This deterioration of the government and aided schools has helped in the growth of commercialisation of education by the private schools. This is the most acute disease at present for secondary education in Manipur. For removing these defects the quality of education in the government schools has to be improved.

Schools and the Type of Management

To understand the growth of secondary education in Manipur in its true perspective, it is necessary to trace in fuller details, the type of management of the secondary schools in the state. Table - 3.4 shows the management wise growth of secondary schools during the period 1921-22 to 1996-97.

From the above table it is evident that there were 11 secondary schools in Manipur during the year 1950-51 as against only one in 1921-22. Among these 2 were government schools, 7 were aided and two unaided schools. Thus though the state government could not open more government schools, private bodies and voluntary organisations played a major part in opening private institutions in the state. Out of the 57 schools during 1960-61, eleven were government, 39 were aided and 7 were unaided. By 1969-70 the total number of government schools rose to 21, aided schools increased to 94 and unaided schools to 8, and the total number of schools becoming 123. In the year 1979-80 the total number of schools increased to 291. In 1990-91, the number of govt., aided and unaided high and higher secondary schools increased to 217, 82 and 131 respectively and by 1996-97, their number in turn reached to 232, 98 and 226.

The govt. schools grew steadily but slowly since Independence, but its rapidity started from 1975-76 onwards, whereas, Private unaided schools rapidly increased since the late 1980's, unaided private schools have increased from only 83 in

1985-86 to almost 226 in 1996-97 making a threefold increased during a short span of 11 years accounting for about 40.65% of total secondary schools in 1996-97. The periodic decrease of aided and unaided private schools are due to their conversion into Government schools where maximum conversion took place during the 1970's.

Table 3.4
Management-wise Number of Secondary Schools (High & Higher Sec.) in Manipur, 1921-22 to 1996-97.

Year	Schools by Management			
	Govt. Schools	Aided Schools	Unaided Schools	Total Schools
1921-22	-	1	-	1
1925-26	-	1	-	1
1930-31	Nil	1	1	2
1935-36	Nil	2	3	5
1940-41	Nil	1	4	5
1945-46	Nil	1	4	5
1950-51	2	7	2	11
1955-56	6	16	1	23
1960-61	11	39	7	57
1965-66	18	88	12	118
1970-71	21	94	8	123
1975-76	51	108	53	212
1979-80	162	62	34	291
1985-86	210	65	83	358
1990-91	217	82	131	430
1995-96	227	82	230	539
1996-97	232	98	226	556

* Johnstone & Tamphasana Girls Schools became the first Govt. High Schools from 1st June, 1946.

Source : 1. Th, Mangoljao Singh, *Western Education in Manipur*, Vol. I & II, 1989.

2. *Statistics of Education in States*, Ministry of Human Resource Development, Dept. of Education, Govt. of India.

Thus there was fairly rapid increase in the number of government schools as well as aided schools during the period 1965-66 to 1996-97. It is interesting to mention here that the state government took more initiative in expanding secondary education after attaining statehood in 1972. Table 3.4 shows that the number of government schools rose more than eleven times during this period while the number of aided schools increased to some extent only. The reason may be that a number of private aided schools were converted into government schools.

It may, therefore, be said that, on the whole, the growth of secondary schools, management-wise, has been quite adequate. Even with the higher rate of progress so far achieved after statehood, the hilly areas are still lagging behind the valley areas to much extent.

Moreover, there is mushroom growth of private schools during the last decade with the sole motive to commercialise education for getting as much profit as possible.

Enrolment at the Secondary Stage

The number of students studying in secondary schools increased trmendously since 1921-22 (Fig. 3.2) The following table shows the enrolment of students at secondary level from 1921-22 to 1996-97.

Table 3.5 shows that the total number of students enrolled in the secondary schools increased by about 40 times during the period 1950-51 to 1996-97. It is evident from the above data that, there has been a steady rise in the enrolment both for boys and girls till 1965-66 followed by alternate gradual and rapid growth. Inspite of gradual expansion of enrolment in absolute numbers the growth in proportion of the preceeding year followed an intermittent trend after 1965-66. From 1970-71 to 1996-97, there was gradual increase in the enrolment. During this period boys' enrolment rose from 25,180 to 111,441 and girls' increased to more than double from 12,826 to 95,504.[8] Although efforts have been made with tremendous enthusiasm to uplift women's education, there have been many obstacles in different forms, e.g., social barriers, religious obligations, idea of thinking girls as less important etc. Hence, there was a long way to go before removing

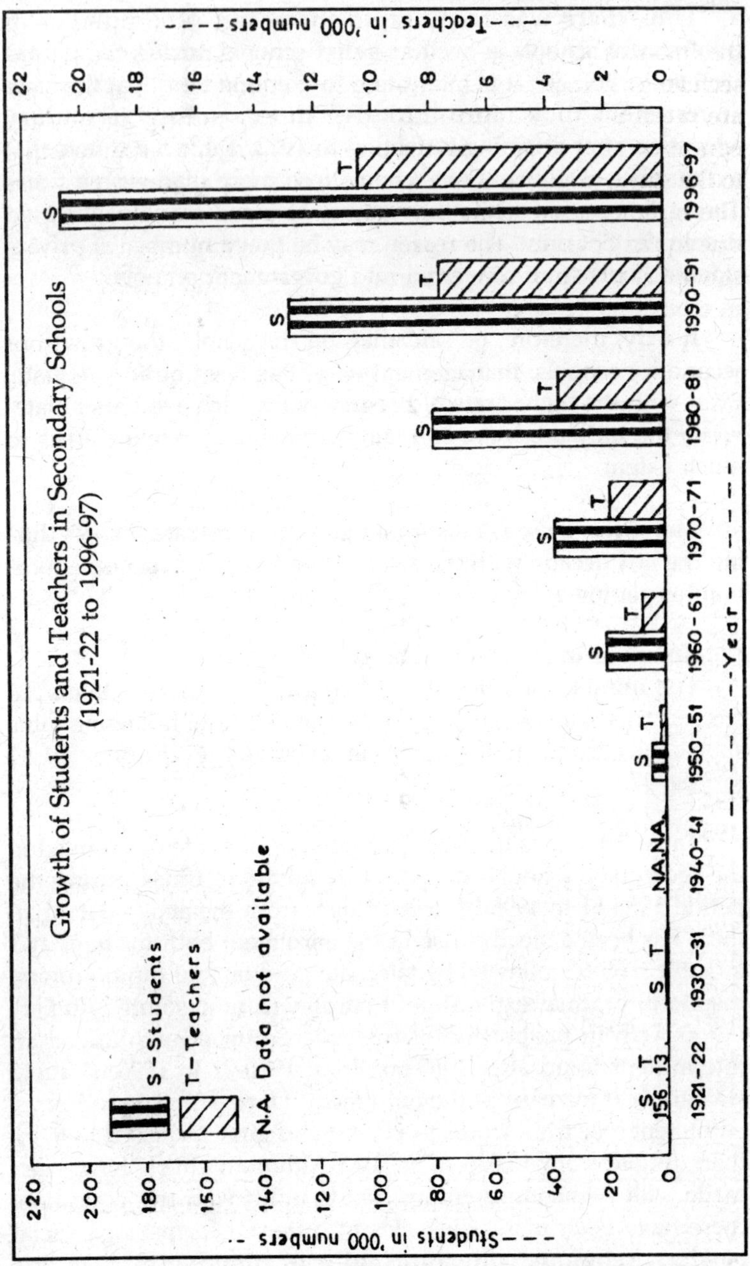
Growth of Students and Teachers in Secondary Schools
(1921-22 to 1996-97)
S - Students
T - Teachers
N.A. Data not available
Teachers in '000 numbers
Students in '000 numbers
Year
1921-22
1930-31
1940-41
1950-51
1960-61
1970-71
1980-81
1990-91
1996-97
156
13
NA
NA
S
T

Fig. 3.2

the imbalances between different religious groups and various sections of the society etc. Moreover a number of other facilities are required for the expansion and improvement of secondary education so that the state of education in Manipur may come up to the status which will be at par with that of the advanced states. The rapid increase in the enrolment of girls after 1971 might be due to the deliberate efforts of the state government after getting statehood to educate the girls and eliminate the gender imbalances in education.

Table 3.5
Students in High/Higher Secondary Schools
(1921-22 to 1996-97)

Year	Scholars					
	Boys		Girls		Total	
	Nos.	In % of total	Nos.	In % of total	Nos.	Growth in % of perce-ding year.
1921-22	N.A.	-	N.A.	-	156	-
1925-26	N.A.	-	N.A.	-	266	70.51
1930-31	N.A.	-	N.A.	-	527	98.12
1935-36	N.A.	-	N.A.	-	N.A.	-
1940-41	N.A.	-	N.A.	-	N.A.	-
1945-46	2172	87.90	299	12.10	2471	-
1950-51	4625	88.60	595	11.40	5220	111.25
1955-56	8251	84.00	1572	16.00	9823	88.18
1960-61	18,084	87.96	2,475	12.04	20,559	109.29
1965-66	25,369	71.51	10,108	28.49	35,477	72.56
1970-71	25,180	66.25	12,826	33.75	38,006	7.13
1975-76	37,202	63.22	21,643	36.78	58,845	54.83
1980-81	46,314	58.04	33,482	41.96	79,796	35.60
1985-86	58,911	55.66	46,935	44.34	105,846	32.64
1990-91	71,451	55.28	57,811	44.72	129,262	22.12
1995-96	106,830	54.18	90,332	45.82	197,162	52.53
1996-97	111,441	53.85	95,504	46.15	206,945	4.96

Source : 1. Th. Mangoljao Singh, *Western Education in Manipur,* Vol. I & II, 1989.
2. Statistical handbook of Manipur, 1992.
3. Statistics of Education in States, Ministry of Human Resource Development, Dept. of Education, Govt. of India.

Alongwith the increase in the total number of students going to secondary schools by about 40 times during the period of 47 years from 1950-51 to 1996-97 the ratio of male and female students also increased from 7.77:1 in 1950-51 to 1.17:1 in 1996-97, which indicates a higher rate of increase in the number of female students as compared to that of males. The total number of female students increased from 595 to 95,504 during the period of 47 years from 1950-51 to 1996-97 whereas the total number of male students increased from 4,625 to 111,441 during the same period.

Teachers in Secondary Schools

Table 3.6 shows the number of teachers serving in secondary schools. During 1996-97 the number of teachers employed was 10,491 of which 6,724 were males and 3,767 females (Fig. 3.3).

It is thus, observed that there were only 13 secondary teachers in the year 1921-22. It increased to 346 in 1955-56 of which 326 were male and only 20 female. This may be due to the fact that the girls' education was very much neglected during the pre-independence period. It may be mentioned that so far the secondary education is concerned, the number of female teachers was too meagre than that of male teachers. Even in 1970-71 their number in schools was hardly 10% of their male counterparts. In fact, higher education for females started very late and only a few of them achieved higher education in Manipur in those days.

The total number of teachers in the secondary schools increased from 346 to 10,491 i.e., by 30 times during a period of 41 years (1955-56 to 1996-97). But the total number of female teachers increased from 20 to 3,767 i.e. 188 times and the number of male teachers increased from 326 to 6,724 i.e. by 21 times. The ratio of male and female teachers in 1955-56 was 16.3:1 and in 1996-97 it became 1.78:1, which indicate a higher rate of increase in the number of female teachers than that of the male teachers in the recent years.

In order to promote secondary education among the girls and for raising the rate of enrolment in the schools, the role of voluntary organisations and local authorities is very important. Over and above, the increase is chiefly due to the extension of the state education system. Therefore, the state government should take

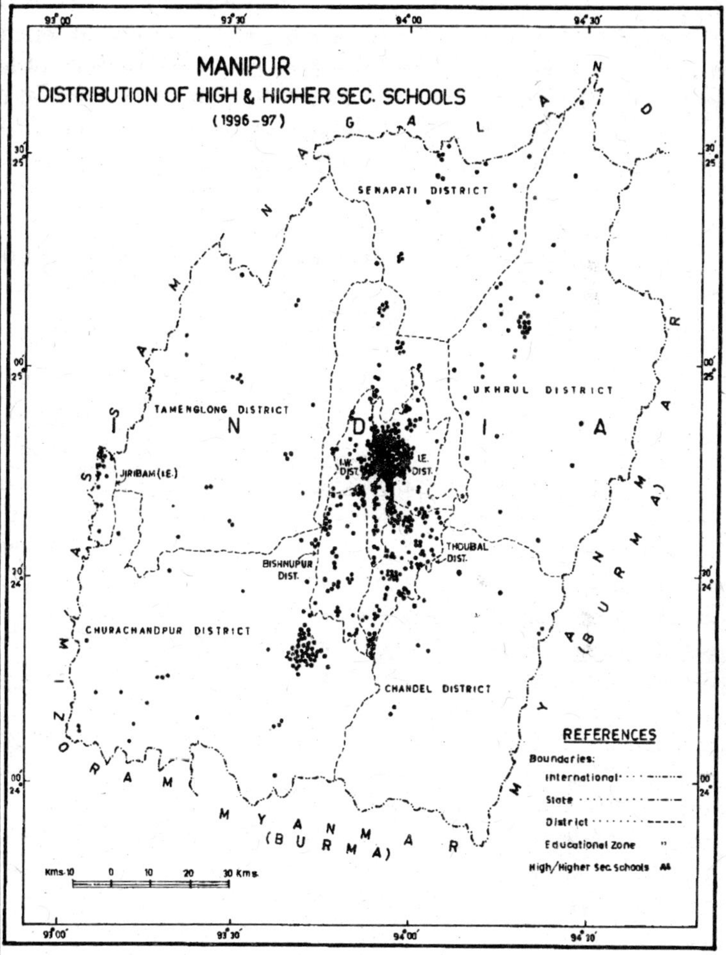
MANIPUR
DISTRIBUTION OF HIGH & HIGHER SEC. SCHOOLS
(1996-97)
SENAPATI DISTRICT
UKHRUL DISTRICT
TAMENGLONG DISTRICT
JIRIBAM (I.E.)
I.W. DIST.
I.E. DIST.
THOUBAL DIST.
BISHNUPUR DIST.
CHURACHANDPUR DISTRICT
CHANDEL DISTRICT
NAGALAND
ASSAM
MIZORAM
INDIA
MYANMAR (BURMA)
REFERENCES
Boundaries:
International
State
District
Educational Zone
High/Higher Sec. Schools
Kms 10 0 10 20 30 Kms.
93°00′
93°30′
94°00′
94°30′

Fig. 3.3.

Fig. 3.3

up appropriate measures to expand the secondary education as far as possible. The Board of Secondary Education in Manipur was established in order to regulate, supervise and develop secondary education in the state. It is responsible for framing the curriculum and syllabus and conducting the examination particularly for classes IX and X standard. Likewise, the council of Higher Secondary Education, Manipur which framed the curriculum and syllabus for higher secondary classes conduct examination for classes XI and XII standard since 1991.

Table 3.6
Teachers in High/Higher Secondary Schools 1921-22 to 1996-97

Year	Teachers					
	Male		Female		Total	
	No.	In % of total	No.	In % of total	No.	Growth in % of perceding year.
1921-22	N.A.	-	N.A.	-	13	-
1925-26	N.A.	-	N.A.	-	14	7.69
1930-31	N.A.	-	N.A.	-	24	71.43
1935-36	N.A.	-	N.A.	-	N.A.	-
1940-41	N.A.	-	N.A.	-	N.A.	-
1945-46	N.A.	-	N.A.	-	64	-
1950-51	N.A.	-	N.A.	-	172	168.75
1955-56	326	94.22	20	5.78	346	101.16
1960-61	757	93.92	49	6.08	806	132.95
1965-66	1,429	41.14	139	8.86	1,568	94.54
1970-71	1,692	90.10	186	9.90	1,878	19.77
1975-76	2,343	86.68	360	13.32	2,703	43.93
1980-81	3,009	82.44	641	17.56	3,650	35.04
1985-86	4,196	78.12	1,175	21.88	5,371	47.15
1990-91	5,230	67.31	2,540	32.69	7,770	44.67
1995-96	6,226	64.25	3,464	35.75	9,690	24.71
1996-97	6,724	64.09	3,767	35.91	10,491	8.27

Source : 1. Th. Mangoljao Singh, *Western Education in Manipur,* Vol. I & II, 1989.
2. Statistical Handbook of Manipur, 1992.
3. Statistics of Education in States, Ministry of Human Resource Development, Dept. of Education, Govt. of India.

Attempts were made to introduce vocational courses in the existing higher secondary schools in 1986-87. FOur trades were selected considering the suitability of the co-educational institutions. The trades were knitting and embroidery, tailoring, short hand writting and electronics.[7]

In order to fulfill the scope of vocationalization of Secondary education in the state, the following courses have been introduced since 1996-97 in different secondary schools. The vocational courses thus introduced are

1. Office management and secretarial practice.
2. Commercial garment designing
3. Textile designing
4. Buiding Maintenance
5. Maintenance and repairing of domestic electrical appliances
6. Medical Laboratory technician
7. Journalism and
8. Inland Fisheries.[8]

Expenditure Incurred on Secondary Education

The expenditure on secondary education in Manipur during the period from 1947-48 to 1995-96 is given in Table 3.7.

From Table 3.7 it is evident that in the year 1950-51 the actual expenditure on secondary education was Rs. 3.55 lakhs only, there were only 11 schools, 5,220 students and 172 teachers. The figure shows that in 1950-51 the expenditure of the state in each of the 11 schools was about Rs. 32,273/- whereas the expenditure per student was about Rs. 68 per annum. However the expenditure per teacher per annum was about Rs. 2,064/- when the actual expenditure is taken together.

During the year 1960-61 the expenditure in this sector rose from Rs. 3.55 lakhs to Rs. 13.25 lakhs. The total number of schools during this period was 57, the number of students 20,559 and teachers 806. Then the expenditure was Rs. 23,246/- per school, Rs. 64/- per student and Rs. 1,664/- per teacher per annum. Likewise the expenditure increased from Rs. 96.72 lakhs in 1970-71 to Rs. 517.39 lakhs during 1980-81 and it further increased to Rs. 2,809.77 lakhs during 1990-91 Finally, the expenditure incurred on secondary education jumped to almost Rs. 5,147.23 lakhs by 1995-96. So, it may not be wrong to say that the expenditure made on secondary education increased many folds since 1980-81 period.

Table 3.7
Expenditure Incurred on Secondary Education
1947-48 to 1995-96

Year	Rupees in thousand
1947-48	125
1950-51	355
1955-56	491
1960-61	1,325
1965-66	3,741
1970-71	9,672
1975-76	16,901
1980-81	51,739
1985-86	111,966
1990-91	280,977
1995-96	514,723

Source : 1. Th. Mangoljao Singh, *Western Education in Manipur*, Vol. I & II, 1989.
2. Statistical handbook of Manipur, 1992.
3. Statistics of Education in States, Ministry of Human Resource Development, Dept. of Education, Govt. of India.

Table 3.8 shows the District-wise distribution of secondary schools in the state. Of the total 556 secondary schools, Imphal West and East Districts (including Jiribam) contains as much as 221 and share more than 39% of the total which is followed by Thoubal District with 89 schools (16.01%). Whereas all the hilly districts (except Churachandpur which has 13.31% of the total secondary schools) together shares only 22.31% of the total secondary schools. In short Imphal West District has the maximum number of higher secondary schools and Chandel has the least (3.06%).

Table 3.8
District-wise Distribution of Secondary Schools in Manipur, 1996-97

Zone District	High Schools	Higher Secondary Schools	Total	In % of total (High & Higher Sec.)
	Total Secondary Schools			
Zone I Imphal West	100	19	119	21.40
Zone I Imphal East	81	9	90	16.19
Jiribam	11	1	12	2.16
Thoubal Dist.	83	6	89	16.01
Bishnupur Dist.	45	3	48	8.63
Ukhrul Dist.	39	1	40	7.19
Senapati (S. Dist.)	20	2	22	3.96
Kangpokpi (S. Dist.)	21	4	25	4.50
Tamenglong Dist.	17	3	20	3.60
C. Chandpur Dist.	68	6	74	13.31
Chandel Dist.	16	1	17	3.06
Manipur	501	55	556	100.00

Source : List of Institutions for Schools (General Education), 1996-97., Planning and Statistics section, Directorate of Education(s).

References :

1. **Singh and Singh** : *Current Problems of Indian Education* (1966), p. 101.
2. *Report of the Education Commission* (1964-66), p.1.
3. *Administrative Report of Manipur Political Agency* (1922-23).
4. *Administrative Report of Manipur Political Agency* (1930-31 to

1936-37).

5. **Th. Mangoljao Singh** : *Western Education in Manipur,* Vol. II (1980), p.1.

6. **N.C.E.R. T.** : *Survey Report* (1972-73), p.9.

7. **Jamini Devi**, *Education in Manipur, p. 68.*

8. *Council of Higher Secondary Education, Manipur.*

4

Higher Education

Realization of the importance of higher education came to the people of Manipur only after the end of the Second World War. Till then, Manipur lived in an age of almost uninterrupted continuity with the past. Though the people of Manipur had some knowledge of schooling, the idea of higher learning was alien to the people and facilities almost absent in the erstwhile kingdom. It can therefore be said that higher education in Manipur started as late as 1946.

This chapter deals with the growth and development of higher education in Manipur with special reference to - (i) a brief history of collegiate education, and (ii) the efforts for the establishment of a University in Manipur.

Collegiate Education

The long felt need of the people of Manipur for collegiate education was partially fulfilled with the establishment of a college in Imphal on 6th August 1946. The college was named after Maharani Dhanamanjuri Devi, who donated a sum of Rs. 10,000 (Rupees ten thousand) only for its establishment. The college was the first of its kind in the state. It started catering to the needs of higher education not only in Manipur but also in other neighbouring states.

Establishment of D.M. College in 1946 marked the beginning of a new era in the development of higher education in the state. The academic activities of the College commenced in August 1946 with 68 students in the first year Intermediate class. Thus Manipur started higher education almost a century after the establishment of institution of this kind in other parts of the country. When the college started, it was affiliated to the Calcutta University upto the Intermediate standard.

The affiliation of the College was transferred to the Gauhati University in 1948. The first batch of graduates in Arts got their degrees from the Gauhati University in 1950. With the establishment of the Manipur Univeristy, the affiliation of the College was again transferred to the Manipur University in 1980.[1]

The establishment of the D.M. College was a landmark in the history of collegiate education in Manipur. Its speedy progress really was an encouraging sign of the development of higher education in the state. The college marched ahead in all aspects of development and became a residential college. Within a very short period, it made quite an appreciable advance towards the direction which is now universally recognised as the ideal at which a college should aim at.

When the improvements in the D.M. College which are now being carried out by the government are completed, this college will be the first government Science and Arts college in Manipur to possess in their totality almost all the facilities like the essential elements of a residential college buildings, houses for professors and hostels for students, playground, gymnasium hall, indoor stadium, common room and library, athletic and social organisations. For various reasons it does not appear that any other college will be able to develop, for several years at any rate, these essential features as fully and completely as the D.M. College. This college started, therefore, with great advantage over all others. Certain distinguishing features of college life and academic activities were also imbibed in the D.M. College. This college has a common hall or auditorium where the students stage dramas and other cultural programmes. They contribute articles in the college magazine. They hold seminars, symposia, debating competitions, quiz programmes, etc.

Co-curricular activities are organised by students union under the guidance of the college teaching staff. They have subject clubs, debating socieities and dramatic clubs; but these activities are organised under the joint auspices of the college management/staff and the students unions. It must, however, be mentioned here that facilities for some of the outdoor and indoor games are found in other colleges also.

The colleges other than D.M. College were private colleges, both aided and unaided. These colleges in Manipur especially the Imphal College (1952-53), the Manipur College (1958), the Oriental College and the Modern College (1963) were established by the people. These colleges were started in response to growing demands for expansion of higher education in the state and with the opening of these colleges, the progress of higher education in Manipur continued in a remarkable way.

The D.M. College continued to be the only college in the state till the year 1951-52. In the year 1952-53, the first private intermediate college, the Imphal College was established with Shri Laishram Achou Singh as the Principal. This college conducted classes in the evening. Such a college was very much beneficial to the working class as D.M. College, the only government college in Manipur became a day college in 1953-54. Manipur College began in a small way in 1958. In the beginning, the buildings of these colleges were inadequate but they had enough land for extension. During the Second Five Year Plan, private organisations in Manipur started playing a vital role for the development of higher education. During the sixties there were several efforts to establish more colleges. This culminated in the establishment of two embryonic colleges i.e. the Oriental and the Modern Colleges in Imphal town in 1963-64. During the same period two other colleges were established, one each at Thoubal and Moirang. The first Arts college in the hill areas was founded in the Manipur South district at Churachandpur in the year 1964-65. The only college having both Arts and Science streams being the D.M. College, yet the College opened B.T., B.Com. and post-graduate classes as its extension programmes. B.T. class was opened in 1959 and the post-graduate classes in 1962. Now a days Imphal College, Manipur College and Oriental College too teach Arts and Science upto Bachelor Degree level. The grant which was given to these colleges were ad-hoc-grant, so they remained under the category of aided colleges. Modern College, Moirang College, Thoubal College and in the hill areas, Seilmat Christian College (Churachandpur) were unaided colleges. In the year 1965-66 the first women's college in the state was established. A sum of Rs. 1 lakh (Rupees one lakh) was donated by Shri Hidangmayum Dwijamani Dev Sharma in the memory of his mother, Smt. Ghanapriya Devi. With the approval of the government of Manipur and by taking the name of Smt. Ghanapriya Devi the college was named as Ghanapriya Women's College. Thereafter Nambol Sanoi College and Maharaja Bodhachandra College were founded as private colleges in the year 1966 and 1969 respectively. During the decade 1960 to 1970 the number of colleges increased to 12 excluding the two government colleges viz., the D.M. College and the G.P. Women's College. According to reports of the Planning Commission, the population of Manipur in the age group of 16-20 was 41,936. According to the same source, percentage of college going students of this age group was 15.62%.[2]

In the year 1966-67, construction of the buildings of Kha-Manipur College, Kakching was started with the donation of a sum of Rs. 80,000/- (Rupees eighty thousand) by the people of the area. In the Sheilmat College of Churachandpur, a hostel which can accommodate 60 hostellers with boarding, lodging and one common room was completed this year. The University Grants Commission also granted some aid to this college. The construction of the building of the Thoubal College also was started in this year and 10 subjects in P.U. Arts and 8 subjects in B.A. were opened. In the year 1969-70, Imphal College, Modern College and Manipur College got "Recurring grant-in-aid" instead of adhoc grant and in other 4 colleges adhoc grant was given. In this year, Sheilmat College was amalgamated to Churachandpur College which was established later on. In the year 1970-71 Honours Courses in English, Education and Political Science were opened in G.P. Women's College, which also started Science stream in P.U. classes. During this period 90% deficit grant was given to 9 private colleges and non-recurring grant to 2 colleges. For Science colleges a special grant was given for purchasing scientific equipments. Thus, at the end of the year 1970-71, there were altogether 12 colleges in the state, of which one college was in the hills and the rest were in the valley. The predominance of colleges in the valley was associated with its importance not only as a thickly populated area but also with large number of towns including the capital of the state. The rapid increase in the number of colleges indicates the growing demand for higher education in Manipur. In this year a sum of Rs. 20,000/- (Rupees twenty thousand) was given as non-recurring grant to the Maharaja Bodhchandra College, Y.K. College and N.G. College. To Moirang, Thoubal and Churachandpur Colleges grant for opening pre-university classes was given as usual in this year. A sum of Rs. 25,000/- (Rupees twenty five thousand) was given to 11 aided colleges and 3 unaided colleges for educational excursion. A sum of Rs. 10,000/- (Rupees ten thousand) by U.G.C. and Rs. 20,500/- (Rupees twenty thousand five hundred) by the Central Government was given for the development of Book Banks in 3 Government colleges and 9 aided colleges. D.M. College of Arts and Commerce was separated from D.M. College of Science in the year 1975. So in 1976-77 there were 19 colleges in Manipur. By 1980-81, there were 24 colleges in the state.[3]

Table 4.1
Growth of Colleges in Manipur*

Year	No. of colleges (including co-education colleges)	No. of colleges for females	Total colleges
1946	1	Nil	1
1950-51	1	Nil	1
1955-56	2	Nil	2
1960-61	2	Nil	2
1965-66	10	1	11
1970-71	11	1	12
1975-76	18	2	20
1980-81	22	2	24
1985-86	26	2	28
1990-91	27	2	29
1995-96	52	7	59
1996-97	57	7	64

* including RIMS, Agriculture College, Polytechnic and CEDT.

Sources : 1. Th. Mangoljao SIngh, *Western Education in Manipur*, Vol. I & II, 1989.

2. Statistical Handbook of Manipur, 1992, Directorate of Economics & Statistics, Govt. of Manipur.

3. College Development Council, M.U.

Manipur has in fact one college student for every 180 of the population compared to about 300 in Assam and 350 in India as a whole. Therefore, it is clear that literacy p.c. in Manipur is higher than that of Assam and that of National average. It is little wonder that the number of High School learners continue to increase and that most of them continued their studies in colleges as they cannot get suitable jobs. This brings in even more difficulties for the existing colleges to admit or educate all the newcomers as there are no plans to reduce the intake. For instance, beginning with 68 students in 1946-47, the number of students rose to about 3,000 in 1975 in the D.M. College, necessiating the separation of Arts and Commerce from the existing college. Thus two colleges were created, namely D.M. College of Arts and Commerce and D.M. College of Science in the same campus. Among the private colleges, particularly Imphal College, Manipur College and Oriental College also felt the similar problems of enrolment in both Arts and Science subjects.

The second women's college was established by the voluntary organisations. It was established in the year 1969-70. It may be noted that due to the efforts of the voluntary organisations during the period 1969-70 to 1980-81, at least one private college came up in the state every year. It may be mentioned that most of the colleges are confined to the valley areas. Tamenglong district does not have even a single private college. Therefore, opening of new colleges though restricted so far, should be taken up on priority basis in the hill areas. Earlier most of the colleges were owned by the voluntary agencies in the state but now most of them have been taken over by the government. Similarly, earlier all the colleges of Manipur were affiliated to Gauhati University. Now all of them are affiliated to Manipur University. Since most of these colleges impart instructions in traditional Arts, Science and Commerce subjects, a situation of severe unemployment has arisen.[4] Medium of instructions and examination at this stage is still English. Only a few colleges offer Honours courses in some subjects. The method of evaluation is the examination after the end of the term. All the colleges hold preliminary tests before the final examinations. Inspite of the growth in the number of colleges, Government as well as private, D.M. Colleges still remain the most developed colleges in the state. Observing of the D.M. College, the N.C.E.R.T. Survey Report says - "The D.M. College, Imphal is the biggest college in the state, offers courses in 23 subjects at the P.U.C. level and 26 subjects at the undergraduate level. It also runs Pre-Medical course. Honours courses in all subjects except Manipuri, Bengali and Anthropology are available there. It is the only college having provision for Anthropology".[5] Most of the colleges are co-educational in nature and there are two women's college *viz.*, G.P. Women's College and Ideal Girl's College, both located at Imphal.

Table 4.1 shows the growthof colleges in Manipur during the period 1946 to 1996-97.

Conversion of Colleges

In the beginning, D.M. College was the only well established and developed college in the state. In the year 1965-66, there were only two government colleges, one of them being a co-educational college and the other exclusively a women's college. The first batch of aided colleges was converted into government colleges in the year 1977-78. The government of Manipur, after having considered the ways and means of improving the available facilities in the private colleges and in order to standardise the teaching facilities in these colleges took over 3 aided colleges. Churachandpur College (hills), Pettigrew College (hills) and Thoubal College (valley). In the following year 1978-79, the government took over 9 more aided colleges, i.e., Imphal College, Manipur College, Modern College, Kha-Manipur College, Moirang College, C.I. College (Bishnupur), Presidency College and Nambol L. Sanoi College. The Government of Manipur further considered the need for the conversion of more private colleges into the government colleges, with the result that Lamka College in the Churachandpur district (hills) and 5 other colleges (Ideal Girls' College, Maharaja Bodhachandra College, N.G. College, Lilong Haoreibi College and Y.K. College) from different areas in the valley were converted into government colleges in the year 1979-80. In 1980-81, Tadubi College was also converted into a government college. Thus, by 1980-81 the number of government colleges increased to 24 in Manipur. The growth of degree colleges was very fast during 1970-71 to 1975-76, after which the growth trend became slightly slow. However, the growth of colleges multiplied by 1995-96 where the total number reached 59 which was only 29 in 1990-91. In the same year, the number of girls' college also jumped to 7. The total number of colleges again increased to 64 of which 7 were girls college in 1996-97. The number of colleges maintained by either government or private bodies in the hill areas is very few compared to those in the valley. Now the Imphal East and West districts have 37 colleges including 17 affiliated private & 2 junior colleges. Thoubal and Bishnupur districts both have 8 colleges including 5 private colleges each. Among the hill districts, Churachandpur District has the highest number of colleges (6 including a junior college) This is followed by Senapati District with a total of 5 colleges of which 2 are Government, another 1 is Affiliated Private college and the remaining 2 being junior college. Chandel district has got three colleges including a Government College at Chandel while Tamenglong and Ukhrul districts have one Government College each.

Inspite of these developments, there are various problems which college education have been facing constantly. The colleges of Manipur have uneven physical, financial and faculty support. Only three colleges are known to have staff quarters and hostel facilities for students. The aided and private colleges have very poor facilities - physical as well as academic. Since most of the colleges in Manipur started as private institutions, their buildings were constructed by the governing bodies concerned according to their own resources. All the colleges in the state, except the colleges established by the government, were funded by the voluntary organisations. The buildings were constructed without proper planning and to meet the requirements at the initial stage only. Like schools, colleges have their own unique problems. There are two types of colleges - the private and aided and government colleges. To the aided colleges 99% non-recurring grant was given. The library and laboratory facilities in the private colleges are not modern and well organised, which lack adequate land and scope for curricular activities. This always results in poor performance of their students in the public examinations.

Another specific problem is about the courses of study. The present curriculum has not relevance with the vocational opportunities as well as day-to-day problems of the society. In this connection, N.C.E.R.T. Survey Report (1972) says,"Courses of study at various levels of the schools and colleges are far from satisfactory. Examinations need reforms on account of constant copying which invigilators fail to check on account of safety of their lives".

Trend in Enrolment

Taking into consideration the enrolment in Arts and Science colleges of Manipur it may be observed that during the period 1947-48 to 1995-96 the growth was about 776 times. This may be due to the fact that as the population increased the percentage of this age group also increased. Table 4.2 gives a picture of the number of students at the college level in Manipur during 1947-48 to 1995-96.

Table 4.2
Students Enrolled in Colleges of Manipur

Year	Boys		Girls		Total	
	Nos.	In % of total	Nos.	In % of total	Nos.	Growth in % of perceding year.
1947-48	N.A.	-	N.A.	-	60	-
1950-51	341	97.99	7	2.01	348	480
1955-56	1,119	93.72	75	6.28	1,194	243.10
1960-61	1,771	87.93	243	12.07	2,014	68.68
1965-66	4,710	81.25	1,087	18.75	5,797	87.84
1970-71	7,767	76.51	2,385	23.49	10,152	75.13
1975-76	11,293	67.98	5,311	32.02	16,584	63.36
1980-81	12,847	62.49	7,712	37.51	20,559	23.97
1985-86	11,816	60.55	9,651	39.44	24,467	19.01
1990-91	22,427	57.47	16,597	42.53	39,024	59.50
1995-96	-	-	-	-	34,568	-11.42
1996-97	-	-	-	-	27,988	-19.03

Sources : 1. Th. Mangoljao Singh, *Western Education in Manipur,* Vol. I & II, 1989.
2. Statistical Handbook of Manipur, 1992.
3. College Statistics, 1995-96 & 1996-97, College Development Council, M.U.

From the above table it is observed that the total increase of enrolment during the period (1947-48 to 1995-96) has been about 576 times. From the data it also appears that there was a sudden increase of enrolment since 1955-56 and the rate of growth was found steady. But for girls, the enrolment increased suddenly in 1965-66. The students passing matriculation examination during these years were few. So the pass percentage at this state was 30-35 during the period from 1970-71 to 1980-81. Once the Board of Secondary Education was established, the pass percentage increased a little. It is because of these reasons that the enrolment in the colleges was found very steady. It is difficult for the colleges to accommodate all who aspire for higher studies. From 1955-56 to 1960-61, there was gradual increase in enrolment. But in 1965 there was a sudden increase in enrolment. In 1960-61 the number of enrolment was 2,014 but in 1965-66, it rose upto 5,797 and during this period boys' enrolment rose from 1,771 to 4,710 and girls enrolment from 243 to 1037. The increase was more than four times. After 1965-66 both boys and girls enrolment increased rapidly. The reason may be that the state government made consistent efforts for the expansion of women's education so that the imbalance between boys and girls education can be eliminated as early as possible. Although efforts have been made with tremendous enthusiam to uplift the women's education, there are many obstacles in different forms. After 1965-66 the rate of growth was found steady but the enrolment showed the peak in 1990-91. When the total enrolment reached 39,024. During this period boy's enrolment was 22,427 and girls' enrolment was 16,597. On the whole, there has been continuous development of college education in general since 1965-66. However, the size of enrolment shows a sharp decline during the year 1995-96. In this year the total number of enrolment was 34,568. There has thus been a steady increase during the past 42 years except 1995-96. There has been continuous growth in enrolment during the last four decades mainly due to the increase in number of students passing the matriculation examination. The number of students qualifying in the matriculation examination would increase gradually if the pass percentage remained substantially the same.

Growth of Teachers in Colleges

Table 4.3 shows the growth of teachers serving in colleges during the period from 1947-48 to 1996-97. (Fig. 4.1).

There were only 7 college teachers in the year 1946-47, all of them being male teachers. Even during 1955-56, there were no female teachers in the colleges whereas 39 male teachers were

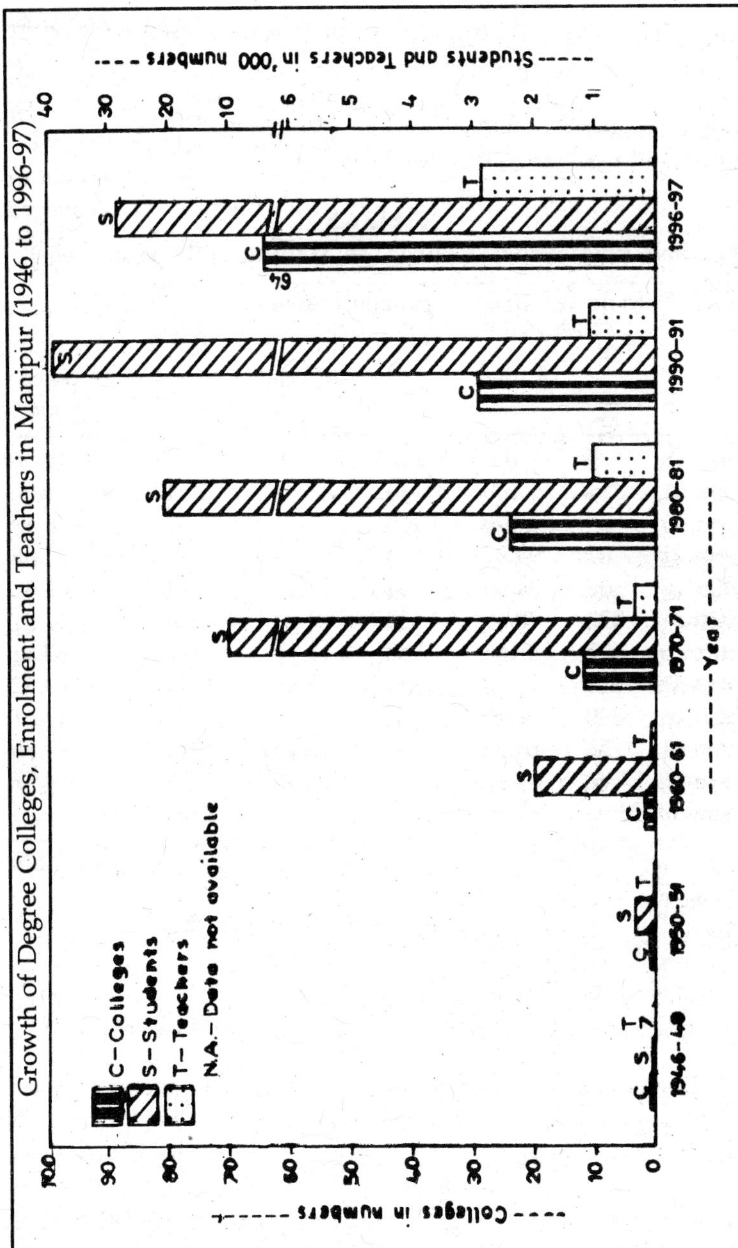

Growth of Degree Colleges, Enrolment and Teachers in Manipur (1946 to 1996-97)

Fig. 4.1

employed. From 1946 to 1960-61, there was gradual increase in the number of teachers appointed in colleges. But in 1965-66 there was sudden increase in the employment of teachers and by this time the number of female teachers also reached 14 and the total number of teachers in this year was 274.

Table 4.3
Teachers Employed in Colleges in Manipur 1947-48 to 1996-97

Year	Male Teachers		Female Teachers		Total	
	No.	In % of total	No.	In % of total	No.	Growth in % of perce-ding year.
1947-48	7	100	Nil	-	7	-
1950-51	14	100	Nil	-	14	100
1955-56	39	100	Nil	-	39	178.57
1960-61	67	94.37	4	5.63	71	82.05
1965-66	260	94.89	14	5.11	274	285.92
1970-71	333	90.49	35	9.51	368	34.31
1975-76	527	85.69	88	14.31	615	67.12
1980-81	811	77.61	234	22.39	1045	69.92
1985-86	890	72.42	339	27.58	1229	17.61
1990-91	753	69.53	330	30.47	1083	-11.88
1995-96	1776*	64.60	976*	35.40	2757	54.57
1996-97	N.A.	-	N.A.	-	2838	-

*Excludes the teachers of Govt. Polytechnics since the data are not availbale.

Source : 1. Th. Mangoljao Singh, *Western Education in Manipur*, Vol. I & II, 1989.

2. Statistical Handbook of Manipur, 1992.

3. College Statistics, 1995-96, College Development Council, M.U.

From 1965-66 to 1985-86 there was a gradual increase in the employment of both male and female teachers. But for females the number was quite low and it was one fourth of their male counterparts. However, total number of teachers employed it colleges was reduced from 1229 in 1985-86 to only 1088 in 1990-91 bringing 11.88 negative growth. But in 1995-96 total teacher employed in college have increased by more than two and a half times (2757) of which female teachers account for about 35.40%

(976). There was a late start as well as a very slow growth in the women's education. Only from 1960's women have been in the forefront of higher education in Manipur. The number of girl students during 1951, 1961, 1971, 1981 and 1991 were 7, 243, 2385, 7712 and 16,597 respectively, and the number of female teachers was 4 in 1961, 35 in 1971, 234 in 1981 and 339 in 1991. The figures corresponding to the above mentioned years for boys were 341, 1771, 7767, 12847 and 22427 while the number of male teachers were 14, 67, 333, 811 and 753 respectively.

From the above table it is clear that the girls education is not upto the level it should be. Till 1956, there were not even a single female teacher in colleges of Manipur. During the period of about 50 years the ratio of female teachers and students are found much lower than their male counterparts. Therefore every possible efforts to promote the collegiate education among the girls are still required to uplift the rate of enrolment of girl students in the colleges.

From tables 4.2 and 4.3 it is evident that the state has maintained stability of teacher-student ratio during the phase of phenomenal increase in enrolment. Data shows that in 1990-91 the teacher-pupil ratio in the colleges was 36 students per teacher, which was just double of the teacher student ratio in Indian Universities of 1:17.

As shown in table 4.4, the district-wise distribution of colleges is highly uneven and larger concentration are found in plain areas. The valley districts of Imphal West and Imphal East (including Jiribam), Thoubal and Bishnupur contains more than 78% of the total colleges of the state in 1996-97. Of them, Imphal-West district alone has 24 colleges (including/junior college) out of the total 69 colleges and accounts for over one-third of the total. Imphal East district (including Jiribam) with 13 colleges (including one junior college) ranks second and shares about one-sixth of the total colleges. Though, Churachandpur, Senapati and Chandel districts have a good number of colleges i.e. 6 (8.70%), 5 (7.25%) and 3 (4.35%) respectively, other hilly districts Ukhrul and Tamenglong have single college each. (Fig. 4.2)

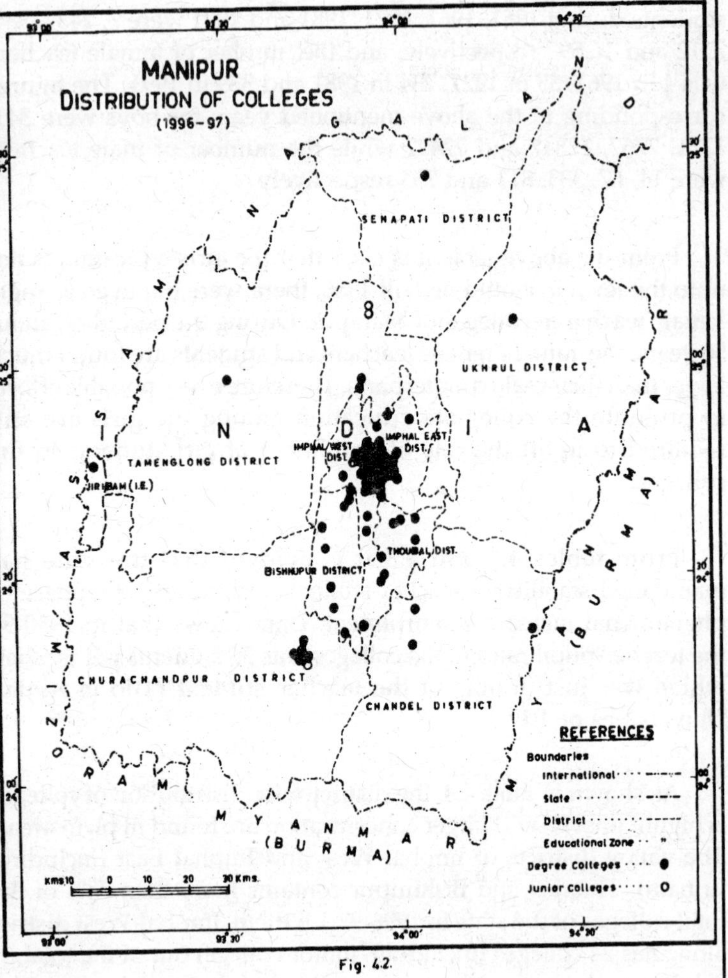
MANIPUR
DISTRIBUTION OF COLLEGES
(1996-97)
NAGALAND
SENAPATI DISTRICT
UKHRUL DISTRICT
TAMENGLONG DISTRICT
JIRIBAM (I.E.)
IMPHAL WEST DIST.
IMPHAL EAST DIST.
THOUBAL DIST.
BISHNUPUR DISTRICT
CHURACHANDPUR DISTRICT
CHANDEL DISTRICT
INDIA
ASSAM
MIZORAM
MYANMAR (BURMA)
REFERENCES
Boundaries
International
State
District
Educational Zone
Degree Colleges
Junior Colleges
Kms 10 0 10 20 30 Kms.
93°00′
93°30′
94°00′
94°30′
25°30′
25°00′
24°30′
24°00′

Fig. 4.2.

Fig. 4.2

The college Development Council also plays an active role in monitoring the implementation of National Education Policy in colleges. It has already iniated the delinking of Pre-university classes from the degree colleges. Consequently, Post Graduate Classes have been opened in D. M. College of Science since 1995-96 in the following subjects :

1. Life Sciences
2. Mathematics and
3. Anthropology

The University Grants Commission has invited proposals from the colleges included under section 2 (1) of the U.G.C. Act for introduction of vocational subjects at the first degree level. The proposals have been invited from the eligible colleges by the university. As a consequence, the following 17 colleges have already introduced vocational subjects since 1996-97.

Sl. No.	Name of the College	Vocational Subjects opened
1.	Kakching Khunou College	Industrial Fish and Fisheries
2.	Thoubal College	"
3.	Oriental College	"
4.	Thambal Marik College	"
5.	Imphal College	Still photography
6.	N. G. College	Tax Procedure
7.	D. M. College of Science	Biological Technique and specimen preservation.
8.	D. M. College of Arts	Functional English
9.	Manipur College	Tourism & Travel management
10.	Moirang College	"
11.	Kha Manipur College	Sericulture
12.	United College	"
13.	Biramangol College	"
14.	Presidency College	"
15.	Modern College	Seed Technology
16.	G. P. Womens' College	Food Science and quality control
17.	Lamka College	Office Management and Secretarial practice.

Colleges Proposed to Provide Vocational Subjects

Sl. No.	Name of the College	Subjects proposed to be introduce
1.	Idial Girl's College	Tourism and Travel management
2.	Nambol L. Sanoi College	Industrial Fish and Fisheries
3.	C. I. College	Sericulture
4.	Pettigrew College	Domestic Animal Farming
5.	S. Kula Womens' College	Food Science and quality control
6.	Mangolngambi College	Industrial Fish and Fisheries
7.	Mangai Lambi College	Science and Art of teaching
8.	D. M. College of Commerce	Office Management and Secretarial practice.

Table 4.4
Distribution of Degree and Junior Colleges (General Education) in Manipur - 1996-97

District	Total Secondary Schools			In % of total (Junior & Degree Colleges)
	Junior Colleges	Degree Colleges	Total	
Imphal West	1	23	24	34.78
Imphal East	1	12	13	17.84
(Jiribam)	-	(1)	(1)	(1.45)
Thoubal Dist.	-	9	9	13.04
Bishnupur Dist.	-	8	8	11.59
Ukhrul Dist.	-	1	1	1.45
Senapati (S. Dist.)	-	1	1	1.45
Kangpokpi (S. Dist.)	2	2	4	5.80
Tamenglong Dist.	-	1	1	1.45
C. Chandpur	1	5	6	8.70
Chandel	-	2	2	2.90
Manipur	5	64	69	100

Sources : 1. College Statistics, College Development Council, M.U.
2. Council of Higher Secondary Education, Manipur.

University Education

During the later part of the sixties, with the increasing number of colleges and students desiring for prosecuting higher studies in Manipur, the need for a separate university in this region was strongly felt by the people of Manipur who have a rich and distinctive cultural traditions. A general consciousness amongst the people arose to get a university of their own so that facilities for extensive research and higher studies are easily made available to the growing number of young scholars. The main objectives of setting up the university were to meet the individual needs of the students and the people, particularly in relation to culture, language and literature. Considering the views of Radhakrishnan, "In India our unity lies in the diversity of culture", Manipur with its unique cultural heritage can make substantial contributions towards the unification and richness of Indian national life. These objectives could be carried out successfully through research and studies in the university or institution of higher studies."[6] So in Manipur there was a strong desire of the people to have a university. Nagar (1978) also strongly emphasised the need of a separate university for Manipur to provide facilities for prosecution of advanced study and research.

It may be mentioned here that a university in Manipur will not only create adequate facilities of advanced studies for the students of Manipur and adjoining areas but will also help satisfactorily to solve the peculiar problems which have a direct relevance to Manipur and its students. Since most of the universities including the universities in Assam have switched over to the regional media, Manipuri students found it difficult to attend classes in these universities. The need of the establishment of a university as such, was very acute to educate the people of the state, who s' ongly advocated the establishment of a university. They further strengthened their demand with the justification that on cultural, historical, geographical, sociological and ethnological grounds Manipur has a different but rich entity and therefore Manipur must have a university of her own to look after her own developments in all these aspects.

It was felt that a separate University would serve and be more solicitous of the welfare of the people of Manipur and that it would provide better opportunities in services, better educational facilities and chances for all round development of their personality. There had been a very remarkable awakening in Manipur and a strong belief had grown up among the Manipuris that Manipur would never develop until and unless there was a separate university.

A Brief History of the Development of Manipur University

Manipur made a tremendous progress in the field of education after the second world war and the institutions for higher education in Manipur grew around the middle of the twentieth century. It was in 1946 that the first college was established in Manipur. Many undergraduate colleges of general education were established in the following years under Gauhati University. In those days, any student of Manipur after graduation had to go outside the state for the post-graduate studies. Several demands for establishment of a university in Manipur had been made since the year 1959. Although the Wadia Committee in 1964 recommended the location of the North Eastern Hill University at Imphal with D.M. College, the biggest and the most well established college in the state as its base. The government of Manipur started a post-graduate centre in the D.M. College. This could not satisfy the desire of the people of the state. So the Government of Manipur, made a proposal to the University Grants Commission to establish a university centre for post-graduate studies at Imphal as an extension of Gauhati University to which all the colleges in Manipur were affiliated. The University Grants Commission appointed a seven members Committee under the chairmanship of Prof. M.V. Mathur, Director, Asian Institute of Educational Planning and Administration, New Delhi to look into the matter. The Committee visited Imphal in April 1969 to make an assessment of the requirements for the establishment of a university. The Committee observed the vast expansion of higher education in the state during the past two decades and remarked that "it would be beneficial not only in this region but to the country as a whole if facilities for higher education are developed in a planned way according to the needs of the people of this area".[7]

After a thorough examination of the resources available in Manipur, they recommended a scheme of developing the departments in D.M. College in a planned manner to enable them to impart effective education at the post-graduate level by engaging qualified teachers available in other private colleges on part time basis. They also recommended for the establishment of a university centre as stop gap arrangement. Both the people of Manipur and the the State Government persisted in demanding a full-fledged university in this state. However, in partial fulfilment of such a demand, the Jawaharlal Nehru University, New Delhi agreed to open a special centre of post-graduate studies at Imphal. The Jawaharlal Nehru University established the centre of post-graduate studies at Imphal in 1971 at the instance of the Government of India.[8]

The Jawaharlal Nehru University Centre was a stepping stone towards the objective of establishing a university in Manipur. The J.N.U. Centre was created with twin objectives of providing facilities for higher education and creating the necessary nucleus for a future university in Manipur.

This Centre was established in 1971 at the Youth Hostel in the D.M. College campus with Prof. Asim Kumar Dutta from the Jadavpur University, Calcutta as the Director of the Centre. The Centre started the post-graduate programmes on the 24th September 1972. It was later on shifted to the present site of the Manipur University in the premises of the then Basic Training Institute at Canchipur. The Government of Manipur offered an area of 317.31 acres for the post-graduate centre. It is situated at the foot of the Langthabal hill. The campus is to the south of Imphal city and on the western side of the National Highway 39.

On the establishment of the Centre, all the four Post-Graduate Departments of D.M. College viz., English, History, Mathematics and Economics were taken over by the Centre. In addition, M.A. courses in Political Science and Manipuri Language and Literature and M.Sc. courses in Applied Biology were introduced.

During the time of the establishment of the Centre, there were 37 teachers in the 7 Divisions. Only a small number of teachers have been recruited through prescribed procedure, while the rest were either on deputation or on contract for a limited period or on a part time basis. Out of 37 teachers 13 were on deputation, 8 were on contract and 4 were on part time basis and only 10 were regular appointees.

The first batch of M.A., M.Sc., students (Mathematics, Economics, Political Science, Manipuri and Applied Biology) came out in 1974.

By the end of the 5th Five Year Plan, the Post-Graduate Centre had 10 (ten) departments (divisions) namely Physics, Chemistry, Mathematics, Life Sciences (originally Applied Biology), Economics, Political Science, History, English Language and Literature, Manipuri Language and Literature and Hindi. The divisions may be grouped into different Schools, *i.e.* School of Language (English, Hindi, Manipuri), School of Social Sciences (Economics, History and Political Science). School of Sciences (Mathematics, Chemistry, Physics and Life Sciences). While the last eight divisions were accommodated in the B.T.I. campus site, separate blocks for Physics Division and Chemistry Division as they are standing at present were erected during that plan period. Moreover construction of the block of Language Laboratory was finished and there was extension for library rooms. Over and above, the construction of a few teachers quarters was started during that plan period. Construction of a hostel for boys was also started during that plan period although it was completed in the early part of the 6th Plan. U.G.C. approved 75 posts of faculty positions during the 5th Plan. The Directors of that P.G. Centre were Prof. Asim Kumar Dutta (1971-72), Dr. D. Shrinivasachari (1973), Prof. C.N. Chakravarti (1973-74), Dr. H.L. Sarkar (from Nov., 1974) and Shri H. Ranbir Singh (IAS Retd.).

The Gauhati University could not conduct its various examinations owing to wide-spread agitations during 1980-81. This acute situation led the Government of Manipur to decide the matter of establishing a separate university of Manipur to save the academic lives of several thousand students in the undergraduate colleges of Manipur from the state of academic deadlock under Gauhati University to which all the colleges including technical colleges were affiliated. The Manipur State Legislative Assembly passed a Bill towards the establishment of a University named the Manipur University which subsequently became an Act called the Manipur University Act 1980 (the Manipur Act No. 8 of 1980). This Act came into force on the 5th June, 1980 which date has since then been observed by the Manipur University as its Foundation Day. With the establishment of Manipur University, the aspirations of the people of Manipur to have a place of higher learning and research have been fulfilled. Shri H. Ranbir Singh (IAS Retd.), the then Director of the P.G. Centre at Canchipur was appointed Acting Vice-Chancellor of the newly established University. He took over the office of the Vice-Chancellor w.e.f the 20th June, 1980 in addition to his normal management duties as the Director of the P.G, Centre. Several Ordinances and Regulations were passed under the Manipur University Act, especially to affiliate all the existing colleges (including professional colleges) and conduct all the examinations of different courses of studies.

In the introduction of Manipur University Act, aims and objectives of university has been described as follows : "To foster the composite culture of India and establish such departments and institutions as may be required for the study and development of language, Art and Culture of India and in particular those of the north eastern region".[9]

In its short life the university has been able to carry this message to a great extent. Though the university has faced with some serious problems, it is expected that the University will be able to promote higher education further and at the same time will play a vital role in preserving and promoting traditional culture. It is also expected that the university will play its role in rapid development of the state and it is hoped that with the promotion of higher education, the university will continue the process of cultural development of Manipur also.

Prof. T. Ratho took over the charge of the first Vice-Chancellor of the University on the 1st December, 1980. The Jawaharlal Nehru, Centre of Post-Graduate Studies was formally transferred to the Manipur University on the 1st April, 1981. Thus, the provisions of the Manipur University Act, 1980 in respect of Post-Graduate education and research came into force with effect from that date.[10]

With the transfer of the Jawaharlal Nehru University, Centre of Post-Graduate Studies, assets in the shape of buildings, equipments, chemicals, vehicles, furniture etc. worth about Rs. 75 lakhs became the assets of the Manipur University. The number of teaching staff and non-teaching staff that was transferred to the

Manipur University were 69 and 77 respectively. All the assets of the Jawaharlal Nehru University Centre were entirely passed on to the newly established Manipur University.

Students Admitted to Post-Graduate Classes

The strength of the students admitted to the post-graduate classes of the University was almost double the strength admitted to the erstwhile Jawaharlal Nehru University Centre of Post-Graduate classes. In the interest of the people of the state and on the abolition of semester system of the Jawaharlal Nehru University Centre, the University decided to increase the number of seats. Selection of students has, however, been made on merit shown by the candidate in an admission test and in their degree examination.

Research Facilities

With the establishment of the Manipur University in 1980-81, as financed by the University Grants Commission, ICAR and CSIR, there have been many research scholars working in different departments of the University. The State Government also finances many junior reserach fellowships in various departments.

With the establishment of a University in Manipur, a new era has heralded in the history of higher education. The long cherished desire of the people to have their own University at Imphal has been fulfilled.

The Academic and Physical Development of Manipur University : The Present Scenario.

Though Manipur University was established very late in the year 1980, the progress and development in every sphere has been very fast and a new era heralded in the history of higher education in Manipur. AT the time of its establishment, there were only 10 departments *viz.*, Chemistry Economics, English, Hindi, History, Life Sciences, Manipuri, Mathematics, Physics and Political Science. These departments were taken over from J. N. U. centre of Post Graduate Students when it was observed in Manipur University. In the first batch of the M.A./M.Sc. programme (1981-82), 435 students were enrolled. The total strength of faculty members at that time was only 70 including three lady teachers. Eleven research scholars were registered for Ph. D. programmes during

1981-82 in different departments. About 23 different subjects were introduced at the University level which were categorised into two different schools i.e., (i) School of Arts and Commerce and (ii) School of Sciences.

The subjects under the schools of Arts and Commerce included English, Manipuri, Hindi, other Indian languages, Philosophy, Economics, History, Political Science, Education, Commerce and Law. On the other hand, Mathematics, statistics, Physics, Chemistry, Botany, Zoology, Anthropology, Geography, Geology, Home Science, Economic Science and Agriculture were classed under the school of Sciences. During 1980-81, the University receives Rs. 2,185,000 as grants from the state Government.

With the opening of four more departments *viz.*, Anthropology, Statistics, Earth Sciences and Commerce in 1984-85 the total number of departments have increased to 14. Since then the University also started teaching programmes in the following diploma courses - Banking, Business management, Educational Administration, Labour laws, Spoken English, Biological Techniques, Computer programming, Electronics, Library Science, Fisheries, Diploma in certain foreign languages etc. In 1985-86, the number of students enrolled increased to 1065 whereas, the number of faculty members increased to 127., Later on, the University started post-graduate departments of Bio-chemistry, Computer Science, Education, Philosophy and Statistics in 1988 and created two new departments of Geography and Linguistics by bifurcating the existing departments of Earth Sciences and Manipuri. The Library and Information Sciences department was created subsequently.

As a centre for the study of Manipuri language, literature and culture, the centre for Manipuri studies started functioning from the middle of 1988. In the following year (1989), the centre for Tribal studies was established on the recommendation of the visiting team of the University Grants Commission with the objective of promoting study and research in history, culture, language and literature of the North-Eastern India, specially of the tribals.

Though Manipuri Studies and Tribal Studies have centralised facilities, they were functioning independently in academic matters.

The Audio-visual Research centre (AVRC) was also established within the University campus in 1989 and Manipur University is perhaps the only University in the North-East having this facility. Since its establishment, the AVRC has produced a good number of films on arts, culture, tradition, environment, flora and fauna and other topics of academic interest in the state. The AVRC periodically telecasts those films in UGC programmes on Doordarshan.

On the another hand, Indira Gandhi National Open University (IGNOU), Imphal centre has been serving the people of Manipur since 1987 with the main aim of providing access to higher education to a large segment of population, specially to the disadvantaged groups. The centre also provides first hand information to the people of remote rural areas. The study centre at Imphal offers twenty different courses of Studies and by 1997, 183 students were enrolled for various programmes of higher studies.

At present, Manipur University provides Post-Graduate teaching and Research in the following subjects under three schools of studies (Table 4.5)

Table 4.5
Subjects at the Post-Graduate Level, Manipur University, 1998-99

Schools of Humanities	Schools of Social Sciences	School of Science
1. English	1. Commerce	1. Anthropolgy
2. Hindi	2. Economics	2. Biochemistry
3. Linguistic	3. Education	3. Chemistry
4. Manipuri	4. History	4. Computer Science
5. Philosophy	5. Library and Information Sciences	5. Earth Science (Geology)
		6. Geography
		7. Life Sciences
	6. Political Science	8. Mathematics
	7. Management studies	9. Physics
		10. Statistics

Table 4.6 portrays a picture of the enrolment of post-graduate students and research scholars in the University besides number

of its faculty members from 1980-81 to 1996-97.

Table 4.6
Growth Profile of Manipur University 1980-81 to 1996-97.

Year	Students			Research Scholars	Faculty Members
	Boys	Girls	Total		
1980-81	-	-	435	11	70
1985-86	660	405	1065	N.A.	N.A.
1990-91	716	585	1301	-	230
1995-96	913	656	1569	62	187
1996-97	870	649	1599	79	187

Source : Manipur University, Annual Report, 1981-82, 1985-86, 1990-91, 1995-96 & 1996-97.

The strength of P. G. Students have increased from 435 in 1980-81 to as much as 1599 in 1997 including 649 girl/women students that shows 40.59% of the total students. Thus a three and a half fold in the enrolment of students in seen during a period of 17 years. The scope of research programmes is also expanding to a great extent by registering almost 79 research scholars under this University in 1996-97 where the number of research scholars was only 11 in 1980-81. Moreover, the number of faculty members also have increased from only 70 in 1980-81 to 187 in 1996-97 and were actively engaged in teaching and research. So far, 1182 students have been registered for Ph. D. degree programmes till date.

The library of this University is fast developing and has a total collection of 93, 992 books on various subjects, Magazines, journals, periodicals, news papers etc. which was 22,582 in 1980. Now, the University library has become one of the 10 selected University libraries in the whole country with internet facility. The library has three main sections : Stacks for reference books, Journal section and reading room. Besides, there are many sub-section like binding and documentation section, text-book section, computer room etc. Moreover, photostate facility is also available within the building at reasonable charges. Manipur Institute of Management Studies (MIMS), sponsored by the central Government within the University campus is the latest addition to Manipur University and is one of the few institutions established for far across the country.

Now, the state has got a second University-Central Agricultural University situated at Iroisemba (on the Western outskirts of Imphal City). This is perhaps the first centrally sponsored Agricultural University in the country and has campus in every state headquarters in the North-Eastern Region, except Assam and in Sikkim.

References :

1. *Statistical Accounts of Colleges under Manipur University:* Manipur University (1987), p.1.

2. **Th. Mangoljao Singh** : *Western Education in Manipur.,* Vol. III (1986), p.43.

3. *Statistical Handbook of Manipur :* Directorate of Economics and Statistics, Government of Manipur, Imphal (1983), p.30.

4. **Kishun Singh** : *A New Approach to the History and Problems of Indian Education* (1982), pp. 177-178.

5. **N.C.E.R.T.** *Survey Report :* (1972-73), p. 67.

6. **R.S. Nagar** : *Development of Education in Manipur from 1891 to 1971,* unpublished Ph.D. Thesis, Gauhati University (1978), p. 130.

7. *Mathur Committee Report* (1969).

8. *University Grants Commission,* Letter No. FS-27/74 (D5a), dated 16th December 1975. Addressed to the Registrar, J. N. University, New Delhi.

9. *Manipur University Act 1980* (No. 8 of 1980), p.13.

10. *Manipur University Annual Report* (1980-81), pp. 6-7.

5

Professional and Technical Education

There was no professional college or any institution of technical education in Manipur prior to 1947. Neither the rulers nor the British Political officers posted at Manipur ever felt the need of such institutions. But it does not mean that there were no arrangements for imparting any sort of professional and technical education in Manipur. Later on due to the growing political consciouness particularly, when India achieved her independence and when Manipur also got her share in it, the people felt the necessity of technical training. Then the administrators realised the need of opening institutions of technical and professional education in this state. Hence, efforts were made in this direction after 1947. Consequently, technical education had a late start in Manipur.

With greater emphasis on vocational and technical education, the state initiated establishment of a network of technical institutions offering a variety of programmes or meeting the technical manpower requirements at the level of skilled workers, technicians, professional teachers, doctors, nurses, engineers and technologists.

Subsequently, institutions providing agricultural, legal, medical and nursing, teacher's training, music and art, and technical and engineering education were established in the state, which impart technical and professional training to the younger generation to a large extent.

Agricultural Education

It was felt that in order to meet the needs of increasing human and animal population, Manipur must achieve self-sufficiency in food, feed, fibre and other agricultural products. To cater the needs of Manipur and its neighbouring states for imparting training in agriculture and horticulture upto graduate level, Manipur Agricultural College was established on 20th September 1979 at Iroisemba situated at the western outskirt of Imphal. At first this college was affiliated temporarily to Gauhati University, then later on to Manipur University since 1980 (upto B.Sc. Agriculture level) The main aim and objective of this college were to impart agricultural training, to encourage agricultural research and to provide for extension education.

Our country is at present in the frontline in many fields of development. The most essential and prime object of our country is to increase agricultural production more and more by employing modern agricultural technology. Manipur Agricultural College, played a vital role in imparting youths of the North Eastern India knowledge about new findings through its very many extension programme.

The courses of study followed at the college lead to the Bachelor's Degree in Agricultural Sciences which is a 4 year programme after the completion of a twelve year school education with Science stream. The annual intake capacity of the college is 40 students only. Out of this, 10 students belong to Manipur and 30 students are the nominees of other states like Arunachal Pradesh (6), Meghalaya (8), Mizoram (3), Sikkim (3) and Tripura (10) subject to their being sponsored by their respective governments for admission. The minimum admission requirement is that a candidate must have passed P. U. Science on 12 year Higher Secondary or equivalent examination in Biological group with minimum 45% of marks in the aggregate. English is the medium of instruction and system of examination is based on the semester system which is followed by the internal assessment in the college.

Since 1990, the college started M. Sc. courses in four subjects - Agronomy, Horticulture, Plant Breeding and Genetics and Plant pathology with an intake of three students in each discipline.

There are two Boys' Hostels and one well protected Girls'

Hostel. The library facilities for laboratory and farm are provided. Extensive development in respect of crop fields and horticultural orchard have been made. In addition to teaching, research and extension education programme, the college is also taking up Lab-to-land programme in collaboration with ICAR. Some projects also are being carried on in collaboration with Manipur University and Government of India. After its take over by the Central Agriculture University in 1992, the college has taken the new nomenclature - college of Agriculture.

Legal Education

Some pioneer gentlemen in Manipur mooted the idea of establishing a Law College and a public meeting was called in 1953 to form a governing body-cum-foundation committee consisting of elected members namely L.M. Ibungohal Singh, Kh. Dhanachandra Singh, Lalita Madhav Sharma, Gourahari Singh. Two other members, Ihobi Singh and Ph. Behari Sharma were co-opted later.

With great enthusiasm and untiring efforts of this body, the Manipur Law College as a private legal institution was started with first year law class and its foundation was laid on Thursday, August 7, 1958.

In Manipur Law College, the first year law class was conducted in the school building of the Ramlal Paul High School, Imphal with the permission of the school authorities. The College was renamed as the 'Lairen Mayum Seibyasachi Law College' (L.M.S. Law College) from July 31, 1963 in the name of the late mother of L.M. Ibungohal Singh who donated a sum of Rs. 15,000 (Rupees Fifteen thousand) for the College fund.[1]

With the untiring efforts of the governing body of the College and from the public help and substantial sacrifice of the-then-teaching and non-teaching staff members, the L.M.S. Law College could improve its premises and land and construct the college building.

The L.M.S. Law College was affiliated first to Gauhati University, but since 1980, it has been permanently affiliated to Manipur University (upto L.L.B. level)[2]. Recently it has started L.L.M. classes also.

The college give instructions through English medium for the three years L.L.B. (professional) degree course and follows the annual examination system conducted by Manipur University at the end of every year of the 3-year course. Courses of studies may be summed up as follows :- In the first year, the following subjects are taught - Land Laws, Family Laws, Legal Theory, Constitutional Law of India. In the second year, Contract and Tort, Labour Law, Property Law, Private International Law and maxims of equity are included in the curriculum. In third year, Evidence Act, Civil Procedure, Arbitration and Limitation, Administrative Law and Indian Legal and Constitutional History, Drafting and Pleading and Law of Taxation, Crime and Procedure are included.

The college continued to function with financial assistance received by public donation till it was taken over by the government in the year 1981.

The following table gives a picture of the number of students in the L.M.S. Law College during the period 1965-96.

Table 5.1
Enrolment of Students in Law College, 1965-66 to 1995-96

Year		Number of students
1965-66	-	203
1970-71	-	717
1985-86	-	612
1990-91	-	682
1992-93	-	1220
1994-95	-	1341
1995-96	-	1063

Source : L. M. S. Law College, Imphal.

Another Law College - L.M.G. Memorial Law College was established at Churachandpur in 1982. In 1995-96, it had 17 teachers and 436 students.

MEDICAL EDUCATION

Regional Institute of Medical Sciences

Regional Medical College, Imphal was started in 1972 to meet the ever increasing need of medical education in Manipur as well as the neighbouring states of Arunachal Pradesh, Meghalaya, Mizoram, Nagaland and Tripura. This College is affiliated to Manipur University since 1980 (upto M.B.B.S. level).[3]

The Regional Medical College, which was established in 1972 as a joint venture of the Centre and the North-Eastern states (through North-Eastern Council) had an intake capacity of 75 students with an attached hospital of 275 beds, which now has been increased to 85 students and 881 beds.

Over and above the course of M.B.B.S., this College had courses of laboratory technicians training and X-Ray Technician course for one year and a two year opthalmic assistant course.

At first this institution was maintained by the Government of Manipur. Since 1976, this institution was under the care of the North-Eastern Regional Medical College Society. Since April 1995, the College has become the Regional Institute of Medical Sciences (RIMS).

The RIMS Hospital is the main teaching hospital. Now, this Institute has earned a name and good reputation not only as a centre of medical education but also as a centre of treatment of many diseases. The Institute building is contiguous with the associated group of hospitals where the clinical departments of Medicine, Surgery, Pathology, Anatomy, Physiology, Gynaecology, Pharmacology, Bio-Chemistry, Micro-Biology, Forensic Medicine, Pediatrics, Opthamology etc. are fully equipped and allied specialists are placed. The North Eastern Council has also adopted a number of schemes for the development of the region. The Council offers considerable financial assistance towards the expansion of the RIMS.

Since 1972, the Institute has produced 1418 medical doctors and 96 post-graduate doctors. It is well equipped for undergraduate and Post-graduate medical education. The Institute also runs Diploma courses in clinical pathology and anaesthesiology.

In the beginning, i.e. in the year 1972, there were 38 teachers only, but by 1980 the number of teachers rose upto 133 and presently the Institute has 197 teachers.

The RIMS has planned to start Dental and Nursing Colleges in the Ninth Five Year Plan besides a training centre in forensic medicine.

Nursing School, Imphal

The need of trained and qualified nursing staff was keenly felt by the people as well as by the Government of Manipur. With intention to provide efficient and qualified nurses to the hospitals, a School of Nursing was established at Imphal in 1970 by the Government of Manipur. The minimum qualification of admission to the General Nursing course is the certificate of P.U. Science or its equivalent. The duration of course of Nursing is three and half years.

In the first year (1970) only 25 candidates got admission but from the next year the enrolment of students was increased to 30. The first batch of the Nursing course passed out in 1974. In the beginning the school was run by 2 tutors only with some part time teaching doctors. But in 1980, the number of tutors rose to 9 and many other part time teaching doctors were also engaged for the smooth running of the school. During the period from 1970 to 1980 this school had trained 222 nurses.

The subjects in the curriculum of the nursing course include Anatomy and Physiology, Physics and Chemistry, Micro-Biology, Pharmacology, Nutrition, Psychology , Medical and Surgical Nursing, Psychiatric Nursing, Community Nursing, Emergency Nursing, Community Organisation, training in Nursing, Midwifery etc.

In 1978 another course known as Auxiliary Nursing and Midwifery was introduced in the Nursing School. It is one and half year course and only the students after passing Class VIII are allowed admission to this course. After two and half years in the year 1981, this course was amalgamated with the Female Health Workers course.

Teacher Education

Manipur is a small state with a small population of little over 18 lakhs. It was thought that all the teachers in schools could be trained within a short period of time. With such an idea the government established training institutes and developed various training programmes. But inspite of government's effort, today there is a great disparity between the number of trained and untrained teachers. In other states of the country, programmes of pre-service training were taken up leaving aside the question of in service training. Further, they have also taken up the programmes of orientation courses to refresh and revitalise their trained teachers.

As observed by the Kothari Commission (1964-66). 'A sound programme of professional education of teacher is essential for the qualitative improvement of education........'[4]

Though the teacher education is so important and essential for the qualitative improvement in educational standard, unfortunately, the professional education of teachers in Manipur had not so far been at par to those of other advanced states of India. Teacher education programme in Manipur started in 1952-53 with the setting up of one normal training institute where 60 undergraduate and matriculate teachers were given training. This institution was closed down in 1955-56. In 1955-56 Basic Training Institute was established at Imphal while teacher education programme of Secondary School teachers was initiated in 1959 starting B.T. and C.T. (Certificate of Teaching) classes as an adjunct to the undergraduate Education Department of D.M. College, Imphal. Prior to this the Government used to depute untrained working teachers outside Manipur and in particular to the Central Institute of Education, Delhi.

The above details of the magnitude of the problem show that the present arrangement for giving training to school teachers needs to be re-organised with a view to getting all the teachers trained within a short period of time and also having an effective check on the growing backlog of untrained teachers. Besides, adequate provisions for the training of fresh graduates or post-graduates has to be made so that trained candidates are available at the time of initial appointment as school teachers. In addition to the above, adequate provisions for Summer School-cum-correspondence Course for the teachers education should be made under Manipur University.

Table 5.2
Teachers' Training Colleges/Institutes in Manipur

S.No.	Name		Level of Training
1.	D.M. College of Teacher Education		Post - graduate and graduate teachers of High/Higher Secondary Schools receive training leading to B.Ed. Degree.
2.	Kanan Devi Memorial College of Education		Post - graduate and graduate teachers of High/Higher Secondary Schools receive training leading to B.Ed. Degree.
3.	Hindi Teachers' Training College	1	Hindi teachers of High/Higher Secondary Schools.
4.	Basic Training College	1	Graduate and under-graduate teachers of Middle/Junior High Schools.
5.	Basic Training Institute	3	Primary School teachers.
6.	Hindi Teacher Training Institute	1	Primary School teachers of Hindi.
7.	Deputation of teachers outside the state- (i) Summer School - cum - correspondence B.Ed. Course of Regional Institute of Education, Bhubaneswar and later on this course was conducted by SCERT, Manipur since 1980. (ii) Sikshan Kala Prabin Course at Agra etc.		

D.M. College of Teacher Education

The secondary school teachers training was started at D.M. College in 1959. This college is a co-educational institution and is partly residential. It was started as an adjunct to the Undergraduate Education Department of the College and continued in such a position for thirteen years. After the attainment of Statehood, the uncongenial atmosphere of the training of teachers came to the notice of Y. Yaima Singh, the then Education Minister. He realised and felt the need of organising teacher training in a right way and took keen interest in the establishment of a full-fledged training college for providing training facilities to teachers, who were already in service and also to those who had aspiration of joining the teaching profession. As such, the Post-Graduate Training College, came in existence on 6th November, 1972. It was later renamed as D.M. College of Teacher Education.

This college has been running only one course viz., B.T., a one year full time course. The minimum qualification for admission to this course is graduation.

Regarding the criteria for selection, the selection procedure is not controlled by the college. The Director of Education (S), Government of Manipur deputes working teachers for training. But in some exceptional cases fresh candidates are also admitted. But both in service and pre-service trainees are allowed to be admitted to the College after 3 years of passing B.A. and B.Sc. The basis for selection is different from year to year. Some of the seats are reserved for private candidates, some for tribals, some for grade seniority and some for length of service. Some seats were reserved for the teachers of the neighbouring states like Nagaland in the past but now that practice has been discontinued. Only in 1973-74, two separate batches of non-teacher candidates were admitted to the college under the scheme of Aid Unemployed Programme in a separate shift. Such candidates were selected on merit basis through written test and viva-voce conducted by the college itself.

In the year 1973-74 the number of enrolled students rose upto 356 but it went down to 154 in the year 1975-76. That is why in this year, Day shift and Morning shift for pre-services students was abolished. So, the number of students also decreased. Table 5.3 Shows the fluctuating trend of trainees in the D.M. College of Teacher Education since 1970-71. There are 17 teachers in the college, which has currently 170 students. English is the medium of instruction and also of examination at the B.Ed. level.

Table 5.3
Intake of Teacher Trainees in D.M. College of Teacher Education

Year	Enrolment of Students
1970-71	107
1975-76	154
1980-81	187
1985-86	174
1990-91	482
1992-93	216
1994-95	199
1996-97	338
1997-98	170

Source : D.M. College of Teacher Education. Imphal.

Kanan Devi Memorial College of Education, established in 1993, imparts B.Ed. training course to pre-service students. It has an intake capacity of 60 students, taught by 19 teachers, most of them employed on part-time basis.

Hindi Teachers' Training College

It was established on 2nd October, 1975. The aim and objective of the establishment of the college is to train the Hindi teachers in the teaching of Hindi as second language to non-Hindi speaking students. This institution was opened under centrally sponsored scheme of the Government of India. The college follows the curriculum prescribed by the Central Institute of Hindi, Agra. Regarding the criteria for selection, In-service Hindi teachers who have passed B.A. or equivalent examinations in Hindi are allowed admission in this institution. It provides one year course. Hindi is the medium of instruction and of examination. The system of examination is 20% internal assessment and 80% external evaluation.

The intake capacity of the students in the college is 60, which has a faculty strength of six teachers.

Basic Training Institutes

There are 3 B.T.I.'s which were established at different places i.e. at Imphal (D.M. College Campus), at Ukhrul and at Kakching in 1966. Formerly there was B.T.I. at Canchipur which was established in the year 1959. But this very institution has been amalgamated with B.T.I., Imphal.

A Hindi Training Institution (Non Basic type) was established at Imphal in D.M. College campus in 1955. These training institutions have the total intake capacity of about 600 (six hundred) and provide one year training course to Class VIII (for B.T.I.s) and Parichay (for Hindi Training Institutes) to the deputed teachers of Hindi.

Basic Training College

It was established in 1955 at Imphal in D.M. College campus. It provides a two years course to the matriculate teachers and has an intake capacity of one hundred.

Examination of B.T.I.s, Hindi Training Institute and B.T.C. are conducted by the Education Department, Government of Manipur. About 87 teachers are serving in these institutes.

State Institute of Education

The State Institute of Education (SIE) started B.Ed. course as a sub-centre of Regional Institute of Education, Bhubaneswar in 1980. The main aim and objective of opening of this sub-centre is to gear up the clearance of the backlog of untrained teachers in the state. At first this sub-centre conducted B.Ed. course for only secondary school teachers but since 1983, this sub-centre has started B.Ed. course for elementary school teachers only. One trainee has to appear in the papers carrying 1000 marks in the examinations. The subjects included in the B.Ed. course are as follows :

i) Teacher education in the emerging Indian society.
ii) Educational Psychology.
iii) Evaluation and Measurement.
iv) Fundamentals of practice teaching.
v) Health, Physical Education and Recreation.
vi) Method subjects.

vii) Internship in teaching.
viii) S.U.P.W. (Practical).
ix) Physical education/working with the community.

Teacher trainees are to attend contact programme of 6 weeks each in two summers. During the intervening period of ten months, teacher trainees have to do correspondence assignments and practice teaching in different schools. At the end of the two summer contact programme, they are eligible for appearing at the B.Ed. examination of Utkal University.

As regard the selection of trainees, Regional Institute of Education (RIE) Bhubaneswar is the final authority. Candidates selected provisionally by the government are required to get final approval of the Institute for enrolment. The pre-requisite for enrolment may be as follows :-

i) The candidate should be a graduate or post-graduate.
ii) At least 5 years teaching experience in case of graduate and 3 years teaching experience in case of post-graduates.
iii) Teachers working in Government schools or recognised private schools are eligible for admission.
iv) There is no fixed number of seats. However, for convenience 100 in each course are selected every year.

The SIE has a small library. Teacher trainees are allowed to borrow books from time to time from this library. All expenditure incurred for running the course is borne by the State Government. Admission fee and examination fee collected from the trainees are sent to the University. The State Government in consultation with NCERT and RIE, Bhubaneswar established this sub-centre.

Vocational and Technical Education

"Institutional training facilities for vocational and technical education have been provided in the state. Besides, Department of Education, providing facilities for technical training, the training facilities are also provided by the Departments of Agriculture, Veterinary and Animal Husbandry, Medical, Health and Family Planning Services and the Industrial Training Institutes. All the training centres and institutes are managed by the State".[5] So far the State provides for facilities for the training of the technicians of the following categories :-

i) Middle level technicians
ii) Craftsmen and mechanics of the lower order.

The middle level technicians are trained at the Government Polytechnic.

Government Polytechnic

Government Polytechnic, Imphal was formerly known as A.T.I. (Adimjati Technical Institute). The Institute was established by the Adimjati Siksha Ashram, Imphal which was a branch of the Bhartiya Adimjati Sevak Sangh. Its foundation stone was laid by late Pandit Govind Ballav Pant, the then Union Home Minister of India on 22nd February 1957 as its original site at Chingmeirong. The function of the institution was to offer diploma course in Civil Engineering to the Schedule Tribe and Schedule Caste students of the North-Eastern Region of the country. The institution got affiliation from the State Council of Technological Education, Assam. Gradually diploma course in mechanical and electrical engineering were also introduced. In the year 1960, the institution started admitting non-tribal students also with its intake capacity of 60 (40 in Civil, 10 in Electrical and 10 in Mechanical).

In the year 1972 the institution was taken over by the Government of Manipur and formally assumed its present name, the Government Polytechnic, Imphal. The first foundation stone of the present workshop building at Takyel was laid in the year 1972. In the year 1977, Government Polytechnic moved from its original site at Chingmeirong to its new and present campus at Takyel about 4 kms. from the centre of the city. The present intake capacity of the Polytechnic is 170 (60 in Civil, 40 in Electrical, 20 in Mechanical, 30 in Electronics and Telecommunication and 20 in Pharmacy).

The Institute has workshop and laboratory, buildings with suitable equipments, lecture and drawing halls, Administrative building, Library, Multipurpose halls, Co-operative store, Canteen, Dispensary building, Branch Post Office, Staff quarters, Hostel for 60 boys and 40 girls and sports complex.

The duration of the courses in Civil, Electrical, Mechanical and Electronics and Telecommunication Engineering is 3 (three) year institutional training and 6 months practical training outside the Institute. The courses framed by the State Council for Technical Education, Assam, in Civil, Mechanical and Electrical are followed in the Government Polytechnic, Imphal. Each year is divided into semesters. A student must pass the examination at the end of each semester before promotion to the next higher class. The medium of instruction is English.

A number of merit scholarships are awarded by the Government of Manipur to students admitted to the Institute. All scheduled caste and scheduled tribe students are given a special scholarships by the Manipur Government and all the lower income group students are given free studentships.

The Ministry of Education, Government of India gives direct financial assistance for the development of the Institute. There is a polytechnic gymkhana which aims at strengthening the tie between the institute and the students through the promotion of social, cultural, educational and recreational activities. At first the college was affiliated to the State Council of Technical Edcuation, Assam. Since 1981, it has been affiliated to Manipur University upto diploma course in Civil, Mechanical, Electrical, Electronics and Telecommunication Engineering and Pharmacy.

Production-cum-Training Centre

In this centre, both the staff and students can work for production and earning during vacation and off time. This centre was established in the year 1976 with the following aims :-

(i) To infuse the spirit of dignity of labour
(ii) To be self-reliant in actual production
(iii) To earn while learning.

A large number of courses of 10 days to six month's duration have been introduced in the production-cum training centre to train the people in trades like blacksmithy, carpentary, turning, moulding, house wiring, television and radio repairing, welding, gold plating, batick painting, computer data entry, soil block making, doll and toy making, tailoring, wool knitting, embroidery, mushroom cultivation, fruit juice extraction, construction of bio-gas plants, chullas, low cost latrines, piggery, cattle rearing, dress making, repairning of electrical appliances etc.

Some more trades like handicrafts, phenyle manufacturing, tiles making, beauty parlour etc. are being introduced in the centre run by the Polytechnic.

College of Technology

With the inauguration of the Government College of Technology on 28 August 1998, a long cherished desire of the people to have an engineering college was fulfilled. The intake capacity of the college is 90 (30 in civil, 30 in Electronics and Telecommunication, and 30 in Computer Science).

Industrial Training Institute

The craftsmen of the lower order are trained at Industrial Training Institute (ITI). Including Imphal ITI, there are 6 ITIs in Manipur which are set up almost in every district head quarters in the state to impart different types of vocational courses. These institutes run the following types of courses (Table 5.4).

Table 5.4
Courses run by Industrial Training Institutes

S.No.	Courses	Minimum Qualification
1.	Draftsman, Electrician, Instrument Mechanic, Radio Mechanic, Pattern Maker, Surveyor and Stenographer. Farm Mechanic, Computer Application	Matriculation
2.	Blacksmithy, Carpentry, Motor Mechanic, Moulder, Construction, Wireman, Diesel Mechanic, Plastic Processing	Class VIII pass
3.	Weaving, Foundry, Blacksmity, Cane and Bamboo, Tailoring and Cutting.	Class VI pass

These institutes impart free vocational training and at the end of the training award National Trade Certificate. The I.T.Is. are financed by the State Government and the National Council for Training in Vocational Trade. The Industrial Training Institutes follow the syllabi for the training courses which have been framed by the National Council for Training in Vocational Trade, New Delhi.

Thus, professional and technical education in the state is in the state of infancy but it definitely has a great potential for future development. In economic planning science and technology have to play a decisive role in increasing agricultural and industrial productivity. The mere availability of science and technology in the country, however, does not ensure its economic development. If science and technology are to contribute to productive processes, special talents have to be developed and people must be trained to apply these techniques effectively on a broad front.

***References* :**

1. *Third Annual Report* : *Manipur University* (1983-84), p. 63.
2. *Statistical Accounts of Colleges under Manipur University* (1987), p.30.
3. *Ibid*, p. 36.
4. *Kothari Commission Report* (1964-66), p. 380.
5. N.C.E.R.T., : *Survey Report* (1972-73), p.84.

6

Women's Education

The women of Manipur have a distinct place in the socio-cultural, religious and economic life of the society. However, inspite of this, the door of education was not open to them in the past. In pre-British Manipur, except a few women of higher strata of society most of them did not get facilities of modern education. The traditional society assigned women only domestic duties like cooking, weaving, spinning, nursing the family members and looking after their children. The women worked in the fields with their menfolks, doing lighter jobs like transplantation of seedling, harvesting of paddy etc. Even the education of women of some enlightened families was not of formal type in the beginning. They received their education in their own household as no school existed in Manipur prior to 1898-99.[1] They got lessons in rudimentary form of reading and writing. But knowledge of reading and writing was not accepted as qualification for a girl in the society. In Manipur skill in weaving, cooking and husking of paddy was considered greater accomplishment for a girl. To be a good housewife, the qualifications that were required for a girl could be acquired from her mother and other elder members of the family. So the guardians felt no necessity of sending their daughters to schools. Besides, the girls were too useful in the household activities, and to that extent it was considered a great loss for the family to send their daughters to the schools. Due to this notion, it was difficult to get students for a girls school. But an enlightened public opinion in favour of girls education developed gradually. English educated youths began to realise the need of women's education and they advocated strongly for the introduction of women education for the welfare of the society. To remove prejudices of the people and to make them understand the necessity of women's education for the welfare of the family and upliftment of society, they took up pen as instrument to create public opinion.

The Government was indifferent to women's education in Manipur upto 1899. This slow progress of women education in Manipur was due to the limited number of educated and enlightened people in the state, who could not succeed initially in removing the old prejudices towards female education. Moreover, some educationists of Manipur also had the orthodox idea that the skill of weaving and other household works is more important for a girl than knowledge in the three R's. Besides, a girl was considered to be a great help to her mother and she could not be spared for school without causing inconvenience to her mother.

The Auxilliary Committee of the Indian Statutory Commission, while reviewing the growth of education for girls and women in British India pointed out three major obstacles to women's education as (i) Conservatism, (ii) *Purdah* system and (iii) Early marriages.[2]

The conservative attitude of even educated fathers towards their daughter's education was simply surprising. The social system in which '*Purdah*' was taken to be a symbol of respectability naturally militated against the education of women. But the most formidable obstacle in the way of women's education and their general progress was the system of early marriages which was a very common practice in India.[3] And such potential obstacles continued in the British India for a long time.

In Manipur slow progress of women's education might be due to the following reasons :-

(a) Historical reason : In the past, education of girls was completely neglected in the State before 1947.
(b) Economic reason : Poverty of parents and usefulness of the girls in domestic chorus.
(c) Social reason : Early marriage and prejudices against girl's education.
(d) Educational reason : (i) Non-existence of schools within a reasonable walking distance in the hills and rural areas; (ii) Irrelevant curriculum; (iii) Lack of facilities for part-time schooling.[4]

Before 1947, education of girls and women in Manipur was completely neglected. This was not very much due to prevalence of ill social customs but mainly out of ignorance of the people regarding the value of women's education. The condition of women in Manipur before Independence of India reflects upon the time honoured tradition of considering women inferior to men. The deep rooted orthodoxy considered the secluded corners of her home as the proper place of woman. Thus, education was confined mainly to the domestic or school education of the girls of the royal or well-to-do families. In 1991 literacy percentage among the males was 71.63 whereas the women literacy was only 47.60.[5] Although the percentage of literacy among the Manipuri women is above the all India average, yet the situation is not quite satisfactory. The Manipuri society is free from many social evils like *purdah* and dowry system which are great obstacles in other parts of India. Women in Manipur conduct most of the economic activities in a better and more efficient manner than the males. So it is quite unreasonable that the literacy percentage of women should be lower than that of males.

Even now many people subscribe to the time honoured conviction of the illiterate parents that women are the properties of men. They cannot be independent at all stages of life - in early years they are under the care of their fathers, after marriage under their husbands and in old age they are subservient to their sons. The idea of giving higher education to girls is still unacceptable to many guardians since girls cannot be considered an asset of family.[6]

Women play a great role in the society. Their purpose in life was to be productive wives, mothers and helpmates who would tend to the domestic needs and moral upliftment of the family. Even advocates of women's education such as Benjamin Rusk, a Professor of Chemistry at the University of Pennsylvania and Emma Willard, an advocate and founder of women's schools felt that women should be better trained in domestic arts. Rusk (1798) called for a feminine curriculum that would teach women to be better assistants to their husbands and better educators of their children in moral and intellectual matters. Men worried about politics, business, war, finance and industry. Women because of their innate biological role as the bearer of children were seen as care-takers of the family, the home and the morals of husband

and children. It was the duty of women to provide a heaven for men in the changing ruthless industrial world. "It is important to note the role of women in society. Many women could not participate in higher education in order to gain these more refined skill. It is important to focus on the progress of women made in obtaining more advanced schooling. Many advocates of women's education felt that if women demonstrated their intellectual abilities, surely the status of women would be enhanced. Education was considered to be the key to job opportunities and social equality. With the advent of women's seminars, academies and colleges, this potential for advancement was enhanced".[7]

Women of Manipur are very hard working and they perform multifarious activities. They weave clothes and sell them in the market. Because of their active participation in trade and commerce, Manipur, particularly, has a good number of separate bazars solely controlled by her efficient and energetic women. They go to paddy fields, sow seeds and reap them and are employed as wage earners in various activities like construction of roads and buildings, digging of tanks etc. Manipuri women had taken the role of leaders in politics whenever the state faced unusual difficulties. The Movement known as *"Nupi Lan" in 1939 is the striking episode of this effect.

It is women who are indirectly responsible for the nation's progress and development. The University Education Commission, 1948 rightly remarks, "if general education had to be limited to men or to women, that opportunity should be given to women, for then it would most surely be passed on to the next generation."[8]

In 1898-99 women's education was started in Manipur for the first time. In this year two girls were admitted in one of the schools of Imphal area. The State Government tried to secure a lady teacher too. The hope of recruiting a lady teacher was fulfilled in December 1899, when a L.P. School for Girls was established at Moirangkhom.[9] On the opening day of the school 12 girls were admitted in the school and the total enrolment of girls rose to 53 by 31st March of 1900.[10] Before this, there were only a few cases of girls receiving education from their male guardians in the form of private tutions. With the beginning of the British occupation in

1891, many primary schools were established. These schools attracted increasing number of students. This also indicates the recent origin of women's education in Manipur. The education of women did not make equal progress with that of men although it was hoped, that in a state like Manipur where woman hold such an important position in the economic activity, the schools would have been attended by greater number of girls than has actually been the case. The main difficulties encountered at the beginning of women's education was due to the rumour that as soon as the girls were satisfactorily taught to read, write and speak English, they were to be shipped off to England where there was said to be a scarcity of marriageable women. The sole basis for this myth lay in the fact that at that time, none of the officers of Government, civil and military, then serving in Manipur, was married.[11] The rumour hampered the attendance of girl students for some time. Further, the dearth of qualified women teacher was another cause of slow progress of girls' education. Another important factor that hampered women's education was the general apathy on the part of parents towards education of their daughters.

According to the Administrative Report submitted by Major A.E. Woods, the then Political Agent of Manipur, after observing the daily attendance of Moirangkhom Balika School, in 1901-1902- "The Girls School can hardly be considered a success, the attendance is very poor and if it does not improve this year, I shall have to close it, as the expense is altogether out of all proportion to the benefit it confers. The Manipuris apparently see no benefit in educating their female children and I am not inclined to disagree with them". It is clear from this report that the older generation of Manipuri society was not so much interested in imparting education to their daughters. So, the position of girls education in Manipur remained very low. In 1900-1901 the population of Manipur was 2,84,465. Out of which 1,44,833 were women. The total number of girls studying in primary and middle schools was only 62 and the percentage of literacy was 0.04. In 1910-11, the number of literate girls increased to 217 and percentage of literacy became 0.12 indicating about threefold increase within a decade. In 1913-14, the Chief Commissioner of Assam, Sir Archdale Earle, came to Manipur to inspect the Johnstone School. During the course of his visit he established one middle vernancular school for imparting education among the Bengali girls and the school was named as Lady Earle Girls School, after his wife's name. In the year 1915-16 one lady teacher was sent outside to receive training for middle vernacular and this lady teacher came back to Imphal in the year 1918-19 after passing the Middle vernacular examination. In 1930-31, the number of the girl students rose to 689, out of the total women population of 2,29,791, making the female literacy as low as 0.30 per cent of the total women population.

In 1932-33 two more L.P. Schools for girls were established making 3 L.P. Schools for them. The fourth girl, school, Sagolband Aided U.P. School was established in 1934-35. The then Maharaja of Manipur, Sir Churachand Singh, was a great patron of learning. It was at his instance that the first Girls' High School was set up at Imphal in 1935 after the name of his eldest daughter, Maharajkumari Tamphasana. For this school, the State Durbar gave Rs. 100 per month in the form of grant. In 1937-38, the number of girls attending primary and middle schools increased to 929 which was the highest in the pre-Independence era and it was only in 1938 that the first Manipuri girl passed the matriculation examination. Subsequently, there was a decline in the number of female students, primarily due to certain rumours about the exporting of educated girls to England and secondly, on account of the Second World War. There had been a decline in the number of male students also during the Second World War. On the recommendation of Manipur State Durbar, Tamphasana Girls' High School was taken over by the Government on June 1, 1946 as a Government School.[12] In 1940-41, out of total women population of 2,62,886, the number of women students was 1,594, which formed 0.61 per cent of the total women population.[13] But women education was mainly academic. There was no separate budget allocation for girls' education in pre-Independence period.[14]

Progress of Women's Education after Independence

In the wake of Independence new hopes and aspirations emerged and new avenues for women were opened by declaring equality of both the sexes. The Constitution of India guaranteed equal status to both men and women. The Constitution of India assumed that there shall not be any discrimination against any citizen on the ground of religion, race, caste, sex or place of birth...... there shall be equality of opportunity to all citizens, in matters relating to employment to any office under the State. Article 45 of the Constitution of India provides that the State shall endeavour to provide within a period of ten years from the commencement of the Constitution for free and compulsory education for all children till they complete the age of 14 years. It aims at the establishment of democratic set up based on adult franchise and where justice, social, political and economic shall govern all activities of life. With this aim the education of women became one of the major responsibilities of the State while formulating its policies.

Manipur turned from monarchy to democracy in 1948. The freedom and right to exercise their franchise was granted to women also. As a result there was an increase in the number of girls in the schools.

From the historical, social and economic reasons, education of girls has lagged behind considerably in Manipur. The overall picture of girls education at the beginning of the first five year plan was very gloomy in the state. In the year 1951 the total population of the State was 5,77,635. The total percentage of literacy was 11.4. Out of which male literacy was 20.77 per cent but female literacy was restricted to only 2.36 per cent. However, there was a progressive development of women's education in the state since 1951 (Table 6.1).

Table 6.1
Progress of Literacy in Manipur

Year	Total population	Total p.c. of literacy	Male	Female
1951	5,77,635	11.4	20.77	2.36
1961	7,80,037	30.4	45.12	15.93
1971	10,72,753	32.9	46.40	19.53
1981	14,20,953	41.3	53.29	29.06
1991	18,37,149	59.9	71.63	47.60

Source : Census of India, 1991.

Within five years of accession to the Indian Union, the number of women students increased by 4.4 times from 1,594 in the pre-Independence period (1941) to 6,696 in 1951. There were 25 girls' primary schools in 1951 against 4 in the pre-Independence era. In the year 1960-61 there was a marked increase in the percentage of literacy reaching 30.4 while the percentage of male literacy was 45.12 and that of women 15.93 and the number of women students being 62,620. During the same period, the number of girls' schools rose to 187 primary and middle schools and 3 high schools as against 30 girls' schools in the year 1951-52. In the year 1960-61, Rs. 3,50,600 were spent on primary, Rs. 1,45,071 on middle and Rs. 1,54,683 on high schools and Rs. 40,918 on colleges.

The year 1961-62 is a remarkable year in the history of education of the state. During this year, for the first time in Manipur a Girls' High School for the Tribal people was set up in the heart of the Churachandpur town after the name of Shrimati Bimala Raina, wife of the then Chief Commissioner, Manipur. The school was awarded 90% deficit grant-in-aid for two undergraduate teachers in the prevailing scales of pay. This was the biggest school for the tribal girls in the state.

In the year under review 1598 boys and 306 girls came out successful in the High School Leaving Certificate Examination, out of 3780 boys and 743 girls who had appeared in the examination. The pass percentage was 42.14.

Some important plans for development of girls' education at the High School stage were : (*i*) award of attendance scholarships to girls, and (*ii*) continuation-class-stipends to girl students who could not complete their studies earlier but were desirous of becoming teachers. In addition to the usual scholarships reserved for the girls, they were paid scholarships out of those reserved for boys if they could list among boy competitors.

Some facilities for girls given to encourage women education were as follows :-

i. Recruitment of qualified women teachers.
ii. Attendance and Merit Scholarships.
iii. Monitory aids.
iv. Scholarship to girls, who wished to be teachers.
v. Facilities for appearing at different examinations as private

candidate.

vi. Sanitary blocks for girl students.

vii. Facilities for undergoing training.

viii. Reservation of special number of scholarships.

In the year 1970-71, out of the population of 10,72,753 the total percentage of literacy was 32.9 while the percentage of male literacy was 46.4 and that of female only 19.53. In this year the number of female students was 1,03,707 and the number of girls schools was 338 against 187 primary and middle schools in 1960-61. The number of girls high schools went upto 19 against 3 in the year 1960-61. But in the year 1969-70, on primary education Government spent Rs. 22,41,778 against Rs. 3,50,600 in the year 1960-61. It means Government paid more attention on primary education than previous years. On high school education of girls, Rs. 13,24,497 were spent against Rs. 1,54,683 in 1960-61, indicating 8 times increase within a decade. On college education of girls Rs. 2,59,552 were spent against Rs. 40,918 in the year 1965-66. In 1981, out of the total population of 14,20,953 the total number of literate male population was 3,84,231 and literate female population 2,03,387 and the total percentage of literacy being 41.5, while percentage of male literates was 53.29 and that of female being 29.06.[15]

With great effort made by the State government in the hope of ensuring cent percent literacy by 2000 A.D., the literacy scene in the state was greatly changed at the close of 1980's. By 1991, Manipur has got 9,16,692 literate persons out of the total population of 18,37,149 and thus literacy rate works to be 59.89, whereas the male literacy increased to 71.63% of the total male population Female literacy too increased to 47.60 per cent of the female population.[15] However, female literacy with reference to male literacy has not yet reached the satisfactory level and as such, the state has to go for a special drive on female literacy so as to make at least 80 per cent of female population literate by 2011.

From the analysis of the above data, it appears that women's education acquired great significance in Manipur after its accession to Indian Union. And steadily the number of girl students and female teachers in various institutions increased, the number of girls' schools went on multiplying and expenditure on girls edu-

Table 6.2
Girls'/Womens' Institutions in Manipur 1950-51 to 1996-97

Year	TYPE OF INSTITUTIONS								
	Primary (Nursery + Primary + Middle)			Secondary (High + Higher Secondary)			Degree Colleges		
	Total Primary	Girls' School		Total Secondary	Girls' School		Total Colleges	Girl/Womens' College	
		Nos.	In % of total		Nos.	In % of total		Nos.	In % of total
1950-51	526	28	532	11	1	9.09	1	-	-
1955-56	966	43	4.45	23	1	4.35	2	-	-
1960-61	1974	187	9.47	57	5	8.77	2	-	-
1965-66	2377	245	10.31	118	14	11.86	11	1	9.09
1970-71	2856	338	11.83	123	19	15.45	12	1	8.33
1975-76	3896	268	6.88	212	25	11.79	20	2	10.00
1980-81	3286	246	7.49	290	32	11.03	24	2	8.33
1985-86	3119	224	7.18	35.8	45	12.57	28	2	7.14
1990-91	3190	204	6.39	430	55	12.79	29	2	6.90
1995-96	3083	83	2.69	539	51	9.46	59	7	11.86
1996-97	2514	148	5.89	556	53	9.53	64	7	10.94

Source : 1. Th. Mangoljao Singh, *Western Education in Manipur*, Vol. I & II, 1989, p. 115
2. Statistical Handbook of Manipur, 1992 pp. 44-46

cation received an impetus. Table 6.2 presents the number and types of girls/womens institutions in the state since 1950-51.

Primary schools for girls (including Nursery and Middle Schools) have increased from July 28 in 1950-51 to 338 of the total 2856 schools during 1970-71. However, the girls institutions were drastically reduced to only 83 by 1995-96. During 1996-97 their number increased to 148. This may be either due to their complete closure or conversion into co-educational institutions.

Thus, the number of secondary schools for girls has recorded continuous increase except for a few years. While there was only one girl secondary school during 1950-51, but by 1990-91 it increased to 55 accounting for about 12.79% of the total secondary schools. However it was slightly reduced afterwards and the state had only 53 girls' secondary schools by 1996-97.

Prior to 1965-66, there was no women's college in the state. The first women's college was established in 1965 with great demand and pressure from the public. However, not much progress was made upto 1990-91, till then the number of womens' colleges was restricted to only 2. By 1995-96, the state had 7 womens' colleges but concentrated mainly in the valley districts. The hill districts are still devoid of womens' college.

As shown on Table 6.3 and the corresponding Fig. 6.2, the girl students enrolled at different levels of education is also increasing continuously both in absolute number and percentage share. The girl students enrolled at primary and secondary schools have increased from only 5341 (15.12%) and 595 (11.40%) to almost 13/473 (47.19%) and 95504 (46.15%) respectively during 1996-97. Inspite of this trend, the absolute number of girl students enrolled at primary level was reduced in 1980-81 from the proceeding year and it may be due to the out break of insurgency and students agitation on foreigners' issue. In the case of higher education, the growth trend of girl students enrolled in colleges was very slow and did not make much progress till 1960-61. After 1975-76 girls enrolled in colleges have increased considerably. They numbered 5311 in 1975-76 forming 32.02% of the total college going students, and increased to 16,597 (42.53%) by 1990-91. Though seperate numbers of girl students enrolled in colleges is not available for the

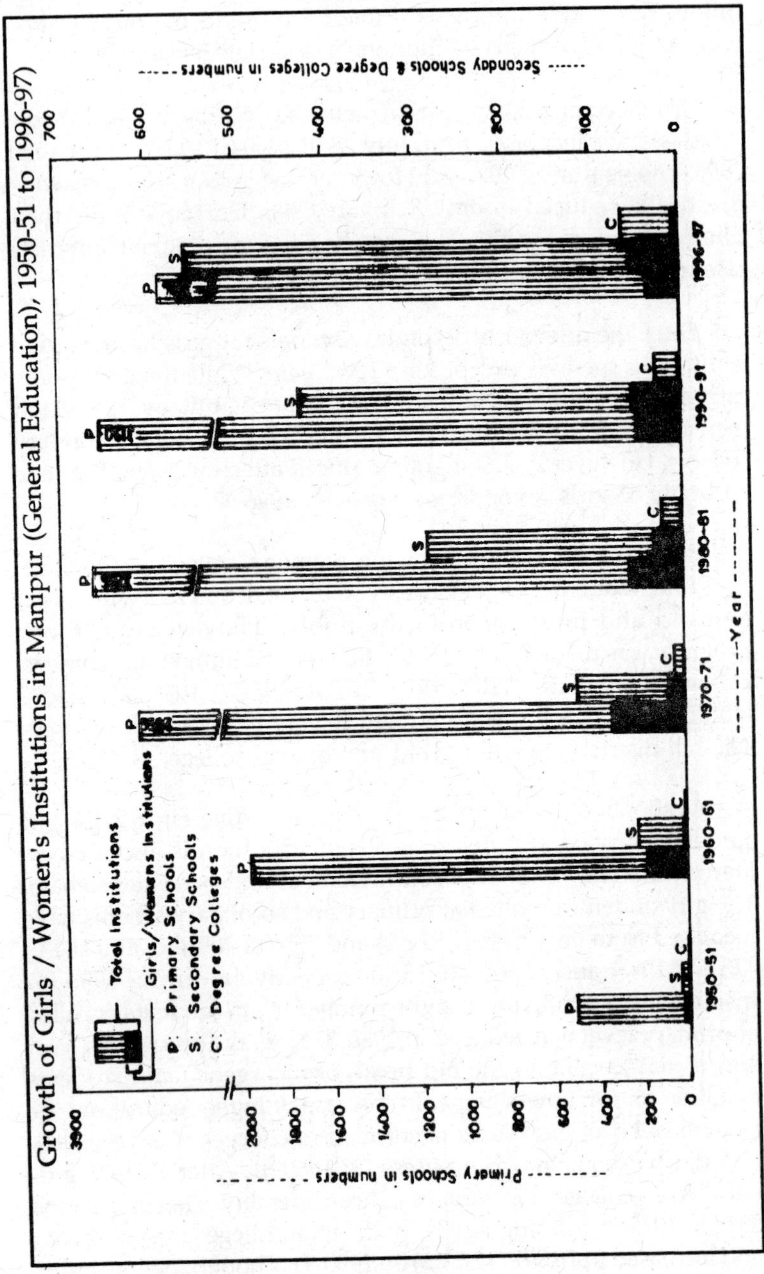
Growth of Girls / Women's Institutions in Manipur (General Education), 1950-51 to 1996-97
Total Institutions
Girls/Womens Institutions
P: Primary Schools
S: Secondary Schools
C: Degree Colleges
Primary Schools in numbers
Secondary Schools & Degree Colleges in numbers
Year
1950-51
1960-61
1970-71
1980-81
1990-91
1996-97

Fig. 6.1

Table 6.3
Girl Student at Various Levels of Education 1950-51 to 1996-97

Year	CATEGORY OF STUDENTS								
	Primary (Nursery + Primary + Middle)			Secondary (High + Higher Secondary)			Higher (Degree Level)		
	Total Primary	Female		Total Secondary	Female		Total Higher	Female	
		Nos.	In % of total		Nos.	In % of total		Nos.	In % of total
1950-51	35318	5341	15.12	5,220	595	11.40	348	7	2.01
1955-56	75679	18963	25.06	9,823	1,572	16.00	1,194	75	6.28
1960-61	131938	43846	33.23	20,559	2,475	12.04	30.14	243	12.07
1965-66	166635	64524	38.72	35,477	10,108	28.49	5,797	1,087	18.75
1970-71	201535	79356	39.38	38,006	12,826	33.75	10,152	2,385	23.49
1975-76	254163	103654	40.78	58,845	21,643	36.78	16,584	5,311	32.02
1980-81	212092	91880	43.32	79,796	33,482	41.96	20,559	7,712	37.51
1985-86	240796	104283	43.31	1,05,846	46,935	44.34	24,467	9,651	39.44
1990-91	264438	120424	45.54	1,29,262	57,811	44.72	39,024	16,597	42.53
1995-96	277965	129985	46.76	1,97,162	90,332	45.82	34,568	-	-
1996-97	278590	131473	47.19	2,06,945	95,504	46.15	N.A.	N.A.	-

Source : 1. Th. Mangoljao Singh, *Western Education in Manipur*, Vol. I & II, 1989, p. 116
2. Statistical Handbook of Manipur, 1992 pp. 48-50.

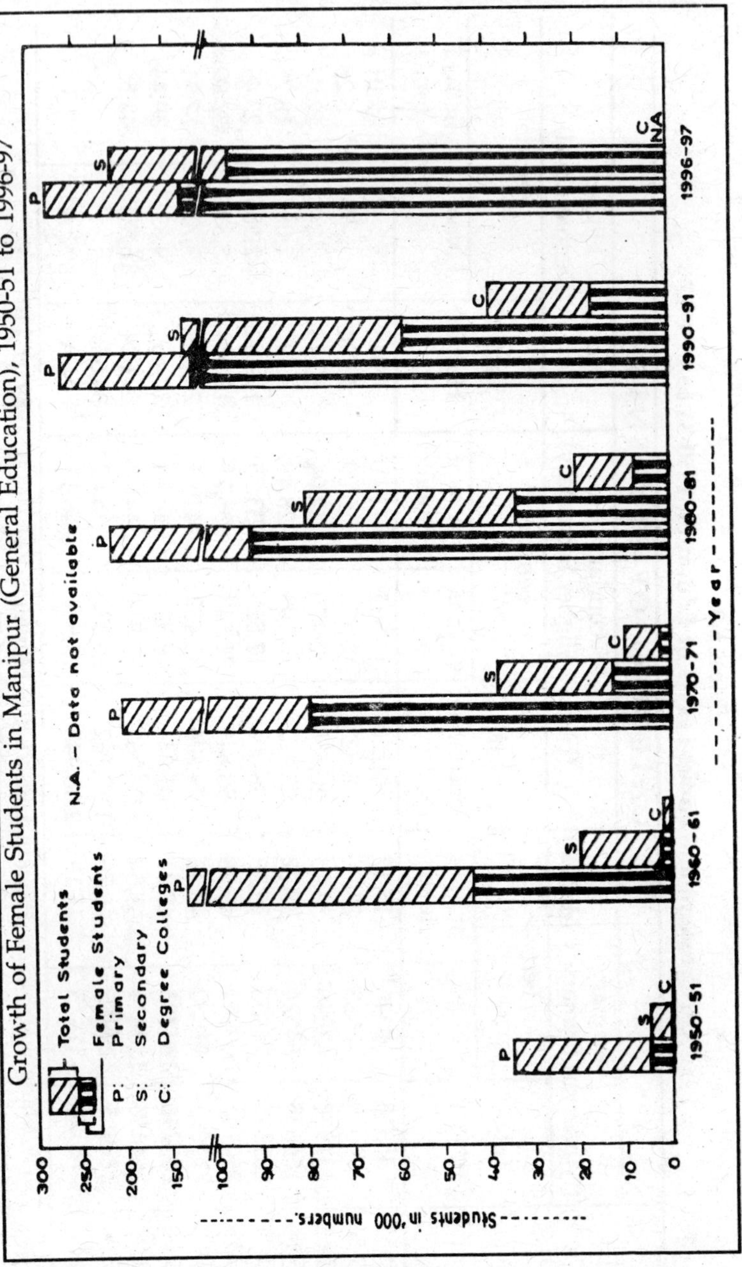
Growth of Female Students in Manipur (General Education), 1950-51 to 1996-97
Total Students
Female Students
P: Primary
S: Secondary
C: Degree Colleges
N.A. – Data not available
P
S
C
NA
1950-51
1960-61
1970-71
1980-81
1990-91
1996-97
Year
Students in '000 numbers.
300
250
200
150
100
90
80
70
60
50
40
30
20
10
0

Fig. 6.2

Table 6.4
Teachers Employed at Various Levels of Education 1950-51 to 1996-97

Year	CATEGORY OF TEACHERS								
	Primary (Nursery + Primary + Middle)			Secondary (High + Higher Secondary)			Higher (Lecturers)		
	Total	Female		Total	Female		Total	Female	
		Nos.	In % of total		Nos.	In % of total		Nos.	In % of total
1950-51	1,233	41	3.33	172	-	-	14	-	-
1955-56	2,444	59	2.41	346	20	5.78	39	-	-
1960-61	5,594	260	4.65	306	49	6.08	71	4	5.63
1965-66	7,828	507	6.48	1,568	139	3.86	274	14	5.11
1970-71	9,145	695	7.60	1,878	186	9.90	368	35	9.51
1975-76	12,800	1,230	9.61	2,703	360	13.32	615	88	14.31
1980-81	12,358	1,547	12.52	3,650	641	17.56	1,045	234	22.39
1985-86	12,822	2,452	19.12	5,371	1,175	21.88	1,229	339	27.58
1990-91	17,734	4,325	24.39	7,770	2,540	32.69	1,083	330	30.47
1995-96	15,351	4,985	32.47	9,690	3,464	35.75	2757*	976*	35.40
1996-97	15,204	5,109	33.60	10,491	3,767	35.91	N.A.	-	-

* Excluding the teachers of Govt. Polytechnic.

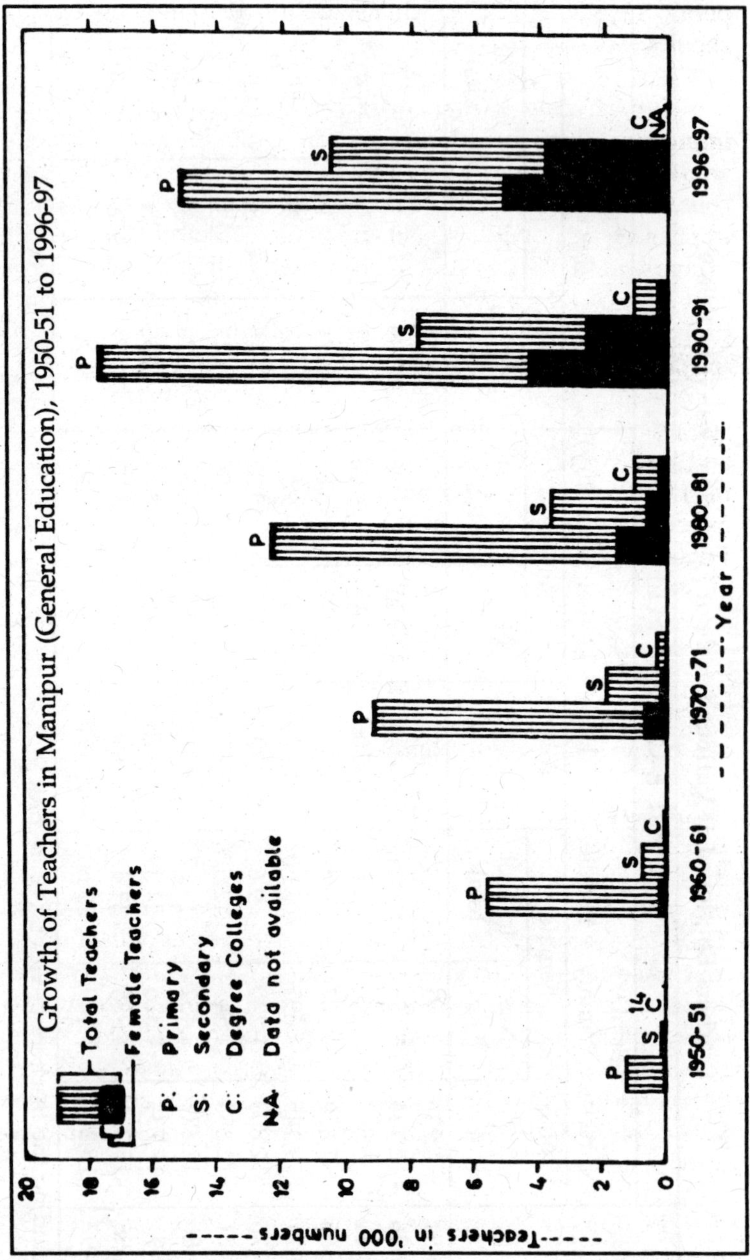
Growth of Teachers in Manipur (General Education), 1950-51 to 1996-97
Total Teachers
Female Teachers
P: Primary
S: Secondary
C: Degree Colleges
NA Data not available
P
S
C
1.4
1950-51
1960-61
1970-71
1980-81
1990-91
1996-97
NA
Year
Teachers in '000 numbers
0
2
4
6
8
10
12
14
16
18
20

Fig. 6.3

period 1995-96 & 1996-97, this share to the total is expected at about 45%.

Though the numbr of girls/students has increased impressively duing the last fifty years or so, the employment of women teachers is still very low in comparision with this male counterparts. In 1950-51 the number of women teachers serving in primary and middle schools was only 41 out of the total 1233 primary and middle school teachers accounting for only 3.33 per cent of such teachers. Now the state is employing 5109 female primary and middle school teachers forming 33.60 per cent of the total. Not even a single female teacher was employed in secondary schools till 1950-51. By 1955-56 there were 20 female teachers in secondary schools. Their number increased slowly and steadily and by 1996-97, reached to 3767, forming 35.91 per cent of the total 10491 teachers in secondary schools. Women could not join as lecturers in colleges at the time of introduction of Higher Education in Manipur and came to the scene after a lapse of about a decade. But now as an impact of development of womens' education, the state has got 976 women lecturers out of the total 2757 lecturers in 1995-96, forming about 35.40 per cent of the total college teachers. Whereas, this number was only 4 in 1960-61 (5.63%) Table 6.4 shows the number of women teachers employed at various levels of education since 1950-51.

After Independence with the increase in the number of educated women, a wide opening of opportunities was created in the field of employment. It is quite evident that western education has made important impact on the life of the women of Manipur. They have come out from the solitary confinement of their houses and have realised the value of freedom by becoming working women. Earlier the girls were given domestic jobs and the married women did outdoor jobs, such as working in the fields, selling commodities and weaving. The educated girls became enlightened. They now have freedom of choice of jobs as well as access to these jobs. Table 6.5 shows the increasing number of women employees in he state.

The number of women employees in 1960-61 was only 159, a meagre 2.42 per cent of total employees under the state government. In next 10 years their proportion increased to 7.87

per cent, and by 1990-91 to almost one-sixth of the total number of employees. During 1997-98, the share of women employees recorded 21.71 per cent share of the total employees in the state, a 110 fold increase over women employees in 1960-61.

Table 6.5
Women Employees in the Government Offices

Year	Total employees	Female employees	% of total
1960-61	6561	159	2.42
1965-66	17554	1443	8.22
1970-71	20428	1607	7.87
1975-76	-	-	-
1980-81	-	3445	-
1985-86	-	-	-
1990-91	55622	8852	15.91
1995-96	78558	15840	20.16
1997-98	80588	17497	21.71

Source : Employment Exchange, Imphal

Maximum number of women are employed in Education (60%) and Medical (23%) departments, and the rest of them in community development, Police, P.W.D., Revenue and other departments.

Steps taken by the Government

The State Government has been trying to popularise and encourage female education. A separate administrative machinery for expansion of girls' education was established in 1972 as a State Council for Women's Education. There is an honorary Chairman and Deputy Director of Education (Women's Programme) acts as ex-officio Secretary of the Council. The functions of the Council are mentioned below :

(i) To advise the Government on issues relating to the education of girls at school level and of adult women.

(ii) To suggest policies, programmes, target and priorities for the expansion and improvement of the education of girls and women.

(iii) To suggest measures for utilising voluntary effort in the field of education of girls and women.

(iv) To suggest suitable measures for arousing public opinion in favour of education of girls and women.

The State Council for Women's Education provides free education to girl students.Following are some of the special incentives provided by the Government of Manipur to attract students and teachers towards women's education :

(a) Facilities for girls to appear as private candidates upto postgraduate level.
(b) Scholarships to girl students who would take up teaching profession.
(c) Facilities for training in tailoring and Home Science in Higher Secondary Schools.
(d) Scholarships to the talented students both boys and girls, for research and further studies.

Role of Central Social Welfare Board :

The Central Social Welfare Board has extended its helping hand for the needy women and launched the schemes of condensed course. Facilities for residential as well as non-residential students are provided to these courses.

These courses have been started for the adult women (in the age group of 20-35 and above) who are literate but could not complete the minimum standard required for any gainful employment such as gram sevika, mid-wife, instructor, teacher etc. Women social education organisers known as mukhyasevikas have been appointed in each block to educate and persuade the people to remove prejudice and eradicate social evils.

***References* :**

1. *Administrative Report of the Manipur Political Agency*, (1898-99), p. 17.

2. *Hartog Committee Report* (1929), p. 152.

3. **Chopra P. D.** : *Social, Cultural and Economic History of India* (1973), pp. 43-44.

4. **Kishun Singh** : *A New Approach to the History and Problems of Indian Education* (1982), p. 194.

5. *Statistical Handbook of Manipur* (1992), p. 15.

6. **M. Purnimashi Devi** : *P.G.T. College Magazine,* Vol. IX, (1977-78), p. 13.

7. *Encyclopaedia of Educational Research* : Fifth Edition, pp. 2014-2015.

8. *Report of the University Education Commission,* 1948, p. 393.

9. **Th. Mangoljao Singh** : *Western Education in Manipur,* Vol. I, (1967), p. 20.

10. *Administrative Report of Manipur Political Agency* (1899-1900), p.13.

11. **T.C. Hodson** : *The Meitheis* (1908), p. 25.

12. **Th. Mangolajo Singh** : *op.cit,* Vol. I, p. 106.

13. *Statistical Handbook of Manipur 1983,* p. 52.

14. **R. S. Nagar** : *Development of Education in Manipur from 1891 1971,* unpublished Ph. D. Thesis, Gauhati University (1978) pp. 93-94.

15. *Statistical Handbook of Manipur,* 1992, pp. 14-15.

16. **Employment Exchange** : Imphal

7

Social Reform Movements

Modern India is the product of many historical forces. Of these the most important was the contact with the western civilization which came in the wake of the British rule in India. The eighteenth century in Indian history was a period of an all round decline. Immediately before the establishment of the British rule, India was a jumble of scattered fragments into which the Mughal empire was gradually dissolving. Apart from political defeat it was also a period of social decadence. Due to lack of inspiration, knowledge and resources, society tended to become narrow in outlook and practice. Blind superstition and inhuman social customs took roots everywhere. Social evils like polygamy, early marriage, *Sati* rites, infanticides became rampart. *Purdah* and vigorous seclusion of women in the houses were strictly observed particularly among the high castes.[1]

Much before the eighteenth century, certain abominable socio-religious customs had entered into the Hindu society, terribly affecting the Hindu women at large. The most unique of these customs were the *Sati* and, *purdah* systems, seclusion of women, child marriage, early marriage, the celibacy of widows, infanticide, caste system, polygamy and untouchability. In eighteenth century India, these customs were, if not universal or widely prevalent, prominent enough to catch the attention of the rulers. They flourished through the eighteenth century but were challenged in the nineteenth both through legislation and reform movements.

***Sati* System** : Among many irrational social customs, the most unnatural was the custom of *Sati* or the immolation of the Hindu widow on the funeral pyre of her dead husband. If a wife lost her husband by death, she was not allowed re-marriage. She had only to choose between two things, either to remain as a widow as long as she lived or to burn herself, and the latter eventually was considered preferable because as a widow she was ill-treated as long as she lived. It was a social and religious imposition on the widows to suffer throughout their life.

***Purdah* System** : With the advent of Islam, new forces appeared on the Indian horizon. Strict veiling of women was the common practice among the Mohammedans in their native lands and absolute strictness was observed to popularise it. Even a liberal king like Akbar had to issue strict orders that if a young woman was found running about the streets and bazars of the town and while so doing she did not veil herself or allow herself to be unveiled she was to go to the quarters of the prostitutes and take up the profession. The *purdah* system was an absolute orthodoxy among the Muslims. However, in many parts of India, the *purdah* had long become an established system both among the Hindus and the Muslims alike.

Seclusion of Women : The position of women of India in the eighteenth century was far from being satisfactory. It was their total seclusion which brought about their physical and mental degradation. It was the complete dependence of women on men which reduced their position to one of abject surrender to man. 'Parents protect women in childhood, their husbands protect them in youth and their sons protect them in old age' such was the ancient saying which dominated the Hindu mind throughout the centuries. It was a system that denied the Hindu women any right to paternal property. This system made the Indian women economically dependent on men. Their economic status was a vital cause of their misery and suffering. The freedom and status which the Indian women enjoyed in ancient times were beyond the scope of human imagination and the sense of insecurity and overall lawlessness which prevailed at that time made the seclusion more tight. There was hardly any opportunity for girls to attend educational institutions.

Child Marriage : There were times in ancient India when girls selected their own grooms, if they were considered sufficiently grown up. Indeed, for considerable period in ancient Hindu society, there was perhaps no system of early marriage, though such marriages were probably exceptions to the rule. Gradually, early marriage became an established custom. Various social factors operated to make the system popular. Child marriage was a widely prevalent system during the medieval period. The Hindus and the Muslims alike practised it. By the eighteenth and the nineteenth century it had become more deep rooted than ever. By giving them in marriage before they were of proper age, people felt assured that society would retain its moral purity.

Child marriage makes the Indian women the epitome of misery and distress due to many sided evils. The greatest evil arising out of child marriage was the growing number of child widows. The child widow had to spend a miserable life, since they could not marry again in their life and they were not taken care by the society they lived in.

Early Marriage : Early marriage was in vogue in almost all parts of India excepting north eastern region like Assam and Manipur. Customs in those days did not allow girls to remain in the house of their parents for more than six to eight years from birth. Due to prevalent social belief, the parents thought that if the girls would be married after their puberty, it would be a great sin. The rigidity of custom together with the celebration of the marriage at a very early age left no room whatsoever, for either the bride or the bridegroom to enable them to think of a partner of their own choice.

Caste System : Hindu society was based on caste consideration and caste system was as old as Hinduism itself. It remains till today as one of the most controversial social institutions of human history. It is the hierarchy which determines the social status in the group. Broadly we can classify these castes into four groups - the highest castes, the upper castes, the lower castes and the lowest castes. They are the Brahmins, the Kshatriyas, the Vaishyas and the Sudras, respectively. The status of an individual is determined by the social status of the group in which he is born. Nothing could alter this, neither education nor wealth.

In the eighteenth century, the caste prejudices were at their highest. In a sense, the rigidity of the caste system attained its strictest form during this period and continued to dominate the scene till the reform movements began in the nineteenth century.

In such a system, the individual's life and occupation were determined at his birth irrespective of his inborn qualities. The most repugnant evil of the caste system was untouchability. Its greatest demerit was that it divided the society into water tight compartments. In the 19th century men's belief in caste system started eroding. The modernism of the 19th century became synonymous with a crusade against caste.

Movements against the Social Evils : English education opened the flood gates of western liberalism and brought about a challenge to many of the social evils, age old ideas and evil institutions of India. Western liberalism kindled the dormant soul of India and she began to tread on the road to modernism.

With the advent of English education social movements sprouted throughout India. The impact of western education had a great influence on different aspects of Indian society. Contact with the western knowledge gave birth to a new awakening in the mind of the Indians. The old orthodox views were gradually replaced by the scientific way of thinking and reasoning. Western education, culture, science and scientific education awakened the people from their long slumber. It enabled them to look at the orthodox beliefs with reason.

The renaissance of the Vedic culture in its purified form took place through the impact of western culture and education. In this respect, it is in the fitness of things to mention the name of Raja Ram Mohan Roy, the pioneer of social reforms. He was a great religious and social reformer. He founded the Brahmo Samaj and worked hard for the abolition of *Sati*, polygamy, infanticide etc., and for the introduction of widow re-marriage. He was deadly against caste system.

The introduction of western education helped the unification of the people of India. The English language facilitated the process of political union of India and it became the official language of India. English education developed a common way of thinking and attitude towards life among the Indians.

The Brahmo Samaj was perhaps the most influencial of all the religious movements of the nineteenth century. Raja Ram Mohan

Roy, the founder of the Brahmo Samaj was the pioneer of all advances in the Hindu communities during the nineteenth century.[2]

But the appeal of the Samaj was mainly confined to the intellectual classes. It was the first important intellectual movement which spread the idea of nationalism and enlightenment of the Indians towards their goal to modernity.[3] The Arya Samaj was another important social reform movement started by Swami Dayanand Saraswati. It affected a massive change in the lives of the Hindus. It was in a position to influence larger number of people than the Brahmo Samaj could, and it had a strong motive force in bringing about a social awakening and even political consciousness among the masses. Dayanand's main aim was to affect a reform in the religious life of the Hindus. He looked at religion scientifically, dispensed with superstitions and aimed at breaking the barrier of the caste system. Its influence was comprehensive, steadily reaching every aspects of social and individual life.[4]

The educational activitiy of Arya Samaj, for example initiated condemnation of the rigid caste system, untouchability, inferiority of women and the custom of the *Purdah*. The Samaj established homes for orphans, widows, destitutes and the distressed.

Through the eighteenth and the nineteenth centuries, a number of movements like Prarthana Samaj and Theosophical Society arose at different places in India. Not only the establishment of such movements, but numerous local organisations and associations also sprang up with some distinctive purpose which left great impact on the social, political, religious and educational life of the people in India.

Social Evils in Manipur and Subsequent Reformation Movement

During earlier days, the people of Manipur lived in a more or less egalitarian society. But after conversion to Hinduism, the Brahmins came to occupy the highest position in the society and their role in the new social set up became highly important. With the increasing grip of Hinduism a number of social evils had been introduced in the Manipuri society as prevalent in other parts of India. One of the most important aspects of introducing the social evils in Manipur is the establishment of an organisation known as

Brahma Sabha. Apart from the evils of the religious organisations, there were certain evils associated with the administration and the king together with other social evils like slavery, polygamy, untouchability and adultery rampant in Manipur as were in other parts of India during this period. With the development of education and growth of social awakening, attempts were made to remove these evils through various organisations, movements and associations under the leadership of the educated elites in Manipur.

Brahma Sabha : It is an organisation which was headed by the king with seven learned Brahmins as its members. The Brahma Sabha's power rose to great heights during the reign of King Chandrakirti (1834-1844) and Churachand (1891-1941). In each village a Hindu temple was built and one or more Brahmins were installed to guide the social and religious life of the people. The village community was ordered to support this financially. People were bound by several rituals and obligations to the Brahmin for family rituals. At the same time only a Brahmin could cook for the feast.[5] The main duty of the Brahma Sabha was to take care of entire Hindu religious matters. It started imposing orthodox customs prevalent in the Hindu society during the eighteenth and the nineteenth centuries. This organisation made various attempts to control the custom of widow re-marriage and divorce. The customs of *Sati* was also introduced in the royal family. However, when two daughters-in-law of King Garibniwaz became *Sati*, he abolished the custom.[6]

When the people of Manipur began to follow all the rules of Brahma Sabha, the Brahmins began to be regarded as deities.

It appears that during the long reign of king Chandrakirti, Hinduism, which had lost its hold during the Burmese occupation was consolidated once more. They enforced the Hindu Vaishnavite value of vegetarianism, the notions of purity, pollution and caste consciousness. Though it was a religious body, yet it worked as a powerful political authority exercising social control over the people.

Brahma Sabha adopted many oppressive methods to enforce rigid norms to maintain social customs. Infact, the motive of the Maharaja was to control the leading educated elite of the state through the Sabha. The religious and social oppressions carried out by the Brahma Sabha on the common people had become unbearable. It ostracised a family or a village at its sweet will, usually sending them to a *Loi* village. They forced the ostracised persons to pay some amount of money, if they wanted to be readmitted into the regular Meitei community by performing *Sudhi* (Purifying ceremony). Hundreds and thousands of poor people suffered under this outrageous ritual. There were punishments for neglecting Vaishnava mark on the forehead, nose and throat in public and people were punished if they ignored the rule of *Chandan Senkhai.*

Administrative Evils : Besides these social and religious injustices the state imposed many levies on the common people e.g. *Pothang Cheithang* (service poster), *Yarek Santri* (night watch or vigil works), *Khewa Lanba* (crossing the river by using boats), *Dolairengi Samasya* (a kind of subscription for using *tilak* marks). Besides, the above instances people in general were not allowed to pluck *simul* cotton even from the *simul* cotton tree grown in their own *patta* land for which tax had been paid by them.

Slavery : In Manipur, slavery system was an age-long institution. It was a social evil of pre-British period. It has been stated that slavery tradition in Manipur existed from time immemorial. But the available records indicate that slavery was introduced for the first time during the reign of Raja Kyamba (1467-1508)[7] and existed till 1891 in Manipur. When the institution of slavery was abolished in British India in 1891 Manipur had her own slave trade.[8] Even after the abolition of slavery its stigma remained in society and an ex-slave could not ordinarily marry a free born girl. He was not allowed to cook or take water in a formal feast of the clan to which he belonged.

There were two kinds of slaves - hereditary slaves and the sold or mortgaged slaves - called '*Minai Channaba*' and '*Minai Asanba*' respectively. The second category of slaves was numerous. There were different kinds of these slaves : slaves out of free will; slaves out of debt; slaves who sold themselves, their children and even wives ; slaves who were sold by their parents (or husband); and thieves who were caught and sold.[9] According to Hodson, of these two kinds of slaves, '*Minai Channaba*' was considered absolute property of the buyer and '*Minai Asanba*' on the other hand was such a slave as remained slave as long as money paid for him (or advanced on him) was not paid back. The latter was like giving work in lieu of the interest of the money paid and should the person who become '*Asanba*' felt ill he was obliged to give a substitute or compensate it in the shape of coin for the labour lost in the interval of sickness. Of course to the *Asanba* no considerable sum would be advanced unless he promised to work for at least for one cultivating season.[10] But in general slavery was the product of indebtedness, laziness, criminal activities, adultery and conquest.

Slavery in a mild form existed in Manipur. The slaves being hereditary ones or people and descendants of people who had sold themselves for debt.[11] They had to pledge for service in lieu of interest for the debt. The use of slaves in Manipur was confined to domestic sphere only. Slavery was neither industrial nor commercial in nature. Slaves were generally treated with kindness and consideration, differing from servants only in that they received no wages.[12]

As described by Col. Mc Cullock, some of them became slaves voluntarily with the view to discharging a money debt which they could not otherwise return and some from sheer laziness. They lived in the same house as their master, ate with him and were altogether like members of the family. Subjugation to abuse or ill treatment of the slaves is an exception. The hill people occasionally sold themselves. But more frequently, they were sold by their relatives. The slaves among hill people were not well treated as the Munnipoorees in a state of slavery[13] but there were many checks on the ill use. If not satisfied with their condition, they used to run to some other house where slaves were better treated. The new master used to pay their prices, however, not in full. The situation of going away of a slave to others' protection is considered a sign of his having been ill treated and so justifying an abatement. Slaves often absconded to the hills too, where they concealed themselves in the hill villages, but as they were likely to be apprehended. They usually preferred passing into the British territory, where they were at once free.[14] Thus, those who had slaves were under the necessity of treating them well. If the party in whose house the slave took refuse was willing to retain him, he might do so on refunding the original price paid. On the other hand, should the slave not be retained, he must be returned to the original owner. Female slaves cost about rupees fifty and male from rupees fifty to rupees seventy.[15]

During the reign of King Chandrakirti Singh, the Raja's slaves numbered about 1,200 to 1,500 among whom were the *Phungganai*-sub-divided into *Hidakphanba* and *Patsangba, Ayokpa, Kei* etc. When the reigns passed from one king to another, it was formerly the custom to seize the slaves of the previous king and to divide them amongst the adherents of the new ruler. This practice, when the changes of rulers became so frequent, was found to entail upon individuals more hardships than the worth of the slave. Slaves, therefore, when seized, were not distributed among adherents, but made to work for the Raja under the name '*Ayokpa*'.[16]

Slaves could be presented by the kings as gifts to anybody whom he like. In case of forced change of royalty, the victorious king could dispose of the slaves among his officers, which caused great hardships to the poor slaves. The chief duty of the Raja's slaves was to cultivate the royal land, retaining for themselves just sufficient of the produce to sustain life and to work for the Raja at all times.[17]

When the British conquered Manipur on 27th April 1891, Major Maxwell, the first Political Agent, counted 1,331 slaves of the king. Individual household slave population could not be ascertained. These household slaves could purchase their liberty but they did not have enough money to buy it. Death alone can liberate such slaves from slavery.[18]

Slavery was in principle abolished by Maxwell in April, 1892, and it was ordered thal all persons called 'slaves' would cease to be slaves within five years from 20th April 1892 or at any previous date on repayment of the purchase money, deducting one-fifth for each year's service effective from the date. In passing this order Maxwell hoped that by offering advances for working on roads etc., many persons would be able to repurchase their liberty before the period of five years as contained in the terms above.[19]

Polygamy : Polygamy is another social evil that attracted the notice of the reformers. The practice of polygamy is one of the aspects of the Meitei society. This practice is followed by those who are economically well off or by those who are unlucky due to the absence of a son or barrenness of the wife. Persons who are adventurous in love affairs and those who seek extramarital relations also join the practice of polygamy.[20]

Polygamy is an accepted custom among the Meitei.[21] It may also be considered that the polygamous society in the present day Manipur is the result of her military adventurism. The male population got depleted and women outnumbered men. In Manipur a man may take any number of wives as he wishes. There is not even the limitations of economic viability insisted upon by certain polygamous societies. It appears that men marry with levity and leave the women if they so choose with impurity. Manipuri society remains as much a man's world as it ever was.[22]

Colonial writers like Dun (1886), Hodson (1908) and Grimwood (1891) have mentioned wide acceptance of polygamy among the royal clan and the urban elite. The Meitei society was polygamous and the Meitei princes were noted for their marriages of polygamous characters. The Raja might have three principal wives with as many as one hundred and eight subsidiary partners. The titles of the Raja's wives in order of precedence were (i) Maharani, (ii) *Apanbi* (which may mean either the preferred one or the one who rules), (iii) *Leimakhubi*. A case in hand is Debindro Singh, who in a short reign of three months, managed to amass ninety six wives, but it is improbable that they were simultaneously members of the royal household.[23]

Polygamy, however, was confined mostly to the richer and higher sections of the society. Today polygamy is most prevalent in urban areas and a rarity in far off rural areas. With their affluence and wealth the rich could afford to become polygamous and licentious. Rather they held that it is a matter of personal pride and social prestige if one could afford it.[24] A few social evils have developed as a result of this superiority complex. Even if a man keeps all his wives, it is clearly beyond his means to provide them with food and clothes and other expenditures involved in the maintenance of such a large family. Under such circumstances, the mother has no option but to take resources to whatever trade she can ply. This in due course, induces in the women a sense of self confidence and being able to stand on their own legs.

The system of polygamy came under critical focus for various reasons. The idea of living together of a man and a woman without performing any ceremony, or, the same being performed after the birth of two or three children, or, before the marriage of their children was regarded as against any moral code sanctioned by religion and the Shastras.[25] People were advised not to involve in such relations.

This male fantasy of a happy polygamous marriage is far from reality in Meitei society. We notice frequent tensions and unhappiness in polygamous homes. When men with children from an earlier wife or wives take new wives, disruption of the family is a common occurrence. The fathers often drift away from their children. Elsewhere, polygamy created various social and domestic complications. It is a social problem because of the bad consequences it entails. The breach of peace in the family, disharmony in conjugal relations and its possible impact on mental health of the family members and other related emotional problems are the consequences of a polygamous family. While eliciting the views of many people in different parts of Manipur, majority of them were found to dislike this practice. There is not much significant variation between the attitude of the less educated and highly educated persons towards this social practice. Inspite of social legislation, hundreds of polygamous marriages are taking place among the people including many educated ones. Therefore, we can say that education has little impact on this spheres of culture. On the contrary, education, like wealth, is a qualification to attract another wife because of the prestigious value attached to its possessor.

It is said that the co-wives in order to control their husband into their personal spell employ a number of weird means. It is believed that administration of excrement of the wife in the food of the husband forms a part of such practice. Jealousy of co-wives in a polygamous family is also expressed by the maxim - "Two tigers cannot live together in the same gorge".[26]

Such proverbs and maxims prevalent in the culture of the people speak out the evil effect of polygamy in the society. Without any sanction of religion, it ruined the lives of innumerable women while causing degradation to the society as a whole.

But with the development of modern education, young boys and girls of new generation gradually have become conscious of the evils of polygamy. A new trend has emerged against the practice of polygamy. Some anthropologists, after interviewing large number of women, have come to the conclusion that most women express deep feeling of injury and loss of honour when their husbands take other wives.

There are visible changes in society. The most frequent tension in conjugal life is caused by the husband's desire for an additional wife and the wife's refusal to take it as a part of her normal life. Among the urban elites, polygamy appears to have a stronger hold. This is probably a result of the adoption of Sanskritized values by women, which inculcate the indissolubility of the marital bond.[27]

Untouchability : Like polygamy untouchability is a vicious evil. On established forms the caste system remained rigid. To the Hindus it was a sure and settled way of existence, sanctified by time and religion. In the eighteenth century the caste system was no problem to the society. But in the eyes of the Europeans of that time, as in the eyes of the Hindu rationalists of the nineteenth century, caste paraphernalia appeared degrading. But at the beginning of the nineteenth century when a rational and secular thinking pervaded all over, the pillars of the caste system were found to be trembling to ramshackles. The untouchables were the outcastes of the Hindu society. The Hindus divided the caste structure of the society into touchables and untouchables in the most irrational way. Untouchability was itself the supreme example of social inequality. But more than that, there was the problem of injustice associated with it. The only redeeming feature of untouchability was that the untouchables belonged to a class of their own. Inside it, an untouchable was accustomed to the traditional ways of his forefathers and did not feel or was not conscious of the injustice to which his class had been subjected to through the ages. But, for centuries, untouchability persisted in the Hindu society as a tradition.

History has known hierarchically graded societies of various types in different epochs and among different peoples. All these societies were based on social privileges and inequalities. However, no hierarchically graded society can be compared with the Hindu society in its extreme gradation of ranks and inequalities of rights. Hardly did any society condemn its section to physical segregation as the Hindu society did in the cases of its untouchables. The mere physical touch of an untouchable was a sin. The untouchables were denied certain basic privileges of living. They could not use tanks, wells, inns and schools meant for upper caste people, not to speak of places of worship or public institutions. An untouchable was punished for a crime by the law of the Hindu state or the village tribunal composed of the caste Hindus, more drastically than a caste Hindu who committed the same crime.

With the impact of western education and the rise of Hindu reform movements in the subsequent century, caste was assailed and there began a slow slackening of right attitudes towards untouchability. It was but natural that the elimination of such an atrocious social phenomenon as untouchability became one of the main planks of the platform of all social reform movements in India. However, inspite of reform movements throughout the nineteenth century, the caste inertia continued without any spectacular improvement in the position of the untouchables. Though different motives and considerations prompted various groups of social reformers in their compaign against untouchability, all recognised it as an institution to be destroyed. When the Chief Minister of Rajasthan led a group of untouchables to the temples in Jaipur city, violent reactions to his action were reported by the press in India.

The practice of untouchability among the Manipuri communities also existed from time immemorial. In ancient times if someone did anything that might displease the king or did not follow the traditional customs he was declared an outcaste and his status in the Manipuri society thus became low. The Muslims and hill tribes were also treated as if they were untouchables and even the people employed for low work were considered untouchables as they did menial works.[28]

On the other hand, the introduction of *Salai* system made a rapid progress in the integration of the state. Powerful and ambitious *salai* chiefs conquered and annexed those who were excluded from the *salai* system and absorbed them into their *salai* and even they became overlord of the neighbouring *salais*. Thus as a case of sub-ordination, Loi community rose up in the Meitei society. In due course *salai* system was replaced by the *yek* system. Under this new system the Meitei society was reorganised and regrouped into seven divisions according to their blood relationships. With the introduction of the *yek* system marriage rule became well established and rigid. Those who refused to observe these rules were treated as outcaste and expelled from the Meitei society. In this way a new section of the people rose up in due course. They came to be known as *Yaithibi*. Thus, a group of low class people was formed in the Meitei society during those days and the problem of untouchability entered into the Meitei society. Their social degradation was so great that, not only were they treated unclean, but also were not allowed to go on the royal roads and to worship the gods and goddesses worshipped by the high caste Meiteis and to live in the type of houses in which the Meiteis normally lived. Their position was not better than that of the 'Dash' or 'Dashu' (Sudra) of the Hindu society.[29]

In Manipur there is a record that the *Yathibis* (low caste community) were treated as the untouchables whenever they went to the market or office. The idea of untouchability gained more momentum with the help of the Brahmins during the beginning of the official adoption of Hinduism by the Meiteis. There existed an old taboo in the Meitei society which forbade all sorts of intercaste marriage strictly and rigidly. The western influence, the popularity of Gandhism and the legislations passed by the Govt. of India through the Hindu Code Bill helped to abolish such an evil practice in Manipur showing the supremacy of public opinion in free India.

Adultery : In the early days the system of both polygamy and polyandry was there in the Manipuri society. But with the introduction of partrilineal society, the system of polygamy became very popular. Polyandry still exists in the Meitei society. A system of having or acquiring more than one husband by a women at a time was known as polyandry. The system of polyandry prevails in the present Meitei society as the present social structure is based on patrilineal form of society. Besides this, polyandry was considered as a kind of marriage under the matrilineal system of society. As a part of its heritage, there were cases of sexual laxity amongst some Manipuri women. Even today there are cases of having secret husbands which are called *Marumba* or *Mawangangnaba*. But the custom dos not permit such laxity, whenever it came to light such woman was either shut up in the house or expelled from the house. The State Government also discourages such a nasty system through punitive steps like causing humiliation (*Khongoinaba*) or forcing the new husband to take the woman and give compensation to the former husband lest both of them should be exiled.

The cases of adultery were very rare as the punishments to adulterers were very severe. The state had a special court for women, i.e. '*Pacha-Loisang*', to deal with all the cases relating to women viz., adultery, insult, beating, divorce etc. A heavy fine was imposed on the adulterer to meet the bride price and it was given to the husband of the woman. The court also took its share of fine. In the 19th century an amount of rupees fifty was levied as fine for *Nupi mamal*, with rupees five being the court's fine.[30] It was considered a heavy fine then. If the offender was not able to pay the said fine he himself along with his family was seized and sold as slaves to the satisfaction of the claimant. Both the male and female offenders were arrested and confined to imprisonment until the claim was satisfied, after which they were freed. For carrying off a women living under a man's protection, but not married, the expenses incurred by the man on the woman must be paid by the party that had taken the women.[31]

Besides the general form of punishment, there were cases of banishment for both male and female by exposing them to the bazar (*Khongoinaba*) and in some cases strictures were passed for the mutilation of manhood too. The punishment for adultery with the members of the royal family by any commoner was usually a capital punishment.[32]

The woman who was involved in adultery was either excommunicated or divorced. Sometimes if the woman was found guilty, she was banished. Some husbands used to cut the hair of their wives instead of taking helps of law courts. So it seems that adultery has been regarded as a social sin and as such the Meiteis despised such women.

Reformation Movements

Though main currents of social reform in India during the 19th century could not reach Manipur, but the spread of education brought a stimulating process of social movements in Manipur. With the introduction of English education many Manipuris came to realise the need for social renovation.

There was no organised social reformation movement as such in Manipur in the 19th century, nor was there any influence of the Indian social resurgence of the period on the Manipuris.[33] Apparently it appears that very few social evils were evident in Manipur even though the social or religious orthodoxy of the upper class Hindus existed since the Brahmins were patronised by the king and the common people. However, the absolutist rule of the monarch and its feudal, social and economic system had their resultant evils against which emerged a consciousness among the educated elite of the kingdom in the middle of the 20th century. Infact encouragement of education by the king himself enabled many young Manipuris to go for higher education to other places, in British India.

Nikhil Hindu Manipuri Mahasabha : The Nikhil Hindu Manipuri Mahasabha was established on 30th May, 1934.[34] The aims and objectives, of the establishment of this organisation were to develop social, cultural, economic and educational spheres of the Manipuri society in order to bring fraternity among the Hindu Manipuris of the state with that of British India and Burma and emancipation of the people from social and religious orthodoxy.[35]

But the leaders of the Mahasabha like Hijam Irabot Singh wanted to use the organisation as an instrument to organise a mass upsurge against the oppressive rule of the British and Maharaja. Some writers regard the establishment of this organisation as a revolutionary upsurge against injustice and oppression.[36] Maharaja was made the president of the Mahasabha and was under the control and influence of the priest of Brahma Sabha.

A determined effort by a few dedicated leaders also helped

to change the outlook of the people. It was directed against social prerogatives of the princes and Brahma Sabha. In this context, the work done by Bankabihari Sharma, Lalita Madhov Sharma and Hijam Irabot Singh will be remembered. The Maharaja's ostracism could produce gruesome situations for the individual and his family even in death. The Dharma Sabha, in the form of Gauriya Sampraday, was taking shelter in the purity and impurity fixed by the Brahma Sabha. As a result of this sometimes the dead body of a man or a woman would remain unburned for two or three days. There was no one to perform the work of cremation. Even Shital Singh, the successor of His Highness, Sir Churachand Singh,was prevented from entering his own house or his wife's house for marrying a '*yek*' (blood relation) and when the bride moved ceremoniously around the bridegroom with a handful of flowers in her hand by singing a marriage song, the singing party went away. The Gauriya Dharma Pracharak Sabha of Mahasabha concluded the marriage ceremony. Regarding the purity and impurity, Atombapu Sharma, Laimayum Leirenjao Singh, Hijam Irabot Singh, Nongmeikapam Nabakishore Singh, Aribam Kunjabihari Sharma etc. submitted an application containing exortion charges to the president, Manipur State Durbar, against the Brahma Sabha. As a response to it a sum of Rs. 81 (eighty-one) was fixed for purifying an unchaste person, and in case of atonement without money, it could be done with three leaves of *tulasi* (Ocimum sanctum). This practice continued even when the Nikhil Hindu Manipuri Mahasabha was established.

Apart from petitioning against Brahma Sabha, educated persons tried to create public opinion through the press. Ningthoujam Leiren Singh published a monthly paper called '*Yaiphakol*' in 1925. It commented sarcastically on the rituals of purity and impurity. This publication was able to create a consciousness among the people. Then some radical members led by Hijam Irabot Singh started a movement against these social evils by convincing the members of the Mahasabha that in the absence of the democratic constitutional reform, the welfare of the people could not be taken care of effectively in Manipur. Hijam Irabot Singh stands as a champion of the masses. With Irabot Singh taking up the anti-monarchical stances, the Maharaja gradually withdrew from the Mahasabha, which, in the Chinga session of 1938, was renamed as the Nikhil Manipuri Mahasabha. The Mahasabha stubbornly opposed the religious exploitation and social persecution carried out by the Brahmins and the king. The Chinga session of the Mahasabha demanded a fully responsible government of Manipur. Whereas the session is regarded as a significant step towards a political change in the history of Manipur on one hand, it also strongly pleaded for the mass-education of children including girls upto primary stage and establishment of an institution of higher learning in the state on the other.[37]

The various works of Mahasabha had far reaching consequences. It included appropriate opportunities for the Manipuri people residing in the valley to establish contacts with the people living at remote places. This would enable them to exchange views with one another. It also strengthened social bond among Manipuris which in turn helped reorganisation of the cultural forces.

'The Manipuri Itihasik Anusandhan Samiti' was established for the discovery of various ancient records which remained unsearched for thousands of years. In this dynamic world, the new flux of developmental currents reached Manipur slowly for geographical reasons. An effort for developing its educational, cultural, economic and political activity and development in respect of its language, its distinct literature, religion, education and science based on equal opportunities for all has been made. Efforts have also been made to keep Manipur's distinct cultural identity recently by the government. Various ventures have also been initiated to ameliorate the distress of women folk in the state by the Nari Raksha Samiti. Women's education receives constant encouragement from the government of the state at present.

Women's Agitation : Women's agitation or *Nupi lan* of 1939 was an important event in the Meitei society. It was carried on solely by the womenfolk. The colonial writers regarded the outbreak of this movement as the most important event of the war of 1939.[38] The deep rooted cause of the movement was directly related to the irregularities and malpractices in the administration of the state.[39] The new administrative system introduced by the colonial authority had caused a widespread dissatisfaction among the people of Manipur. This dissatisfaction was first expressed in the movement of 1904, which was also launched by the women of

Manipur, who always played a vital role in the economic life of the state, as a protest against injustices of the British authority. This was a striking feature of political awakening of Manipuri women. The women of Manipur take a major part in the economic life of the state in which they enjoy maximum independence. This high status accorded to the womenfolk is regarded as one of the greatest prides of Manipur.

The colonial writers were impressed by the contribution of women in Meitei society. On the women's important role in the economy, it is stated that women perform every kind of work except the heaviest and form the mainstay of their family.[40] The Manipuri women are also called "the great traders".[41] "Apart from the economic activity the market is also an important venue of social and political interaction. It was this aspect of Khwairamband bazar which played a crucial role in the outbreak of the Nupi-lan".[42]

But from the year 1891, i.e., after the introduction of direct colonial rule the whole traditional economy of the state changed. The British authority introduced a free trade policy which ultimately gave a great economic benefit to the British. Under the colonial economic policy, the British officials began to control the trade and industry of the state. The main aim of the colonial conquest was to satisfy and enable British government to secure for themselves the most advantageous strategic economic position.[43] This colonial policy was one of the main causes of the outbreak of the Nupi-lan or women's agitation of 1904.

It was directly related to the existing political, social and economic condition of the state which developed after the introduction of colonial administrative system. Regarding the colonial economic policy of the British, it is said that the development of the colonial economy almost invariably began with the distruption of the static, low level, self sufficient economy of the village communities based on the integration of local agriculture with handicraft and small industries.[44] Further reactions in the form of an agitation by the women against the government imposition of water tax were witnessed in 1925. Once again the women of Manipur launced a widespread movement in the year 1939, which is known as women's agitation of 1939 and it was led by Hijam

Irabot Singh. He became a pillar of strength of this movement. The tradewomen organised a massive demonstration against the official policy of exporting rice outside Manipur by the Marwari merchants. As a result of it, there was a sudden increase of the price of rice and Manipur was fast approaching near famine. On the other hand, merchants from outside the state began to set up rice mills. They purchased the paddy as much as they could get, milled it and exported to other states. As the price of rice started soaring posing the conditions of acute scarcity the women tried to check up such milling of rice and tried to prevent the export of rice outside Manipur. This led to the outbreak of the movement of 1939 and it gave a serious blow to the economic policy of the feudal and colonial authorities. Moreover, this movement brought a new reform into the Manipur state.[45] This movement was a great landmark in the colonial history of Manipur. It brought drastic change in every aspect of life of the people of Manipur. It brought social and political consciousness and a movement for the constitutional and administrative reform in the state which resulted in the emergence of a new Manipur. The vanguard of these changes were the women who had launched a massive movement against feudal and colonial rule.

Once the women succeeded in controlling the economic catastrophe, several male leaders like Hijam Irabot Singh, Ngangom Tompok Singh and other members of the Mahasabha appeared on the scene and raised many other grievances against the government. Their demands were now geared towards the change in the Durbar and other administrative policies. This movement was mainly due to the growth of the social consciousness of a group of educated elite who supported this agitation behind the scene. Similarly several other collective movements have also started during the past few decades. Women of Manipur took up many vital constructive works. Women of several urban localities organised protest against liquor sale, drinking being a major social vice which has affected the lives of a large number of Meitei males. Mature women organised themselves into groups of night patrollers and guarded their neighbourhoods against any man consuming liquor, and risking addiction to excessive drinking. Apparently, a collective spirit rather than a single individual is the main force behind the women's upsurges. A number of associations known as 'Meira Paibi' and 'Nisha Bandh' were formed in several districts of Manipur to liberate people from this dangerous habit of intoxication and using liquor which have been causing immense harm to the poeple and society. The women started giving illustrations from the lives of a number of persons who had lost their property, health and morality and gradually had marched towards death in an early age due to such habits of using liquor.

Some of the important women's associations in Manipur are All Manipur Women's Social Reformation and Development Samaj. All Manipur Rural Women's Welfare and Upliftment Association and Manipuri Women's Society. They try to find out the evils of the society and attempt to safeguard the women's community and also promote welfare of the humanfolk as a whole.

The establishment of All Manipur Students Union was a major step towards the path of social development and progress. The main aim and objectives of this organisation is to achieve common ends through equality, fraternity and justice and promote and protect educational, social, cultural, physical, moral, intellectual and scientific advancements of the general public and the students in particular. Similarly many associations were formed in order to create conditions favourable to reform through the education of public opinion for social progress and national development. The growth of education brought new ideas to these groups of men and they tried to act against social evils and prejudices. Thus there came about a new change in the social life of the Manipuris where greater emphasis is laid on the acquisition of education for all round progress of one's personality.

It can be safely concluded that the present Manipuri society marching thr ugh the dynamic path of modernism owes much to the rise of education and secular forces that shattered the foundation of injustice and orthodoxy. The popularity of education through various schools and colleges in Manipur has added new dimensions to the society and dynamic roles to the youth of Manipur. Like various movements for reforms through which the Manipuri society has passed, the day is not very far away when the state might attain the stage of maximum educated population in India.

References :

1. **V.A. Narain** : *Social History of Modern India* (1973), p.5.
2. **J. N. Farquhar** : *Modern Religious Movements in India* (1915), p.21.
3. **K. P. Karunakaran** : *Religious and Political Awakening in India,* (1965), p. 50.
4. **Har Bilas Sarda** : *Life of Dayananda Saraswati* (1946), p. 255.
5. **Nobinchandra Singh** : *Ethnographic History of Brahmins in Manipur,* Regional Integration Vol. 8, No. 15, pp. 31-32.
6. **L. Ibungohal Singh and N. Khelchandra Singh** : *Cheitharol Kumbaba* (1967), p. 74.
7. **Minai phunga punba shillon (MS)** : *Manipuri puya.*
8. **N. Ibobi Singh** : *The Manipuri Administration* (1709-1907) (1975), p. 216.
9. **Gangmumei Kabui** : *Social and Religious Reform Movements in 19th and 20th Centuries* (Edited by S.P. Sen, 1979), p. 412.
10. **T.C. Hodson** : *The Meitheis* (1908), pp. 90-91.
11. **James Johnstone** : *My Experience in Manipur and Naga Hills* (1896), p. 117.
12. **B. C. Allen** : *District Gazetteer of Assam, Naga Hills and Manipur,* Vol. IX, Part 4 (1905), p. 97.
13. **N. Ibobi Singh** : *op.cit.,* p. 223.
14. **T.C. Hodson** : *op.cit.,* p. 91.
15. **R. Brown** : *op. cit.,* p. 47.
16. **E.W. Dun** : *Gazetteer of Manipur* (1886), p. 25.
17. **Gangmumei Kabui** : *Op. cit.* pp. 413- 414.
18. **Robert Reid** : *History of Frontier Areas Bordering Assam,* (1942), p. 75.
19. **M. Bhattacharjee** : *Gazetteer of Manipur State* (1963), p. 298.

20. **S. Gyaneswar Singh** : *Impact of modern Education in Manipur,* unpublished Ph. D. thesis, Gauhati University (1979), p. 225.

21. **Manjusri Chaki Sircar** : *Feminism in a Traditional Society* (1984), p. 80.

22. **R. Constantine** : *Manipur Maid of the Mountains,* (1981), p. 145.

23. **T.C. Hodson** : *op.cit.,* p. 76.

24. **Puri Das Chopra** : *Social, Cultural and Economic History of India* (1974), pp. 86-87.

25. ***Arunodoi*** : Vol. II, No. 12 (1947).

26. **S. Gyaneswar Singh** : *op. cit.,* p. 226.

27. **Manjusri Chaki Sircar** : *op. cit.,* p. 202.

28. **M. Kirti Singh** : *History of Journalism in Manipur (in Manipuri)* (1980), p. 69.

29. **N. Birachandra Singh** : *Socio-Religious Life of the Meitheis in 18th Century, unpublished Ph. D. thesis, Manipur University (1987), pp, 95-96.*

30. **T. C. Hodson** : *op. cit.,* p. 92.

31. **E.W. Dun** : *op.cit.,* p. 18.

32. **N. Birachandra** : *op.cit.,* p. 118.

33. **Gangmumei Kabui** : *op.cit.,* p. 411.

34. **L. Yaima Singh and R.K. Maipaksana Singh** : *Nikhil Hindu Manipuri Mahasabha* (1983), p. 2.

35. **Gangmumei Kabui** : *Leftiest Movement in Manipur, A Case History of Comrade Hijam Irabot Singh* (A paper presented to the 35th session of the Indian History Congress), Jadavpur (1974), p. 2.

36. **Soyam Chhatradhari Singh** : *Manipur Itihasta Irabot* (1972), p.8.

37. **Th. Bira Singh** : *Comrade Irabot* (1983), p. 18.

38. *Administrative Report of Manipur Political Agency* (1939-1940), p. 1.

39. **N. Joykumar Singh** : *Social Movements in Manipur,* (1987), p. 14.

40. **E.W. Dun** : *op. cit.,* p. 17.

41. **James Johnstone** : *op.cit.,* p. 134; T. C. Hodson, *op. cit.,* p.23.

42. **Manjusri Chaki Sircar** : *op.cit.,* p. 34.

43. **Georgy Rudenko** : *Colonialism and Neo-Colonialism,* p. 17.

44. **B. N. Ganguly** : *India - A Colonial Economy 1757-1949,* published in "Enquiry" 1958.

45. *Administrative Report of Manipur Political Agency* (1940-41), p. 1.

8

Social Development

A New Trend in Social Life

Social progress is indicated by the level of intellectual development of the people. Educational backwardness is the main factor of social degradation. The role of English education introduced by the British people in bringing social changes in the twentieth century cannot be denied. The object of some of the British officials behind the move for the spread of education in India might not have been purely humanitarian. The British introduced and encouraged education to get a better class of subordinate staff for administration. But no one can deny that it unfolded before the Indian youths the vista of a new world and sowed in their minds the seeds of an intellectual revolution pregnant with mighty consequences. In Bengal Raja Ram Mohan Roy, with the support of a section of the society pleaded for English education and took the lead in the spread of English education in the nineteenth century. Thus the demand for English education came from Indians themselves.[1]

But in Manipur the case was quite different. Here the desire to learn English could be found in fewer instances. English education in Manipur was in fact misconstrued as it received little encouragement in the days of the native rule in Manipur. It is reported that there were no schools and any sort of assistance in the formation of schools were not forthcoming. The rate of illiteracy was so high that even officials could hardly read and write without any display of apparent shame.[2] People did not like to take western education on religious grounds. As the political agent was a Christian, they also did not like to have social contact with him. It was thought in those days that anybody who would receive western education might be excommunicated.

In the history of progress of education in Manipur, perhaps, pioneering work was done by Major General Sir James Johnstone, the then Political Agent in Manipur. He established a school at Imphal in 1885.[3] Before 1885, formal schooling on the western model was unknown in Manipur. Only indigenous education consisting of literacy, physical education, health and hygiene, games and indigenous medicine etc. was conducted by the *Pandits* and *Maichous*. The Survey Report of Education prepared by National Council of Educational Research and Training Team in 1972-73 stated that, "Inspite of their constant pre-occupations with military exploits, Manipuri kings were great patrons of art and learning as is evinced by the ancient literature in subjects like history, astronomy, medicine, moral instructions etc. Learning of Sanskrit was popular in earlier ages and was imparted through the indigenous schools called '*Tols*'.[4] Again while studying the educational history of a country we cannot undermine the importance of socio-cultural, economic and political aspects of the people. A feudal state, situated at the confluence of three great civilisations of India, China and Burma, agrarian in economic foundation, but in hostility with her neighbours, Manipur had not a peaceful past. Not only the external threat from her powerful neighbour, Burma, but also the internal strife among the different principalities namely, Ningthouja, Moirang, Khuman, Angom, Luwang and Khaba-Nganba to dominate the political scene in the valley was also her problem. In such a political atmosphere the people had to exert their energy for the defence of the country as an utmost priority. As such, excellence in the art of fighting with the sword and spear and keeping fitness of physique - all these dominated the whole educational scene.[5] In the past, people were highly patriotic and were noted for chivalry and gallantary. A handful of men with conventional weapons fought the mighty British in the battle of occupation in 1891. The people and rulers were concerned more with military education than formal education. As mentioned earlier, inspite of their constant occupation with military activities, Meitei kings were great patrons of learning, too. The few who devoted themselves to liberal education, received sufficient royal patronage and public recongition. Only those persons who could show merit in the war and hunting of wild animals were highly honoured by the kings by giving respectable posts and their daughters in marriage irrespective of caste.[6]

It should, however, be noted that, long before the arrival of the British in Manipur the Meiteis (Manipuris) had their own system of literary education. But it was considered to be of secondary importance. For literary education the princes were sent to the house of the learned *Gurus* (*Maichous*) to learn the art of royalty and administration. For example, prince Naothingkhong (663-763) was sent to the house of Luwang Ningthou Punshiba to receive education in different arts.[7] Similar was the case with the commoners also. The pupils had to go to the house of the learned teachers for receiving instruction. The guardians of the students had to pay the teacher in money or in kind. There was also a custom to do menial work for the Guru by the pupils. Vaishnavism made an important contribution to the intellectual life of the people before the advent of western system of education. Vocational subjects like music, dance, etc. were also studied by the people.[8]

Schools on the modern lines were first introduced by the officers of the British Political Agency in Manipur in order to impart instruction to their own children. Earlier a primary school had been established by Capt. Gordon but it soon died out. In 1872 a vernacular school was established in Manipur at the suggestion of the then Political Agent, Major General, W.F. Nuthall. But, for want of encouragement on the part of the authorities, it was nearly closed.[9] During his tenure in Manipur, Johnstone had made repeated efforts of the establishment of an English School at Imphal. After a good deal of persuasion, a Middle English School was established at Imphal in 1885. This marked the beginning of general English education in the state.

The Christian Missionaries played an important role in the education of the hill tribes. Mention may be made of Reverend William Pettigrew of the American Baptist Mission and his contribution in spreading western education in the hill areas. Along with their missionary activities they started many schools. As stated in the Administrative Report, the quality of education imparted by Mission Schools was superior to all other primary schools established by the government.[10]

The Christian Missionaries were interested in education only in so far as it served the purpose of enabling them to convert the people to their faith.[12] Both the agencies of missionaries and government went hand in hand in the spread of western education in the formative period of educational development in the hills. Hill people had been very much influenced by western education. It brought a change in their social life while Christianity brought changes in their customs and traditions.

According to the Government Report, women were not educated during the pre-Independence period. The advantages of domestic or school education were open to the girls of the royal families or to the children of the affluent families. Of course, the Manipuri society was free from many social evils like child marriage, dowry system and *purdah* which were great obstacles in the progress of women's education in other parts of India. But these customs were known to Manipur where women hold such an important position and play a better and more efficient role in the economic activity of the state than their menfolk. And in the family also a girl was given more responsibilities than a boy. This led to the neglect of girl's education and early drop-out of girls from schools. The Survey Report found that percentage of girls enrolled was always lower than those of the boys at every stage in every district of Manipur. Another obstacle to women's education was the wrong notion prevalent among the common masses that educated girls became more independent than the uneducated ones. So, it was believed that education spoiled a girl. Thus common people did not like to select educated girls even as their brides. Knowledge of three R's was not accepted as a desirable qualification of a girl in the society. In Manipur state, weaving, cooking, husking of paddy etc. were considered greater accomplishments for a girl. To be a good housewife - that was required of a girl and they could be well equipped in these arts by their mothers and other members of the family. So guardians felt no necessity of sending their daughters to school. Mr. A.E. Woods, the Political Agent of Manipur wrote in his Administrative Report that the Manipuris were not much interested in imparting education to their daughters as to their sons.

Western education made important impact on the life of the girls. They came out from solitary confinement of their houses and realised the value of freedom by becoming 'working girls'.

Another significant feature of the last decades of the twentieth century is the entry of women into the professions.[13] Earlier, the girls were given domestic jobs and married women did outdoor jobs such as working in the fields, selling of commodities and weaving. The educated women became enlightened and with the advance of time people realised the importance of their education.

Later on in 1945, Maharani Dhanamanjuri Devi took keen interest in spreading western education in Manipur and she established the first college in Manipur, Dhanamanjuri College after her name. Subsequently many colleges like Imphal College, Manipur College, Oriental College, Moirang College, Post Graduate Training College, G.P. Women's College etc. have sprung up at Imphal. With the growing appreciation of the advantages of higher education by the Manipuris, a new orientation in their general outlook appeared. Till Manipur's merger into India in 1949, progress of modern education was quite slow in the state mainly because of the fact that the British rulers were more interested in the spread of Christianity than in the spread of education. The number of intelligent persons in the society who could understand the importance of an extended system of education was very few and therefore support from the public for a well developed educational system was non-existent. It took many years for the people to change their attitude to education and realize its importance. It gradually dawned upon the mind of the pople that alongwith the improvement of physical health, the mental or intellectual development was of great importance for the progress of the society.

The role of modern means of transport in the consolidation of the people into modern nation cannot be ignored. The pre-British India could not develop a large-scale, unified economic, social and cultural bond in the country due to hopelessly bad transport system. In the absence of any appreciable social exchange among the people, they could not develop national consciousness and outlook.[14]

The development of modern means of transport and communication established after the British regime paved the way for bringing a closer social and economic integration and more rapid cultural advancement of the people.

Formerly, people of Manipur used boats, horses, elephants and bullock carts as means of bringing commodities and goods from one place to another. With the improvement of transport and communication system, mobility of men and goods was accelerated. As transport system developed, the people of the state were also exposed to the highly developed social system of other advanced states.

With the advancement of science and technical education, there have been great changes in the society. After the British conquest, the flow of European technology greatly increased; introduction of modern means of communication, telegraphy, wireless, printing press, construction of roads and mechanised means of transport (cycle, motor, vehicles etc.), introduction of electric power, modern medicine and modern health services, water supply and Civil Engineering constitute the new technology.[15] These are some of the factors which are responsible for bringing a vital change in the state of education and social life in Manipur.

When society becomes modernised its members are motivated to raise their social status. Emerging factors like urbanisation, industrialisation, spread of education and specialised training motivate the people to send their children for higher education in order to raise their social status.

With the improvement of the transport and communication system came great changes in the economic aspects of agriculture in the state and increased the economic well being of the people. Modern educational system, which trains the individuals in different vocations and allots different occupational roles, played vital roles in the advancement of the society.

In primitive societies, the only means of production was the hand and the hand made tools. However, it gradually transformed to the use of modern machines for large scale productions. Factories, well organised transport and communication system and electricity are the blood veins of modern society. They are the gifts of the present day education to society. In the past, people did not make any earnest effort to promote education among themselves since it was an entirely new thing. It was supposed to be superfluous and wasteful. With the change of time and subsequent spread of education, this adamant attitude towards education changed and society reaped a rich harvest from a highly developed educational system.

During early days in Manipur, the people living in valley had more or less an egalitarian society.[16] But after conversion to Hinduism, the Brahmins came to occupy the highest position in the society and their role in the new social set up became highly important. With the increasing grip of Hinduism the Brahma Sabha became very powerful. Attempts were made to impose orthodoxy and conservatism in the valley. The society began to change and hierarchical order of castes, sub-castes and privileged social position were established. The most dominant position was that of the Kshatriyas among whom the royal class held the supreme position. At the lowest strata were the *Lois*. It appeared to be a rigid caste system in practice in the state. But this was quite different from caste system prevalent in other Hindu areas of India.[17] It was the privilege of king to admit any person as a Hindu on payment of certain nominal fees.

The Brahma Sabha enforced the Hindu Vaishnavite values of vegetarianism, the notion of purity, pollution and caste consciousness. Besides being a religious body, it worked as a powerful political authority exercising social control over the people. There were punishments even for neglecting Vaishnava mark on the forehead, nose and throat in public.[18]

One of the changes that have been taking place during the later part of the present century is the gradual breakdown of the age old distinction in society, the two classes of people - the royal aristocracy and the common people. There were certain restrictions in dress and ornaments, type of house, the use of means of transportation etc. of the common people. A man of lower status was not permitted to sit in front of a person of a higher class in a social gathering. In the recent years the distinction in the society has been maintained more or less according to the merit and qualitative rank of the people rather than the earlier class practice.

Western education and the policy of a secular democratic government opened the scope for everyone, irrespective of caste and creed to get education. In such a free atmosphere, the Christian missionaries played a successful role in the conversion of the tribals to Christianity and spread of education among them. The tribals came to be attracted, under the influence of Christianity, to western culture and as a result changes in their dress, living style, behaviour and outlook occurred. Their material well being also considerably improved.

During the sixties and seventies of the 20th century many people came forward to champion and promote higher education in Manipur. With the object of a wide diffusion of higher English education among the people of Manipur and to bring it within the reach of the common people many educational institutions were opened. The demand for higher education led to the opening of more colleges through public contribution by the middle of the present century. Manipur has been experiencing increased modernisation since the end of the World War II with the introduction of public transport, schools and colleges, movie houses, roadside hotels, telephones, air transport and a tremendously improved transportation system. It illustrates the changing pattern of a society accommodating the advent of modern facilities. The advent of modern education has ushered in a rapid rise of literacy. These attempts led to the emergence of a group of educated persons who were eager to adopt the modern way of life.

After getting modern education people in Manipur began to use modern equipments and implements. Earlier for measuring seasons they used to observe the waxing and the waning of the moon, the sunrise and the sunset which were too crude. In the ancient time the Manipuris had a traditional technique for measuring time by using a simple instrument called *Tan* which was just the reverse of the principle of Clepysdra.[19] The use of *Tan* which was introduced in Manipur during the 2nd century A.D. continued with great sincerity till 1891. However, after the British rule the outlook of the people changed and they came to rely more and more on watches and clocks. People started using wrist watches to keep their activities syncronised. Hours of meals and rest were fixed. Urban life is an adaptive society. Life is symbolised by the clock, the traffic light, the hooter, the time table, the shift system and warning notice. Until people know how to use leisure time wisely, spend money efficiently, learn the new concept of time and space and to relate cause and effect in a rational way, disorganisation persists. In fact there has been streams of changes in the whole gamut of one's life and one has to try hard to adjust and adapt himself to the new and changed situation. Every adjustment to this change has evolved from the surrender of old loyalties, relationship and life style and the learning of new ways.

Educationists have been emphasising the role of education as an instrument of change. Any society which is interested in the welfare of its members cannot afford to ignore this important role of education in life. In order to remove the deficiencies in the current system, the Government of Manipur appointed a committee of experts to consider the educational system in Manipur and to recommend to the government a suitable educational policy which would serve best the interest of education and its development in the state. "Education is an important means of ensuring social, cultural and technological continuity and yet at the same time a means for ensuring readiness of citizens to change in response to new needs".[20]

In a modern society, knowledge increases at a terrific pace and social change is very rapid. This needs a radical transformation in the educational system. To modernise itself, a society has to educate itself.

Modernisation can be achieved through social reforms which transforms the traditional society, by expanding the educational system, by creating a modern system of administration and state authorities, by disseminating the achievements of modern scientific knowledge and by organising more productive process in rural areas. By and large, the objective of English education was to induce a social and intellectual change. In Manipur also, the educated Manipuri middle class became the most vocal element in society. Education is a vital input in the modernisation and development of the state. It must help in illuminating the young mind, unfolding of creative powers and developing the students' moral, intellectual, aesthetical and practical capacities. But this is only possible if the environment in which they work is sympathetic and conducive to intellectual and social activity.[21]

The growth of education brought new ideas among the educated people. Thus there came about a new trend in the social life of the people of Manipur. Educated persons of different ethnic groups began to raise their voices against social prejudices like slavery, polygamy, clean and unclean, untouchability etc. Several local organisations were formed by enthusiastic Manipuris.

Among the Manipuris, marriages are mostly settled by the guardians but very often boys and girls reach an understanding before involving the guardians.[22] Such boys and girls meet and exchange their ideas through social gatherings like *Likkol* (a cowrie game), *Thabal Chongba, Kang, Sinaipham Kabi* at community *sangoi* or *mandops* in presence of other people. If a boy and a girl happen to fall in love such occasions serve as means of communications for them.[23]

In order to meet girls, sometimes, boys visit their houses and sit at the verandah of house when the girl is seen weaving but they are not usually permitted to enter the house.

Modernisation has brought some changes. The romantic boat-rides and collection of water lilies, and outings are things of the past. A boy does not go to a girl's house for his daily meetings with her. Movie houses, walks to colleges or the village corners have replaced the former rendezvous.

With the advancement of society and progress of western education there has been certain changes in marriage system also. In addition to the traditional system of marriages, court marriage and advertisement in matrimonial columns also have become popular these days.

Progress of education and concerted efforts of many organisations have raised the marriageable age of boys and girls also. In India, every year about 3 million brides out of 4½ million marriages are in 15-19 age group. The salient reasons behind early marriages are pressures from elders, customs and anxiety of parents about the grown up marriageable girls. Customs and traditions play a major role in determining the age of marriage.[24] Education helped many individuals in raising their social status through marriage. Those who were economically hard pressed were sometimes forced to delay the marriages of their daughters because of their inability to meet heavy expenses of a marriage. On the other hand it has also benefitted young women in many ways, as for example the agonies of child birth are to some extent lessened in the grown up women.

With the spread of education there is an awareness of population control and family planning and adequate health services among the masses. Awareness of family planning is fairly widespread and over 60% people have attitudes favourable to restricting and spacing births. They realise the difficulties of more children which require more food, more clothing and more space for living. And the concept of small family has taken deep roots among the educated.[25]

As such, there is the rapid growth of population in Manipur. It is attributed to the low death rate because of improvement in health and medical facilities. The control in the infant mortality may be taken as an indication of the progress of society.[26] Apart from low infant mortality, other conspicuous achievements of modern health programmes are - low death rate and prolonged life span.

The educated and resourceful persons of Manipur like Hijam Irabot, Sri Atombapu Sharma edited *Meitei Chanu* and *Dainik Manipuri* which show a clear picture of religious, cultural and social aspects of the Manipuris and the *Manipuri Matam*, the daily paper of the time, also reflected the aims and objectives of the Mahasabha and expressed the opinion of the Mahasabha against social prejudices and propagated new ideas. Besides, many monthly magazines of 1950's like *Yaiphakol* and *Lalit Manjuri Patrika* may be mentioned for the vital role they played in propagating and creating public opinion against social prejudices. Such periodicals and newspapers dealt with public opinion of that time and played a vital role in promoting Manipuri language, literature and patriotic feelings among the masses.

The era of Manipuri journalism and free press played a great role in social development. When western education came to India, there came free expression of public opinion which was not possible earlier and a more remarkable progress in it could be seen during the post-Independence period. These were the reflections of the progress that society has been making.

The growth of literacy led to the rise of the press, journalism and periodicals both in English and the vernacular and free expression of public opinion which helped to accelerate the pace of social reforms and national consciousness among the masses of Manipur.

Social Consciousness

The beginning of the twentieth century saw the continuation of the trend that had started in the last two decades of the nineteenth century. With the establishment of a Middle English School earlier and D.M. College later, Manipur entered into the stream of modernity and thus a new phase in the history of its society started. A group of educated men emerged who showed leaning towards new ideas. Naturally enough attempts were made by a few enlightened persons of Manipur to encourage this education. Educational institutions received support from many local bodies also. There were efforts and interest for the establishment of colleges. People came forward to champion and promote higher education in Manipur.

Educational endowments to promote education in different classes were a common phenomenon during this period. Perhaps the endowment by Maharani Dhanamanjuri was the earliest in Manipur.[27]

In the beginning a demand for education in English arose among those who were accustomed of taking government jobs. They desired to learn English because it was the only language of administration. In the Hindu society, the Brahmins being the superior caste, occupied a high status and the nobility and the royal families being the highest class, not only occupied a position of dignity but also enjoyed certain privileges in the society. Naturally at the beginning of the twentieth century almost all the leaders of educational development belonged to these classes. In fact, the educated group of Manipur mainly comprised of members of these sections and classes, and the doors of education were opened commonly to them only.

During this period the government was approached by various private agencies and local bodies to help in spreading education. In regard to education, there were several other matters which engaged the attention of the enlightened leaders of the people.

The educational progress naturally led to the removal of many social evils. Many local associations were formed by the educated people with a view to reform society. Encouragement of education by the king of Manipur enabled many young Manipuris to get higher education from outside Manipur and these people came back with new outlook.

Western education in its wake, like in every other places of India, brought a wave of change in the social values in Manipur, too. People began to value the idea of liberal humanism brought by the new education and they began not only to appreciate it, but also to adjust their lives with the changing envrionment. After this the old taboos started declining. More and more Manipuris started getting western education, which revolutionised their life.[28]

A political organisation, named Nikhil Hindu Manipuri Mahasabha was set up in 1934. The Maharaja himself took the leading part in its deliberations. Indian National Congress was the guiding force behind it. The Mahasabha followed the ideology and the policy of the Indian National Congress but the programme was modified to suit the local needs. The political consciousness of the people was indirectly aroused by Maharaja Churachand himself.

In the meantime, the religious and social oppressions carried out by the Brahma Sabha on the common people were unbearable. They used to ostracise a family or a village at their sweet will. However, the king had the power to declare such people, in return of a payment of a certain amount of money, clean and allow their readmission to Hindu society. These people would be allowed to wear the sacred thread again and was known to have enjoyed a second birth. The practice however grew oppressive and many poor people suffered. Besides these social and religious injustices, the state imposed many levies on the common people. Some prominent leaders of the Mahasabha had started movements against these excesses.

Politically, women took the leading role in showing the people's discontent against various injustices of the British administration. *Nupi-Lan* (women's war or agitation) in 1939 against transportation of rice outside Manipur which gave rise to unprecendented price-rise in the local market, is unique in the history anywhere in the world. It brought a new political awakening which gave rise to several mass organisations during post, 1940 period. The vanguard role played by the toiling women to rouse the people, had no parallel anywhere in India before 1947.

A group led by Irabot Singh, called Praja Sammelini, was formed to press for constitutional reform without which the social and economic ills of the people could not be redressed. A non co-operation movement was started as a result of which the religious levies and other necessary taxes were abolished.

The tribal revolt in Manipur was the expression of resistance against imperialist exploitation. Unable to bear the tyranical exploitation of colonialism, the Kukis rose to open rebellion against the British in 1917. This rebellion was an open challenge to British imperialism and is a great watershed in the history of Manipur.

The Kuki uprising (1930-32) was another major rebellion in the history of the state. Although it could not materialise, it marked the beginning of political movement and national consciousness among the hill people of Manipur. After 1930, the impacts of national movements were visible in Manipur.

With the increasing social and political consciousness, many associations and organisations were formed by the educated people of Manipur which took major steps forward in the path of social development. The youths formed powerful organisations to fight social evils effectively.

By and large they were active on the social and economic fronts also. They were equally vigilant against the anti-national elements who did not enjoy any respect in the eyes of the people. There arose sentiments against exploitation done by the business community and others, too. For this the credit goes to western education which brought new ideas and novel ways of thinking.

Over and above, the establishment of All Manipur Students Union was a major step forward in the path of social development. The main aims and objectives of this organisation were to achieve common ends through equality, fraternity and justice and to promote and protect educational, social, cultural, physical, moral, intellectual and scientific advancement of the general pulbic and the student in particular through the spirit of unity, co-operation and selfless service. Besides it, there were many other associations which helped to a great extent in the progress and development of the social life of the people of Manipur.

The All Manipur Women's Social Reformation and Development Samaj also played a vital role for the safeguard of the women community as well as for the improvement and advancement of women's education.

In the three decades between 1950 and 1980, many colleges had been established from the sympathy and support of the public.

Many scholarships were also awarded to encourage education in Manipur. The pupils who secured first division in the lower primary examination were awarded state scholarship of Rs. 3 per month by the state for two years. And the others who passed the primary examination and joined the Johnstone Middle School were awarded Rs. 2 each. In 1901-10, one pupil was sent to Sylhet (Bangladesh) to appear at the Matriculation examination and was successful. He received the special government scholarship of Rs. 10. Under the State Government Scholarship Scheme, deserving students were sent outside Manipur to receive professional education like Engineering, Medicine, Veterinary and Higher Sanskrit education.

For the first time in Manipur, in 1914-15 the first boy came out after passing his medical examination. He was not only married to the kings daughter, many other favours were bestowed on him by the king. Before it, people used to get treatment of the diseases by applying various herbal medicines. Fortunately a change was visible in the attitude of the Manipuris. A group of educated middle class emerged who came to assert interest in modern education. Most of them belonged to those groups of people which first took the initiative to take the new education.

Hijam Irabot Singh, Bankabihari Sharma, Lalitamadhob Sharma, Dwijamani Dev Sharma, Elangbam Tompok Singh, Nongmeikapam Gopal Singh, Ningthoujam Leiren Singh, were some of the prominent persons among the educated Manipuris. They constituted an elite, the vanguard of social and political movements in Manipur. They began their work during this very period. Many of them went outside for higher studies. Coming back, they acted against social ills and taboos.

The publication of journals in Manipur also helped in bringing about a new outlook. The first periodical in Manipuri Language *Meitei Chanu* was published and edited by Hijam Irabot (1896-1951) in 1921. This journal started taking up the cause of educational and social development. With its birth may be said to have begun the period of renaissance in Manipur. The magazine was fairly well established and was recognised as the accredited exponent of Manipuri public opinion. This was largely possible due to the great personality of its editor, Hijam Irabot Singh, who was well versed in politics also. Atombapu Sharma edited *Dainik Manipur* which showed a clear picture of religious, cultural and social aspects of Manipur and the *Manipuri Matam*, the daily paper also reflected the aims and objectives of the Nikhil Hindu Manipuri Mahasabha and expressed the opinions of the Mahasabha against social prejudices and inhibitions and started propagating new ideas.

Besides these, many monthly magazines like *Yaiphakol* and *Lalit Manjuri Patrika* started campaigning for educational development and social change. Almost all the publications after 1949 focussed on social development. A press club was established in Manipur and the Association of journalists carried out these objectives for the development of the society. These vernacular journals also helped in the awakening of the national feelings.

Education plays a vital role in effecting changes in human society. Things which cannot be foreseen, which cannot be forced by royal will or which cannot be suppressed by bayonet are effected by education. Inspite of many defects in English education, it has helped a lot to think in terms of democracy and individual liberty. Liberal ideas of the west have affected the people with a new social consciousness. Thus, education endeavours to lay firm foundation in national consciousness as well as social consciousness in the minds of the youths of Manipur.

Structure of Society

The people of Manipur consists of various ethnic groups. The Meiteis who predominate the plain people in the valley are the largest group. The people inhabiting the hills surrounding the valley consist of about 30 hill tribes[29] with differences in languages, customs and modes of dress.

Meitei society was divided into seven groups. Each group was known as *yek*. The system is still in vogue in the present Meitei society. Just before the introduction of *yek* system, there was a system known as *salai* system which divided the Meitei society broadly into nine divisions. In course of time, these nine groups merged into the seven *yeks* and *salai* system was replaced by the *yek* system. The Meitei society was reorganised into seven divisioins (*yeks* or *salais*) according to their blood relationship[30] : various clans fought for the supremacy in the valley; all these were closely allied although constantly at war. Of these clans, that called Meitei, came out the conqueror and that name is now applied to all clans. But besides the clans known now collectively as Meiteis, there were other clans in the valley whom Meiteis conquered but did not admit into Meitei confederacy. They are now known collectively as *Lois*.[31]

Thus, there developed a stage of groupism and social divisions. Some of the powerful local tribes also shared political privileges along with the Meiteis who respected them in their society e.g. the Purum tribe.[32] Thus many local tribes and ethnic groups were assimilated into the Meitei society, but the system of social division was there even at the tribal stage in Meitei society. With the establishment of *yek* system, marriage rules became well established and rigid. Those who refused to observe were treated as outcastes and expelled from the Meitei society, which formed a new section of lower caste people known as *Yaithibi* . Thus, the question of untouchability came into the Meitei society. The Yaithibi group, besides being treated as unclean, were not allowed to walk on the royal roads. Their position was not better than that of the

Sudra of the Hindu society.[33]

During early days people living in the valley had more or less an egalitarian type of society. But after conversion to Hinduism, some changes were introduced in the social customs and the Brahmins came to occupy highest position in the society. The role of Brahmins to the new social set up became highly important. Broadly after conversion to Hinduism, there came the caste divisions in Meitei society i.e. the Kshatriyas and Brahmins.

The two hundred years of Brahmin influence brought adoption of caste consciouness in the habit and life style of the people.[34] In the beginning of this new current of social life there was not much difficulty. In fact the new converts derived tremendous spiritual benefits under the guidance of the Brahmins who came from outside and got settled ultimately to become Manipuri in every respect, except their appearances. Thus the earlier migrants (pre-Brahmin) were also generally assimilated into Manipuri society. They were assigned one or the other of the *yeks* according to the area in which they had settled to their family names by the terms Nongchupharam (migrants from the west) and Nongpokharam (migrants from the east). Subsequently all immigrants were to some extent integrated into the Manipuri community.

Apart from Brahmins, there were lower caste Hindus who migrated from outside into Manipur. They were called Bishnupriyas. They also went through the same process of integration into Manipuri society.

Inspite of the Brahmanical influences, the occupational caste remained conspicuous by its absence in Manipuri society. This fact has helped the Meitei society to develop a community life based on co-operative labour. The trades of blacksmith, goldsmith, brass-worker and work in bell-metal and copper are each restricted to a particular family, but there is nothing to prevent a member of one of these families from engaging themselves in a different occupation. It is almost certain that all these were brought by former rulers or persons who were sent to Cachar and Assam to learn trade. Likewise the barbers were also brought. But the indigenous trades like carpentry, fishing, weaving are open to all. The four trades mentioned above like blacksmith, goldsmith, brass-work and work in bell-metal and copper were very close to the life of the people.[35]

The group division in society indicates the different professional classes among the people in the valley. It is also stated that in the Manipuri population, there were four great divisions in order of seniority namely, Laipham, Khabam, Ahallup, and Naharup. related to the service of kings. Different groups were assigned with different works of the king or royal family.[36] But, caste system in Manipur is not based on any trade. The community had no *dhobi* caste, no barber caste, no cobbler etc. Now under the pressure of modernisation *dhobis* and barbers have become established.[37] The acceptance of equality between man and man was the outcome of the flourishing Manipuri culture. The absence of casteism is the second feature of Manipuri society. With the introduction of Hinduism the society began to change and hierarchical order of castes, sub-castes and privileged social positions were established on the grounds of qualitative merits of the man in the society.

Development of Various Agencies for Social Changes

Various agencies have taken up the work of social development. The introduction of modern education, the improvment in the means of transport and communication and the establishment of central political authority, have all been helping in the process of nation building. Contacts with the west and transformation of the country from the subsistence agriculture, handicraft and commerce to modern industry have been accelerating the pace of development from the primitive to a more modern evolution of villages and towns. This building up of a national outlook is a long and difficult process embracing many generations.[38] When illiteracy is one of the major problems facing the country, it is impossible to educate the masses without the help of the mass-media. It is not always possible for the policy makers to reach the people through mass contacts and oral communication. Since Independence, the country has witnessed the growth of various media of mass communication. With the development of mass communication during the last five decades, it has been generally felt that mass-media can help in effecting a social change towards development. Education and mass communication help in accelerating the pace of change. This is the reason why education including mass communication was looked upon as an investment for social development during the recent years.

It is stated that modernisation and economic development involve three phases - growth in urbanisation, growth in literacy and finally growth in mass-media. All these three are linked together in the modern society. On the other hand, the function of mass communication is to open up the large masses in society to new information, new thought, new attitudes and new aspirations which lead them to new achievements.[39]

During the last one hundred years reasonable changes have been observed in the Manipuri society, associated with the modernisation in the life style of the people. These are no doubt influenced directly or indirectly by the various agents of social change. Dance and music, press, radio, literature etc. can be considered as the main agents of social change in Manipur.

Development of Dance and Music

Manipur is a land of music, dance and drama. The artistic urge is strong. In the region, the people express themselves mostly through music, dance and drama.[40] Manipur today is best introduced through her dances, which are part and parcel of Manipuri culture.

The people of Manipur, through the ages, evolved and preserved their distinct traditions of art and culture, including a variety of dances and related rituals which is collectively called the Manipuri Dance. Dance and music run in the blood of Manipuri people and it is rare indeed to find a Manipuri who cannot dance and sing.[41] Over and above, the Meiteis are a religious minded people, emphasising to dancing and singing as a form of religious expression. With indigenous Manipuri dance many rituals are associated and people performing the dancing feat do it as a part of religious rituals. As such, these dance forms are perfected through regular practice and performances. From very early times people of Manipur loved dance and music and pleaded for themselves as the descendants of the Gandharvas. Though remote, Manipur was influenced by the strong currents of Indian culture and incorporated into its dances the themes of Hindu epics and mythology. In course of time, medieval Vaishnavism penetrated into the valley with its devotional songs, music and dance. By the eighteenth century, the Bhakti cult was deeply rooted in Manipur patronised by the ruling princes and it became a popular form of religion. The traditional dance and music of the area came under the influence of the new cult and adjusted itself to the spirit of the times.[42]

The credit for reviving and systematising the dance of the soil goes to King Bhagyachandra who became the ruler of Manipur in the beginning of the 18th Century.[43] With utmost devotion to Lord Krishna he dedicated himself to the cause of the Bhakti cult. He built the temple of Govindaji at Imphal, developed the Ras Lila on the techniques of Lai Haraoba dance and finally patronised it. The king's whole hearted encouragement to music and dance finally culminated in the revival of the Manipuri dance.

In the nineteenth century, rulers like Gambhir Singh (1825-1886) and Chandrakirti Singh (1850-1886) rendered valuable service to the Manipuri dance. Chandrakirti Singh himself composed as many as 64 drum dances, besides many other compositions.

Till 1855, no formal schools were established in Manipur. Education was given through military training and women had to learn singing and dancing.[44] Manipuri dances are inseparable from its music and the music aspect occupies an important place in the total structure of a Ras.[45] Music in Manipur may be broadly divided into folk music and classical music. The folk music includes the type of songs like Khullang Isei, Lai Haraoba Isei, Pena Isei and Khongjom Parva. The classical music includes Nat Pala and Kirtan.

Dances of Manipur may broadly be classified under two heads - folk and classical. The folk group includes Thabal Chongba, Lai Haraoba, Naga dances etc. and the classical group includes Ras dances. Lai Haraoba and Ras dances are the most important types of Manipuri dances. The former is performed by worshipping the pre-Vaishnavite deities and the later is for worshipping the Vaishnavite gods.[46]

Among the various types of dances, Thabal Chongba may be regarded as a community dance. There is no distinction between the dancers and spectators here as in Lai Haraoba and others we find the distinction. The spectators themselves can join in the proceedings of the dance.

With the British annexation of Manipur in 1891, the dance art of this small state suffered neglect and was also in a state of decline. The dancers, who performed a religious duty in the temples and served an aesthetic purpose in society came to be looked down upon as unwanted and destitute by others. There was no understanding of the spirit which the dances represented and no recognition of their artistic values. In this way, dancing as an art began to decline rapidly.

It was in the early years of the twentieth century that the Manipuri dance captured the attention of Rabindranath Tagore. He, for the first time witnessed Manipuri dance at Sylhet and Agartala in 1926 and was deeply charmed by it. The mode of dance, the melody of the music, the emotions represented and the artistic value of the performances appealed the Tagore's imagination in a profound sense. Shortly after that, he introduced the teaching of Manipuri dance in his Vishwabharati at Shantiniketan.[47] At Shantiniketan he initiated the study and performance of Manipuri dance till the art was restored to its original value. That was the beginning of the modern phase in the history of the Manipuri dance. Very quickly its fame spread and wherever it was performed there was a deep appreciation of the art. The gurus of the Manipuri style - Nabakumar, Sanarik, Nileswar Mukherjee - developed the dance in various ways. Tagore gave his touch of validity to Manipuri dance to keep it abreast of the times. He supplied themes for the dance dramas in Manipuri technique and his Rabindra Sangeet made the dance specially charming in every respects.[48]

While Manipuri dance was cultivated at Shantiniketan, other centres sprang up for its promotion and spread. Bipin Singh carried it to Bombay while Nabakumar taught it at Ahmedabad. Imphal, the traditional centre of classical Manipuri dance developed into the greatest centre of dance under the gurus - Amubi, Amudon Sharma and Atomba Singh. The renowned exponents of dance like Javeri sisters, Savita Mehta, Nirmala Mehta, Thambalyaima, etc. have successfully spread the name of this art far and wide in India and abroad.

Role of Education in the Development of Dance and Music

The early pre-Hindu dances of Manipur were of animistic nature and then came the dances associated with the worship of Shiva and Parvati as rather the native counterparts of these details.[49] With the introduction of Vaishnavism in Manipur, a new wave came to Manipuri dance with the development of the classical form of Manipur Ras dance. With the introduction of the western education in Manipur, new techniques of Manipuri dancing have been developed. As for instance, the dance techniques normally composed of the traditional forms of dance and music were usually performed in front of Sylvan deities or Ras mandals etc. came to be introduced on the stage for demonstration to the general public by using special dance compositions with modernised stage techniques. Lai Haraoba dances, Naga dances, Rasa Leelas etc., which were usually performed in the open gatherings for longer durations of several hours have been composed specially for short durations as stage performances. There has been a gradual transformation of the usual dances from ritualistic aspects to more and more techniques of stage performances for entertainment of the people.

More and more institution of dance and music have been established for proper training in the art of dance and music. With the influence of the techniques of Indian art and western dances new techniques of Manipuri dances like dance dramas, ballets etc. have become popular during the last two decades. Classical form of dance, music, painting and drama with the modern aspect of the art and culture have been established. People have been trained in the art of dance, music, painting and drama. Many of the traditional arts like Manipuri Ras dances, martial arts, Manipuri Mridanga, Sankritans etc., which were considered to be traditional folk art of Manipur, have been claimed and recognised as well established classical arts of the Manipuris.

Impact of Dance and Music in Social Development

With increasing popularisation of the traditional arts of Manipuris like dance, drama, music, painting etc. many educated young people of Manipur took lessons and training in the traditional arts as a profession in the various institutions established for the purpose. The status of artists in the society has improved to a great extent during the last two decades. Various courses of certificates, Diploma and Degree have been introduced in the institutions of Manipuri dance and music and they are well recognised by the Universities and Governments inside and outside the state. These helped the artists in making a career of their own as well as job opportunities inside and outside the state. During the recent years, the educated young artists from Manipur have been able to introduce the age-old traditional Manipuri art of dance and music not only to the other states of India but to foreign countries as well. Thus, the development of modern education in the state had a great impact on the popularisation of the traditional Manipuri arts of dance, music, drama, painting etc., which subsequently played an important role in the social development of Manipur.

Development of Press and Journals

Manipuri journalism had its first beginning from outside Manipur with the publication of such journals as *Meitei Leima*, *Jagaran* etc. in Cachar and Pratapgar. These publications were started by the Manipuri students who read outside. But in Manipur also five or six issues of one journal called *Meitei Chanu*, edited by Hijam Irabot Singh, were published during the period between 1925 to 1926. These issues were all hand written and not printed.

In course of time, Manipur also had her own printing press, which was started in 1910. In 1918-19 the Government of Manipur also set up a printing press and published all papers related to the Government. The Churachand Printing Press of Atombapu Sharma took an important role in the history of printing and journalism. As a result of which magazines, weeklies and dailies began to appear. Thus, Manipuri journalism began to advance with the passage of time. It was mainly due to two reasons, one due to the coming of the western education and the other, due to having good number of educated who felt the necessity of the Manipuri journals. The period from 1920 to 1949 may be known as the first period of the Manipur journalism. The daily newspapers, weeklies and monthly periodicals published during the period were the *Dainik Manipur*, the *Manipuri Matam*, the *Manipur Paojel*, the *Ngasi* and the *Praja*. They were influencial organs which dealt with social, religious, political and cultural aspects of the Manipuris. A number of pamphlets, booklets and journals dealing with social and political life of the people of Manipur also appeared. The main dailies today are the *Prajatantra*, the *Anouba Samaj*, the *Simanta Patrika*, the *Khollao*, the *Sanaleibak*, the *Ihou*, the *Paojel*, etc.

Monthly Magazines

Yaiphakol - It was a montly magazine edited by Dr. Leiren Singh. It dealt with the public opinion of the time and played a vital role in promoting Manipuri language. It reflected different political facets of Manipur, emphasized the patriotic feelings of the masses and condemned the despotic attitude of the ruling Maharaja.

Lalit Manjuri Patrika - This magazine was edited by Atombapu Sharma in 1933. It tried to popularise Meitei tradition and made Manipuri poetry and drama more interesting. It had its social, educational, historical, cultural and religious aspects. It was an important organ of the Indian National Congress and was sympathetic to the Nikhil Hindu Manipuri Mahasabha.

The other journals that could be mentioned were *Meitei Leima, Khonjel, Naharol, Jyoti, Gouranga, Satramacha, Bhagyabati Masik* and *Bhagyabati Lalit Kala*. These journals dealt with different aspects of life. During the period from 1948-75 the number of printing presses in Manipur rose up gradually. More profits could be made from printing, because of the high literacy percentage of the Manipuris. Now-a-days there is a great demand for printing all over Manipur because printing has been popular not only in the urban areas but also in the hill regions. The Christian missionaries also issue a number of Christian journals.[50]

The press alone made possible the large scale, swift and constant exchange of views among different social groups inhabiting various parts of the state. It brought about a closer social and intellectual contract among the provincial population.[51]

The journals and newspapers published and edited by the local people and articles written by them not only acted as an effective weapon in the hands of the social reformers to expose social evils and abuses, but also reflected the changing aspect of the people, their outlook, social, political and economic life. A number of articles stating the serious affects of addiction to intoxicants, drugs etc., essays on the necessity of female education and higher education for the youths of Manipur showed clearly the development of consciousness about the welfare of their society and the people of Manipur.

The women of Manipur also took initiative in developing Manipuri journalism. For example in 1969 one Manipuri journal known as *Yaipha Yumbalda Nupi* (role of women in family planning) was published. One monthly journal called *Macha Leima* continued its regular publication and the sole responsibility of its publication was taken by an association called Chanura Marup. All writers and editors of this journal are women and all articles are directly or indirectly related to the affairs of women. The Family Planning Association, Manipur and the Mahila Kalyan Samiti published souveneirs and many social issues in relation to the International women year. It can be proudly said that such a publication specially meant for women began a new era in the journalism of Manipur. So, not only men but women also played great roles in developing journalism in Manipur. The progress of vernacular journalism is a sure index of the progress of education in Manipur.

The development of journalism is the direct outcome of the development of western education and ideas as well as advancement of science and technology. It has played a vital role in the progress and advancement of our society.

Radio

Radio broadcasting through the All India Radio was introduced in India as a major item for mass communication. A separate Station of All India Radio was inauguarated at Imphal by the then Chief Minister, M. Koireng Singh, on the 15th August, 1963. The studio of A.I.R. at Konung Lampak was commisioned in 1981 along with a high power transmitter at Mayang Imphal, raising the total annual transmission hour to 45,000. The programme of the Imphal Station is now distinctly heard in Cachar district of Assam and other adjoining States of Manipur.[52]

The Radio began to provide educational information and entertainment programmes to the people of Manipur. While newspapers are read by 4%, the radio programmes reach 10% of the population. Moreover, literacy is not a bar to getting entertainment and information through the radio. Further, it serves a medium of mass communication which offers the solution to the three problems of inaccessibility, illiteracy and lack of properly trained and motivated extension personnel, faced by the communicator in enlisting the co-operation of the rural community in India with respect to the programme of economic and social development.[53]

For speedy communication and for imparting to millions a sense of participation, the radio is the only effective mass-media available to the rural people[54] and it is perhaps one of the most important media whose effects reach both the urban and rural audiences. The impact of the broadcast on the general habits and social development of the people, the influence of the rural programmes on agricultural practices and so on are innumerable.

Being one of the most powerful media in Manipur, the Imphal Station of All India Radio has been able to play an important role as an agency of social change specially in the field of education and socio-economic development of the state. It also has been able to play an important role as an entertainer and people's main source of information on day to day happenings around the world. Through rural programmes, Radio has been playing a significant role in bringing the new technology in agriculture to the door-steps of the farmers by giving support to the various farmers trainings and functional literacy programme of the Ministry of Agriculture. The Farm and Home Unit of All India Radio, Imphal has also started intensive agricultural programme of the government. Through this programme, varieties of high yielding rice have been introduced to the farmers along with the day to day guidance for fertiliser application and use of pesticides. Recently a lot of stress has been given on soil and water management, the need for social forestry and environmental protection and ecological balance in addition to family welfare programmes on nutrition, eradication of social evils etc. which have been well received by the rural listeners.

The Rural Programme which is known as Khungangi Thouram is so popular not only among the rural listeners but also among the urban dwellers as it deals with a wide range of subjects like health, nutrition, rural development and agriculture besides entertaining programmes like Jatra and Khongjom Parba. Presently, the regular drama programme 'Family Serials' play a very important role in educating the people to solve various family and social problems like alcoholism, drug addiction, mass copying in examinations by students, quarrels between daughter-in-laws and mother-in-laws and between brothers on the instigation of wives etc.

However, the educational programmes of the All India Radio appear to have little impact on the listeners. This is because the programmes coincide with the school working hour and the schools generally do not have a listening set.

In the field of games and sports, radio has been able to popularise certain indigenous games, e.g. Kang and Polo programmes, along with international games. The press interview of some young talents also give a new impetus to the youth in their particular fields. When the radio broadcaste their names, the players feel that their efforts have received social recognition. So the radio has been able to play role in the drive for a sports movement as well as in catching young talents. From the available official records and letters written by the listeners to the Station Director it has been observed that the women's programme of the station has been able to deal with the multifarious social problems relating to women. The bigamy system which has been practised for generations in the state has been effectively countered since the inception of the station. Besides, the station has been able to provide a forum for women to interact themselves about social problems as well as their own problems.

Literature

Literature portrays society and records yearning, aspirations and doubts of the people. It is, therefore, an invaluable record of the changes through which society passes.[55] The development of education that has taken place in Manipur during the 20th century has also its refletion in contemporary literature, and literature in its turn makes a significant impact on the social transformation. In fact literature as a social document mirrors the contemporary social reality and reflects the spirit of the age. It is conditioned by the prevailing institutional and social ethos and gives interpretation of the contemporary reality.[56] The pattern of literary development is interwoven with the fabric of the society. The history of literature cannot, therefore, be essentially different from any other aspect of social history.[57] In fact the history of literature of a nation may be said to be the record of the march of its civilisation and culture. Manipuri culture and civilization find vocal expression in the literature of this tiny state.

The literary history of Manipur can be divided into three parts; i.e. the Ancient (from the earliest upto 17th century), the Mediaeval (from 18th century upto the end of the 19th century) and the Modern (from the time of the British rule in Manipur upto the present day).[58] Further, researches have divided it into four parts; Prachin, Adi, Madhya and Bartaman.[59] In another effort it has been divided into three groups i.e. (a) the old literature (from the earliest upto 1074), (b) the Mediaeval literature (from the accession of king Loyumba upto 1891) and (c) the Modern (from 1891 onwards).[60] Some scholars have divided it into two parts i.e., the ancient and the modern.

After the British occupied Manipur in 1891, the British administration gave a great impetus to the quickening of the Manipuri intellect and widening of their mental horizon. The Manipuri writers at the beginning of the 20th century were scholars who were also acquainted with the old literature and thus they played a great role in maintaining the age old literary traditions for a long time. With this heritage the creative talent of young writers is now expressing itself in various forms : lyrics, novels, dramas, short stories, etc.

The literary scene in Manipur before the Second World War was dominated by three personalities like Chaoba, Kamal and Angahal. The Manipuri literature blossomed with their work. It aroused a new consciousness in the people with the richness of their own language and a fine taste of literature.[61] There were many prolific writers who made their contributions to all forms of modern Manipuri literature.

The modern form of writing was found in some early works like '*Chandrakirti Jila Changba*' (King Chandrakirti's meeting with the Viceroy on the bank of the Barak river) and *Khongjom Parba* (battle of Khongjom in 1891). Here the writers selected for their description the patriotic deeds achieved by king Chandrakirti and the heroic and patriotic deeds of prince Koireng alias Tikendrajit in ballads.

Chaoba (1896-1950), a teacher by profession was primarily a poet. But he was equally great as an essayist and a novelist. In his early years he composed melodious lyrics. He took poetry seriously and in his composition he adopted as far as possible the form of old ballads. Chaoba was also a humanist. Many of his poem bear the mark of philosophical query about the transitoriness of life.[62] He was also equally adept in the writing of prose and is even regarded as the father of modern Manipuri prose. His historical novel *Labangalata* is a classic in that field. All his essays are excellent in form and content among the modern Manipuri essays. But most of his important works, like poetry, novel and essays saw the light of day before the war.

Kamal (Dr. Kamal Singh), a contemporary of Chaoba, was the favourite writer of the people. His *Lei Pareng* (a garland of flowers) is a collection of beautiful poems. His *Madhavi* is a novel so sweet and poetic that he won a place of love and esteem in the literature of the state. He was an idealist. In his poems there is a feeling of disappointment at the imperfections of human life and yearning for the perfection. His early death was a great loss to the literary galaxy of Manipur. He could have contributed much more if he had not died in the prime of his youth.

Hijam Angahal Singh was another pioneer in the field of modern Manipuri literature. He was also a poet, an essayist and a novelist. He prepared the formidable and serious task of compiling the scattered fragment of the epic poem *Khamba Thoibi Sheireng* in blank verse of fourteen syllable lines. This was a great contribution to the richness of literary heritage. His ability to narrate and describe in poetic form is of a high order. His *Shingen Indu* is a narrative poem of love. He was equally adept in the writing of prose as well. As a novelist he showed his ability in *Jahera*. The theme of this story is the love between a Muslim girl and a Hindu youth. Nabadwip and Dorendra were the other two figures of modern Manipuri literature. Nabadwipchandra was one of successful translators. With his knowledge of Bengali language and poetic genius he translated Michael Modhusudan Dutta's *Meghanad Badh Kavya* without losing expression of the original version. This shows the confidence in the capacity of the Manipuri language in expressing complex, rich thoughts and lofty imagination. Dorendrajit Singh shows his ability in his compiling of *Kansha Badha Kavya*. His contribution to Manipuri epic and drama is considerable. Thus, modern Manipuri literature took its shape at the hands of the above writers, who served the subject with dedication before the war.

In the post Independence period, the literary scene in Manipur has gone a drastic change. And the war produced a tremendous impact on the life of the Manipuris and many changes took place in the society. Modern literature witnessed such great changes. Manipuri literature of the post Independence period has been marching ahead in the field of poetry and novel as well.

Poetry and novel which dominated the pre-war literature yielded now to drama. People sought diversion in performing arts particularly the theatre. Now-a-days there has been a mushroom growth of playhouses, theatres etc. which produce hundreds of plays and dramas in Manipur. Manipuri drama entered into a new phase during the Second World War. The immediate post-war period was a boon to dramas. The modern Manipuri theatre, had its inspiration from the Bengali dramas, which were played in Manipur since 1903. For the first time in 1914, a Manipuri drama *Arjungi Maithiba* (Defeat of Arjun) was staged with success. It was translated from the Bengali *Partha Parajay*. Later on others like *Devala Devi, Karnarjuna, Savitri* etc. came out successfully on the stage. For the first time in 1925, the original Manipuri play *Nar Singh* written by L. Ibungohal Singh came out with success. Besides the creative poets, novelists and story writers, some others have enriched Manipuri literature by translating selected works from Sanskrit, Bengali, Hindi and English literature.[63]

The most popular form of entertainment in the form of performing art, however, is the age old *Shumang Leela* also known as *jatras*. It does not require any stage. It is very popular in Manipur and rather plays a more important role as an agent of social change because the plays in *Shumang Leela* are mostly social and various aspects of society are presented in it. The identity of the society exhibited by it could make all the persons know clearly about the life and conditions of the society of that time. With the increasing popularity, the quality of *Shumang Leela* has also much improved during the recent years. The relationship between *Shumang Leela* (plays) with the social, political, economic and religious life of the society is very close. All the images of the society are reflected in it.

In the field of drama, quite distinct from all the rest, the most interesting figure was Tongbra, who, with a shavian stance exposed the social prejudices and shallow human relationships with a subdued reforming zeal. All his plays are characterised by witty humour and racy prose. His plays like *Mani-Mamou,* dealing with the incompatibility of the temperaments of an illiterate and orthodox mother-in-law and an educated daughter-in-law with modern outlook and *Chengi-Khujai*, an allegory on the revolutionary movement, speak eloquently of the writers commitment to social and human problems and maturity of his craft. He was a prodigious writer, who wrote over one hundred plays. The notable writer of the nineteen sixties considered as pioneering playwright of the Manipuri novel was Pacha Meitei. He first proved his narrative skill in his two early works *Haj* and *Hayad Begum* set in the midst of Manipuri Muslim society. One critic observes him in this way, 'A young writer, Pacha Meitei exposes the rottenness of our society with vigour and cruelty in an idiom allied to that of Virginia Wolf.........The novel *Na Thathiba Ahal Ama* first of its kind in Manipuri gives impression of a slow motion camera at work.[64] With the publication of two novels of Pacha Meitei, *Na Tathiba Ahal Ama* (1969) and *Imphal Amasung Magi Ising Nungshitki Phibam* (1972) a new turn has been set in the domain of Manipuri novel.[65] All his novels try to show the selfishness, meanness and shallowness of society. Biren, Ibophishak and Brojen are other important writers. *Hallakpa* by Shri Biren Singh is an attempt to point out the absurdity of human life in the context of a rootless and materialistic society.

Literature, as an important social force has been playing a significant role in bringing about changes in the folk culture also. It brings changes in the values, attitudes, ideas, customs, rituals and ways of life of the people.[66] Thus, growth of literature played a great role in the social development of the state.

References :

1. **S.N. Pandey** : *Education and Social Changes in Bihar* (1975), pp. 156-157.

2. **R. Brown** : *Statistical Account of Manipur* (1974), p. 93; **E.W. Dun**, *Gazetteer of Manipur* (1891), p. 26.

3. **James Johnstone** : *My Experience in Manipur and Naga Hills* (1896), p. 144.

4. **N.C.E.R.T.** : *New Delhi Survey Report* (1972-73), p. 8.

5. **S. Gyaneswar Singh** : *Impact of Modern Education in Manipur*, unpublished Ph. D. thesis, Gauhati University (1979), p. 30.

6. **L. Ibungohal Singh** : *Introduction to Manipur* (1963), p. 75.

7. **N. Khelchandra Singh (ed)** : *Coronation of Naothingkhong* (in Manipur) (1967), p. 1.

8. **L. Ibungohal Singh** : *op.cit.*, pp. 213-214; **M. Kirti Singh**, *Religious Development in Manipur in the 18th and 19th Centuries* (1982), p. 183.

9. **R. Brown** : *op.cit.*, p. 93.

10. *Administrative Report of the Manipur Political Agency* (1898-99), p. 17.

11. **Th. Mangoljao Singh** : *Western Education in Manipur* (1967), Vol. 1, p. 22.

12. **H.R. James** : *Education and Statemenship in India* (1911), p. 13.

13. **B. Kuppuswamy** : *Social Change in India* (1986), p. 267.

14. **O' Malley** : *Modern India and the West* (1941), p. 855.

15. **Gangmumei Kabui** : *Modernisation in Tribal Manipur*, Souvenir, The Third Annual Conference, North East India History Association (1982), p.48.

16. **Manjusri Chaki Sircar** : *Feminism in a Traditional Society* (1984), p. 23.

17. **L. Nobinchandra Singh** : *Ethnographic History of Brahmins in Manipur*, Regional Integration, Vol. 8, No. 15,, p. 34.
18. **Manjusri Chaki Sircar** : *op.cit.*, pp. 29-30.
19. **R.K. Jhaljit Singh** : *A History of Manipuri Literature* (1976), p. 98.
20. **M.S. Gore** : Universities and Government, *University News* (1986), p. 1.
21. **S.M.H. Burney** : Education and Social Change, *J.N.U.* News, p.7.
22. **T.C. Hodson** : *The Meitheis* (1908), p. 115.
23. **Manjusri Chaki Sircar** : *op.cit.*, p. 68.
24. **H. Lalmohan Singh** : *Role of Family Welfare Programme in achieving Health for all by 2000 A.D.* (State level Seminar, R.M.C.) (1987), p. 18.
25. *Manipur Mail*, 7th May, 1987.
26. **L. Krishnamangol Singh** : *Economic Changes in Manipur*, An unpublished Ph.D. Thesis, Manipur University (1987), p. 30.
27. **H. Dwijamani Dev Sharma** : *My Reminiscences* (1986), p.22.
28. **N. Tombi Singh** : *Manipur, A Study* (1973), pp. 67-68.
29. **B.K. Roy Burman** : *Demographic and Socio Economic Profiles of the Hill Areas of North East India* (1969), pp. 27-28.
30. **N. Birachandra Singh** : *Socio-Religious Life of the Meiteis*. An unpublished Ph.D. Thesis, Manipur University (1987), p. 95.
31. **J. Shakespeare** : *The Religion of Manipur* (1913), p. 420.
32. *Thirel Nanamba* (unpublished), p. 13.
33. **N. Birachandra Singh** : *op.cit.*, pp. 94-96.
34. **S.N. Parrat** : *Religion of Manipur* (1980), p. 3.
35. **J. Shakespeare** : *op.cit.*, p. 420.
36. **R. Constantine** : *Manipur, Maid of Mountains* (1981), pp. 52-

53.

37. *Ibid.*

38. **B. Kuppuswamy** : *Social Changes in India* (1986), p. 402.

39. **Daniel Lerner** : *The Passing of Traditional Society*, (1964).

40. **B.K. Ahluwalia and Shashi Ahluwalia** : *Social Change in Manipur* (1984), p. 60.

41. **Mohan Khoker** : *Myths, Legends and History of Manipuri in Classical and Folk Dances of India* (1963), p. 3.

42. **Puri Das Chopra** : *Social, Cultural and Economic History of India* (1973), p. 381.

43. **N. Tombi Singh** : *Manipur the Mainstream* (1975), p. 54.

44. **L. Ibungohal Singh** : *op.cit.*, p. 74.

45. **N. Tombi Singh** : *op.cit.*, p. 69.

46. **A. Atombapu Sharma and M. Amubi Singh** : *The brief description of Manipuri Dance* (1957), pp. 1-2.

47. **J. Roy** : *History of Manipur* (1973), p. 185.

48. **Puri Das Chopra** : *op. cit.*, p. 383.

49. **Mohan Khoker** : *op.cit.*, p. 3.

50. **M. Kirti Singh** : *History of Journalism in Manipur* (1980), p. 61.

51. **A. R. Desai** : *Social Background of Indian Nationalism* (1948), p. 218.

52. All India Radio, Imphal.

53. **B. Kuppuswamy** : *op.cit.*, p. 421.

54. *Ibid.*, p. 424.

55. **Tarachand** : *The Freedom Movement in India* (1972), p. 582.

56. **Jyoti Swarup Saxena** : *Modern Essays* (1956), pp. 52-53.

57. **B.R. Mullick** : *Literary Essay* (1953), Vol. II, pp. 25-26.

58. **N. Khelchandra Singh (ed)** : *Ariba Manipuri Sahityagi Itihas* (1970), p. 2.

59. **Kalachand Shastri** : *Asamba Manipur Sahityagi Itihas,* (1976), p. 3.

60. **R. K. Jhaljit Singh** : *op. cit,* p. 13.

61. **Ch. Manihar Singh** : *Post War II Manipuri Literature,* Souvenir in the Seminar on post war poetry in North Eastern India, (1988), p. 18.

62. **J. Roy** : *op. cit.,* p. 180.

63. **J. Roy** : *op. cit.,* p. 182.

64. *Indian Literature,* December (1971).

65. *Scale* (1973), Vol. II, No. 2.

66. **S.L. Srivastava** : *Folk Culture and Oral Traditions* (1974), p. 344.

9

Conclusion

The main objective of the present study has been to trace the growth of modern education in Manipur and evaluate its impact on the society. English education came to Manipur very late in 1885 with the establishment of the first English school at Imphal by the then Political Agent Sir James Johnstone. But till the first decade of the present century no tangible progress in education could be seen as the general public looked upon the English and anything associated with it with suspicion and hatred. Besides that, the English and their education system were regarded as something impure that would defile their sacred being. As a result, the progress of education was very slow indeed.

Gradually, the, public interest began to change. In 1907, Maharaja Churachand Singh, came back after completing his education at Mayo College, Ajmer. The Maharaja had seen the advantages of English education and was keen to introduce it to his subjects. He devoted his time for its promotion among the public. As a result the number of primary schools increased from 72 to 93 in the decade 1910-20. After that the progress has been tremendous. The number of pupils rose tremendously since Independence.

People gradually began to see the benefits that English education brought to them. Moreover, English education assured a job in Government offices. Government schools were no longer enough to satisfy the growing demand for admission and private schools had to be established. Moreover, the general public also felt the urgent need of the introducing secondary education to improve the academic standards and the subsequent introduction of University education to produce the intellectuals, scholars and leaders in various fields. During 1931-41, five High Schools were established through public initiative. The real progress was, however, made only after 1947. The need for new schools grew so strong after 1948 that many secondary schools were established through private and voluntary efforts. The Government also gave all possible assistance in the establishment of these institutions. Consequently the number of secondary schools increased from five in 1940-41 to 123 in 1970-71and 556 in 1996-97.

The number of students increased from 5,220 in 1950-51 to 206945 in 1996-97, almost 40 fold growth in a time span of 46 years. Girl's education, too, received a tremendous boost during this period. From one Girl's High School in 1934, their number rose to 19 in 1970 and 53 in 1996. The total number of girls students in Secondary Schools grew from 595 in 1950 to 95504 in 1996, a 160 fold growth during the period. The growth rate of boys during the corresponding period was 24 times only.

Higher or collegiate education began in Manipur with the establishment of the D.M. College on 6th of August 1946, which marked a new phase in the history of education in the state. This was the only college in the First Five Year Plan but the progress of collegiate education was so rapid that by 1996-97 there were 64 colleges in Manipur with 27988 students on their roll. Population-wise this represents one college student in every 80 of the population, while the corresponding ratio for Assam and India are 1:300 and 1:350 respectively.

With the growth and expansion of collegiate education, the Manipuris felt the urgent need for a University of their own to (i) help in the all-round development of the state, (ii) provide better educational facilities and therefore better job opportunities, (iii) solve the problem of a large number of the youths going outside the state for higher education, and (v) look after its rich and unique cultural heritage.

The demand grew stronger, the post graduate classes in certain subjects were introduced in 1959 in D. M. College. But it fell far short of the people's aspirations. Meanwhile, the Wadia Committee which was constituted by the Government of India to look info the problem of opening a University in the North Eastern region recommended a Central University, not in Imphal, but in Shillong. This disappointed the Manipuris to a great extent.

The people, however, continued to demand for a separate University for Manipur. In partial fulfillment of the public demand and the proposal made by the government of Manipur on the recommendation of a Committee, the University Grants Commission agreed to open, in 1971, a Centre of Post Graduate Studies in Imphal, of the Jawaharlal Nehru University, New Delhi. Though it was short of a full-fledged University it was an important step towards the object of establishing a University in Manipur. This Centre took care of post graduate studies for ten years.

The long cherisheddesire of the people of Manipur to have a university in the state was, however, fulfilled in the year 1980 with establishment of Manipur university at Imphal. All the degree colleges which were till then affiliated to Gauhati University were transferred to the Manipur University. The post Graduate centre of J. N. U. was formally transferred to Manipur University on 1st April, 1981.

Prior to 1947, there was no professional college or institution of education in Manipur. The people felt the necessity of imparting technical training and the administration also realised the urgent need for establishment of technical and professional institutions in the state. Subsequently, an Agricultural Collage, two Law Colleges, Regional Institute of Medical sciences, Nursing schools, college of Teacher Education, Hindi Teacher's Training college, Basic training colleges Government Polytechnic, Industrial Training Institutes, college of Technology and Central Agriculture university etc. were established in due course. These institutions impart technical and professional training to the people.

The women of Manipur have a distinct place in the social, cultural, economic and religious life in Manipur. However, the Manipur women could not receive formal education. In its traditional society, the girls were not allowed to go to the school and kept confined in the domestic works. Women education started in 1898 with only 2 girls entering the school. The number of school going girls however increased tremendously in the Post Independence period. The percentage of literacy for female increased from 2.36% in 1951 to 47.60% in 1991, while the total literacy percentage increased from 11.4% to 59.9% during the same period. With the increasing trend of educated women in the state, the number of employed women in the government and private sectors has immensely increased in the recent years. In fact, the development of women education in Manipur has brought a significant change in the states of women in the society.

Education is the single most important factor in bringing social change. In Manipur, after the initial hesitation to accept English education due to suspicion of the motive of the foreign rulers and also due to the superstitious belief that English education will defile ones body and soul, people began to appreciate its real value. The pioneering work in this respect was done by Maharaja Churachand Singh. He had received western education with great zeal. The ground work for the development modern education was initiated during his regime.

After Manipur's merger with the union of India in 1949, the pace of education was accelerated with significant changes and modernization of Manipuri society. The merger also brought democracy to Manipur. The people began to participate in the democratic process of decision making. As was happening in the rest of the country, western education brought the ideas of nationalism, secularism and democracy accompanied by an all round social development in Manipur, too.

Among the important social changes that came to Manipur, mention may be made of the gradual breakdown of distinction between man and man in accordance with one's birth. No longer was there any difference between the royal aristocracy and the common people. Educational qualification and not birth became the measuring rod for one's social position.

Western education, with its scientific outlook, brought about a new life style, too, in the Manipuri society. The Christian missionaries played vital roles in changing the outlook and life style of the tribal people. Under the influence of western liberal education, many Manipuris began to decry the evils like slavery, polygamy, untouchability etc. in traditional society. Associations like the Nikhil Hindu Manipuri Mahasabha (1934) with aims to fight social evils and exploitation came up. Under the leadership of men like Hijam Irabot Singh, Dwijamani Dev Sharma, Banka Bihari Sharma and Lalita Madhob Sharma, these societies fought against religious exploitation by the Brahma Sabha. Many educated persons, too joined hands with the Maha Sabha in these reformatory work. Under their concerted efforts gradual change in the society came in. The *Nupi Lan* (women's war) of 1939 against the price rise and rice export may be cited as the example of the enlightenment that came to Manipur.

The Mahasabha was converted into a political organisation in 1938 and its name was changed to Nikhil Manipuri Mahasabha. It fought for the political and economic reformation as well as for the constitutional reforms that followed on later years. The limited constitutional monarchy that Manipur enjoyed as early as in 1947 was the result of the work of the Mahasabha.

Women's education was almost non-existent till 1949. after wards, women were given the right to exercise their franchise and the following years witnessed great progress in women's education. The government, too gave special attention to the development of women's education. Consequently, far reaching changes were seen in the life of women,who refused to remain within the four walls of their home. They began to take active parts in politics, fought against exploitation of women by men and competed with men in every walk of life.

Western education also helped in the emergence of a new class of people in the society, i.e. the middle class intellectuals, who were well educated, imbibed with modern ideas and thought. A new literary group also emerged who ennriched the literature of Manipur by introducing new style of writings. Their writings, fraught with new ideas, spirit, liberalism and modernism showed to the general public the evils of the early traditional society.

In this way, since beginning of the 20th century, western education brought great changes in Manipuri society. Superstitious, religious orthodoxy and the evils associated with feudal system were the bane of Manipuri society. Humanistic and enlightened education that the English brought, opened the eyes of the Manipuri people and they successfully got rid of these social evils. The process of modernization was accelerated by the introduction of democratic way of life, a highly developed communication system including mass- media.

The impact of modern education on the traditional habits, ideas, life style and mode of thinking of the people have been tremendous. Its effect on the society and culture of the people too has been quite significant. The traditional society once governed, guided and goaded by caste considerations, superstitions, taboos and several other local belief has emerged into a modern society ready to march ahead with the main national stream into the path of progress and development.

Problems

Education plays a vital role in national progress and re construction. Success of democracy depends largely upon the diffusion of knowledge among the masses. It appears that significant progress in education has been made both at the national level as well as in the state. However, the progress of education still remains unsatisfactory. The main problems of education in Manipur are detailed below.

A. **Problems of Primary Education**

1. The curriculum of the primary school is unsuitable to local needs. In the curriculum of the primary schools emphasis is given on bookish knowledge and theoretical lessons, ignoring the principle of"learning by doing" to develop the constructive power of the students. It is unsatisfactory, one sided and unrealistic and has very little attraction for the common pupil and people.

2. There is an acute shortage of trained teachers in primary schools. Recently, the teachers training programme has been taken up in the state to a great extent, still there is a huge backlog of untrained teachers. As majority of the primary school teachers lack proper training,they are not intellectually alive and keen on their duty. Besides this, the primary schools are not using the proper tools and techniques of teaching due to shortage of fund. Consequently the present system of education has failed to attract the children.

3. About three fourths of Manipur's population live in villages.

Besides the general lack of roads and other means of communication, villages do not have sufficient number of schools. So many children have to attend the schools situated in the neighbouring villages.

4. The unfavorable environment in the schools is responsible for the children leaving the school before completion of their courses. Many schools in the state lack in teaching aids, facilities for practical classes and practical demonstrations etc., making the school teaching a dull affair.

5. Primary schools in the state usually receive inadequate funds from the State Government. It received an insignificant share of the total educational expenditure. The slow progress literacy is to a great extent due to the meagre funds allotted to it.

6. Education is essential for the harmonious development of an individual in the various phases of life. School education is supposed to be the pre-requiste of all the children upto 14 years of age to become a true citizen of the nation. The present society assumes widespread participation of the people in all activities and constructive leadership at various levels. It is the most important factor in achieving technological progress and quality education in the school. All these things will be possible when we are able to give a sound system of primary education. "The State shall endeavour to provide within a period of ten years from the commencement of this constitution for the free and compulsory education for all children until they complete the age of fourteen years" (Constitution of India, 1950).

Education at the primary level is not only concerned with expansion but also at its quality. The Education Commission (1964-66) has also given much importance to the qualitative improvement of primary education.

7. In most of the states of the country including Manipur, the responsibility of primary education is entrusted to the municipalities and Zilla Parishads. These institutions could not speed up the work of expansion of primary education due to the lack of working capacity, interest and resources. In fact, primary

education should provide the basic training to all the young children to become good citizens.

8. Another great obstacle in the expansion of primary education in Manipur is wastage and stagnation. Many students are droped out before completing primary stage. Premature withdrawal of children from school at any stage before the completion of the primary course has been defined as "wastage". While the "stagnation" refers to the retention of a child in a class for a period of more than one year. According to a sample survey conducted by the Directorate of Education(s) in Manipur the rate of wastage and stagnation in class I to V was 42.80 percent in 1995-96, Out of which the percentage of boys dropouts was 41.52 and of girls dropouts 44.21. Even though there is the provision of universal, free and compulsory primary education, the percentage of wastage and stagnation in primary education is very high.

B. **Problems of Secondary Education**

1. In Manipur, the progress of secondary education has been very rapid since Independence. Its qualitative growth has not been impressive. Qualitative improvement is a very important factor in Secondary education as most of the students after completion of the course enter into a vocational or professional career. In order to enhance the quality of secondary education a variety of improvements like the construction of suitable classrooms, hostels, libraries, laboratories, staff quarters, practical training, regular assessment of the student's progress in study and monitoring their knowledge etc. are required. In order to improve educational standards, the improvement of proper study atmosphere, dedication of teachers, maintenance of strict discipline among the teachers and students, improvement of library facilities with sufficient books and magazines, improved methods of teaching with laboratory and practical classes etc. will be necessary.

2. There is the lack of diversification in the curriculum of secondary schools. Inadequate provision for vocationalisation of secondary education is one of the major problems. So there is the need to diversify secondary education and prepare the children for different vocations. In addition to core-curriculum, provision should be made for students to select vocational subjects relating

to agriculture, industry, technology etc. which could provide self-employment or better job oppurtunities to the students apart from general groups such as science, arts, commerce etc.

3. Defective examination system is also responsible for various problems of secondary education in Manipur. There is the pre-dominance of matriculation examination over the whole objective of secondary education. A school, its teachers and its students are tested in accordance with their success in the examination. The faulty examination system encourages mass copying and use of unfair means etc.

4. The curriculum of the secondary education is narrow and one-sided, which fails to develop the personality of the students. There is need for the diversified courses of instruction at the secondary stage, in order to meet the needs, interests and aspiration of the society for its children.

5. There is general shortage of trained teachers in secondary schools. Untrained teachers are not properly acquainted with teaching methods. Due to shortage of funds and lack of trained staff, most of the schools in the state are not using proper teaching aids.

6. The curriculum in our schools as formulated and taught through the traditional methods of teaching does not give the students insight into the everyday world in which they are living. In the secondary schools of today, there is absence of well-organised community life.

7. Physical facilities include spacious classrooms, well equipped libraries and special rooms for music, art and audio-visual aids. A large number of schools lack facilities for indoor and outdoor games while many others do not have even playgrounds.

8. There are different types of secondary schools in the state. Some of them are government schools, directly managed by the state government. The private schools are run by the managing committees. Majority of the private schools are government aided and the rest are unaided. There are also several schools managed and controlled by missionaries. There is lack of coordination

among the government, aided, unaided and missionary schools.

9. The Hartog Committee devoted its attention to wastage and stagnation that was taking place at the stage of the secondary education in Manipur. As in the case of primary education, there is huge wastage and stagnation in secondary education also. But what is still more regrettable is the serious wastage of time, energy and resources of the students and their parents or guardians while losing all their ambitions and aspirations.

C. **Problems of Higher Education**

1. The success of education depends upon the quality of teachers to a great extent. There are difficulties in getting qualified teachers to teach different subject efficiently in various colleges of the state. Moreover, there has been a shortage of women teachers in the institutions of higher education. In the absence of female teachers, male teachers have been appointed in the women's colleges. It is essential to encourage the female education and to raise the quality of teaching and standard of education.

2. Some of the colleges are functioning without material facilities like proper staff, buildings, hostels, libraries, laboratories, staff quarters etc. There can be improvement in the standard of teaching if such material facilities are provided in the colleges. The ill-equipped institutions will enhance wastage of time, money and energy of the students and dilute the quality of education in the state in general.

3. In university education, emphasis is given on the specialization in different subjects. Consequently, when the student complete the university education they acquire special knowledge and skill in the particular subjects. However the area of specializations in the colleges of Manipur are very much limited and the students cannot go for higher studies in the subjects of their interest and compelled to take up the available area of studies and subsequently their viewpoint remain illbalanced and narrow.

4. The quality of education in the colleges in Manipur has deteriorated due to the mushroom growth of colleges without proper facilities, irregular admission under pressure, recuitement of incompetent teachers, financial hardship to make payment of

teacher's salaries and essential infrastructures, lack of library and laboratory facilities, etc. The colleges do not have any atmosphere for higher learning and research except the classroom teaching.

5. Defective examination system is also one of the main causes leading to the decline in the standard of higher education. In the present system of examination too much importance is given to the easy type of examination. The students think that by preparing some selective question they will achieve success. So most of the students do not devote themselves whole heartedly to learn and study the entire course prescribed in the syllabus and try to pass the examinations by studying only a part of it.

6. The number of students of receiving higher education has increased considerably and it is likely to increase more in the near future. But the necessary facilities and the number of teachers in the colleges have increased proportionately.

7. Indiscipline among the students is one of the root causes responsible for the decline in the standard of higher education. It includes various activities of students like absence from class, poor teacher taught relationship, use of unfair means in the examination, and lack of interest and aptitude for serious studies. The students aim at getting a degree by any means and subsequently get a job. Majority of the students lack interest in studying and learning. The problem of indiscipline among students may be solved by diverting their activities to the healthy channels like sports, games and other co-curricular activities. Better facilities for teaching will develop their interest in study, which in turn, will make them more responsive to academics and well disciplined in life.

8. The curriculum of the higher education, being old and outdated, fails to cope with the recent advances in the area of studies in different subjects. Moreover it fails to instil interest among students for serious studies and consequently the intellectual development is checked.

9. Manipur has witnessed a fast expansion of facilities for scientific and technological education. It has a Medical Institute, an Agricultural University, and an Engineering College besides a

large number of colleges imparting Science, humanities and social sciences education affiliated to Manipur University. The state has now to aspire for qualitative growth of these institutions to check the exodus of good and serious students to the colleges and universities throughout the country and even outside.

D. **Problems of Technical and Professional Education**

1. The curriculum of the technical and vocational institutions appears to be defective. It lacks diversified courses and the institutions do not impart training to the variety of trades, as per social needs.

2. During the post independence period many technical and professional institutions have been established. However, these institutions cannot accommodate more than 50% of the interested students who are interest for admission to these institutions. The people now-a-days realised that those persons receiving technical education have a bright future. But due to the lack of proper facilities and shortage of such institutions more than half (50%) of the students are unable to get admission and they are very much disappointed.

3. Shortage of teachers is one of the main problems of technical and professional education. As most of the brilliant students after completing their education go for better jobs and employment, and least interested in working as teachers in technical and vocational institutions. So there is shortage of teachers in professional and technical institutions.

4. In technical and professional institutions more importance is given to the theoretical education rather than to practical education. Hence, the products of these institutions lack in practical experience and face problems when they take up employment. Hence, the technical and professional institutions in Manipur need to improve the facilities for practical training so that the products of these institutions may have better job opportunities.

5. All India Council of Technical Education have the academic control over the Engineering college, Govt. Polytechnics. While

the Medical Institute is controlled by the Medical Council of India. Moreover, the technical institutes are affiliated to the Manipur University and the rules and regulation of the university as well. Thus the dual or multiple control of the institutions sometime create problems in their administration and academic affairs.

6. The mother tongue has been accepted as the medium of instruction in the stage upto university stage. When the students takes admission in some technical institutions, he is given training through English because standard text books are not available on the subjects in the local language. Translation of the text books to the local language, Manipuri has been difficult since there is no proper terminology for the scientific and technical terms. Hence, it will be better to take up steps to translate the books on technical subjects in the local language.

7. We have made quantitative improvement in our technical and professional education, but we have not paid adequate attention to its qualitative improvement. Consequently many of our technical and professional institutions are being run in a very bad condition. There is lack of goodworkshops, laboratories, libraries and buildings in the technical institutions.

8. In Manipur there is lack of employment prospects for the technical graduates and diploma holder in absence of industries. There is very little scope for self employment also due to the nature of training imparted in the technical institutions. Efforts have to be made to provide self-employment facilities to the technical manpower.

E. **Problems of Women's Education**

1. The national as well as the state government have not been devoting their full attention towards the expansion of women's education. Sufficient funds are not allotted for the education of girls and women as compared to the education of boys. Besides this, the administration of women education is also defective because the administrators are not properly acquainted with the problem of women's education. So proper development and significant progress of women's education could not be achieved in the state In order to encourage women's education, able and talented women should be given responsible and administrative

positions in Education department.

2. There is acute shortage of trained women teachers in the schools of Manipur. Although teachers training programme has been taken up in the state, still there is huge backlog of the untrained women teachers.

3. The financial condition of the people of Manipur are not very sound and majority of the people in the rural areas are so poor that they cannot afford even the basic necessities of life. So, many parents are unable to send their daughters to educational institutions. The low enrolment of girls in the educational institutions is mainly due to the poverty and ignorance of the parents. In the early Manipuri society girls used to be engaged in domestic and household works by their parents. The society never gave emphasis on the women education. Even now majority of the people in the rural areas do not favour education of the girls and majority of women are illiterate. National Committee on Women Education had demanded that government should take up serious steps for development of women education on priority basis. Further the government should pay special attention to the upliftment of rural people with emphasis on women education in their development programme.

4. Lack of separate schools for girls is also responsible for slow growth of women's education in Manipur. Co-education is an obstacle in the expansion of women's education because many parents are strongly against co-education and do not like to send their daughter to school where girls have to study with boys. Mudaliar Commission also emphasised on the establishment of seperate schools for girls. So the government should pay special attention in the establishment of separate schools for girls.

5. Prevalence of age-old superstition, customs, traditions, orthodoxy and conservatism have all affected the development of women education in the state. It is believed that if the women are educated, they will be liberated which is not encouraged by the society. These social evils are great obstacles in the expansion of women education. As such unless this attitude of the people is changed, sufficient expansion of education of women will not be possible. These social evils have to be removed and concerted efforts

made for the development of women education.

6. At all the stages of education curriculum for both boys and girls are almost the same. But significant changes are necessary in the curriculum of girls at the stage of second secondary and higher education because of the variations in the physical, social and cultural needs of the boys and girls. So the curriculum for the girls education should be framed in order to meet the needs of the girls. There is the lack of awareness regarding the introduction of significant changes in the curriculum for women . Mudaliar commission has also recommended diversified courses of study for the boys and girls. Fine Arts, Craft and Home Science should be made compulsory for girls with view to increase the utility of women education.

7. The rate of wastage is more in the field of women's education as compared to the boys. Many girls leave the schools before completing their studies because of the social evils, financial problems, poor communication system, etc. Many parents never give emphasis on the education of their daughters.

8. The quality of education has suffered considerably due to poor instruction system in the schools, unsuitable curriculum for girls and shortage of competent female teachers. It is desirable that girls get a broad liberal education which should be the same as that of the boys. Subjects like nutrition, home science, home economics, child development and fine arts (music, dancing, panting), and hygiene etc. should be included in the curriculum of women education. Various committees have examined the problem of women's education. They are of the opinion that the education of women should be regarded as a major programme in education and a bold and determined efforts should be made to close the existing gap between the education of men and women as early as possible.

PROSPECTS

For qualitative improvement of education at different levels, a number of measures have to be adopted and programmes have to be initiated.

A. **In field of Primary Education**

1. The curriculum at the primary stage should be reformed and modified as per needs of community.

2. For raising the quality of teaching at the primary school level well trained and efficient teachers should be appointed. The existing untrained teachers can be given teachers training through refresher courses.

3. School buildings should be constructed before establishment of schools in both rural and urban areas. The buildings should be in open and healthy environment with provision for blackboards, furnitures, equipments and teaching aids.

4. The primary education should lay emphasis on qualitative improvement alongwith universalization of education. Besides, fees may be charged from the children of rich persons in order to reduce the expenditure on compulsory education at the primary level like private primary schools.

5. The primary schools should be within the easy reach of children in order to make them easily accessible to the young children.

6. For the qualitative improvement of primary education, a number of innovative programmes like creation of school complex, programme for part time schooling and ungraded system etc. should be taken up, number of primary schools should be attached to the middle schools for general guidance in instruction. Programme for part time schooling will help children who are not able to attend school for the whole day. The ungraded system is very useful to reduce wastage and stagnation at this stage.

7. Primary education should be made compulsory for all children with provisions for mid-day meals, uniforms, free medical service, free text books and transportation for relieving the economic hardship of the parents who could not provide these facilities to their children.

Measures should be adopted to enforce compulsory attendance with better methods of teaching and motivation of children. Proper and effective inspection and supervision in primary schools are important to improve their efficiency.

B. In field of Secondary Education

For the qualitative improvement of secondary education a variety of programmes have to be taken up. The construction of suitable classrooms, hostels, libraries and staff quarters must be undertaken. In order to improve the standard of education, the existing curriculum, text books, and teaching methods should be improved. For effective teaching, of science subject, the laboratory facilities should be improved with proper scientific equipments, chemical and teaching aids. Facilities of field work and practical training should be provided for all the subjects wherever necessary and these should be incorporated in the curriculum.

2. In the syllabus and curriculum of secondary education, vocational subjects related to the local needs should be introduced. Secondary education should be vocationalised in a large measure and enrolment in vocational course rest to 20 percent of total enrolment at the lower secondary stage and 50 percent of total enrolment at the higher secondary stage.

3. The existing examination system should not be accepted as a tool for measuring the academic achievement of students and need reformation and improvement. The existing essay type question in the examination should be supplemented by short answer and objective type test. While making the final evaluation of the academic achievement of the students, importance should also be given to the internal assessment, periodical tests and attendence record in order to remove some of the defects of the present system of examination.

4. The curriculum should be made more practical and useful. It should be diversified and flexible to cater the interest and aptitude of the students. The curriculum should be closely related to the social life of the students so that it may help in developing the capabilities of the students.

5. The teachers are like the spinal cord of the school. The schools should employ trained teachers for the vocational courses. only qualified and trained teachers should be appointed in secondary schools. Untrained teachers should be sent to training colleges from time to time in order to acquaint them with latest teaching methods. Short term training courses summer schools and workshop, orientation courses etc. should be organised by the State Council of Higher Education, Manipur.

6. Education during the secondary stage should be planned for

citizenship and leadership training with emphasis on the development of personality and enhancement of professional skill.

7. The school should be the centres of community life. It must reflect the experiences gained by the society. In fact, school should be an idealized epitome of community life.

8. In all the secondary schools provision should be made for suitable buildings for proper accommodation, library facilities, sanitary arrangement, laboratories and equipments, Science laboratories should be provided in selected model schools at each district headquarters, to begin with and later on to other schools.

9. For over all improvement of secondary education, measures such as training of teachers, introduction of vocational subjects, examination reforms, improvement of curriculum to cope with the local needs and demand, use of innovative methods of teaching, etc. should be taken up.

C. **In field of Higher Education**

1. In most of the colleges in the state the shortage of qualified teachers has been a major problem. The college teachers should be encouraged to attend refreshers courses, workshops and training programmes in the related field of studies. Moreover there has been a shortage of qualified women teachers in the colleges. Efforts should be made to attract women teachers, particularly for the women's colleges.

2. Sufficient grants should be provided to improve the material facilities in the colleges like buildings, library, and laboratories etc. The non-government organisations and rich section of the society should donate liberally to raise the standard of higher education.

3. Different branches of knowledge and experience should be interlinked at this stage. Interdisciplinary studies should be encouraged. Therefore, there should be programme for imparting certain degree of general education so that the student of humanities and social sciences may acquired the knowledge of science and the students of science and commerce may acquire the knowledge of the subjects of art and literature. By establishing harmony between general education and specialization; the defect of narrow

specialisation can be removed. The university has made efforts in this direction by introducing certain elements of science, humanities and social sciences in the general foundation course at the degree level.

4. The present system of examination should be supplemented by objective type test with short answer and very short answer type questions covering the entire syllabus. Efforts have been made to improve the examination system by the Manipur University in the recent past.

5. Selective system of admission should be adopted in the universities. The number of students in the educational institutions should be determined keeping in view the facilities available in the institutions concerned and the number of teachers.

6. The best way of solving indiscipline is to divert the activities of young students into healthy channels like sports, and games, co-operative living in hostels, self management of mess, debate and extension lectures symposium etc. under the guidance and assistance of the teachers. Efforts have to be made to inculcate a strong habit of discipline among the students.

7. There should be diversification of courses in the curriculam at the university stage with enough dynamism and flexibility. Inlight of the needs and aspiration of society the curriculum of the universities should be under constant modification and improvement.

8. In order to solve the problem of wastage and stagnation, innovative methods of teaching, curriculum reform, and in examination system, are necessary.

D. **In field of Technical and Professional Education**

1. Appointment of sufficient number of teachers should be made in technical and professional institutions. The curriculum of technical courses should be modified to cater the need of the people, with emphasis on vocational subjects.

2. More technical and vocational institutions should be established

to meet the demand of the people.

3. Sufficient number of qualified and talented teachers should be appointed in these institutions.

4. Technical and professional institutions should give importance to practical training as done in such institutions in the other states. The students should be sent to various workshops and factories etc. for such training to provide them proper insight in work experience and work culture.

5. The state government in consultation with the All India Council of Technical Education should take up the responsibility of proper administration, control and improvement of technical and professional education in the state.

6. Attempts should be made to change the medium of instruction from English to Manipuri in the technical institutions of the state. Of course, it will be a complicated process to change the medium of instruction from English to Manipuri as there is absence of books on technical subjects in local language.

7. For qualitative improvement in the professional and technical education, institutions which do not fulfil the minimum conditions as prescribed by the Indian Council of Technical Education should be derecognised. The institutions following the rules and regulations should be encouraged and given incentives like financial assistance for improvement of workshops, laboratories and libraries etc. Co-operation of the industries is necessary for vocational and technical education in the state. The improvement of technical institutions in the state is possible by appointing well qualified teachers, who may impart best type of education and training to the students.

E. **In field of Women's Education**

Expansion of education in Manipur has been fast enough since Independence. The population of men and women is almost equal but the number of educated men is more than the number of educated women. The state government did not take proper attention towards the expansion of women education in the past. For the development of women education, specially trained women teachers, administrators and resource persons are required. Women should be trained in different professional courses and institutions should be established to provide training programmes for them. Reservation of seats in various institutions for the girls will facilitate the growth of women education in various areas. Women study centres should be established in the institutes of higher learning. Seminars, conference and refresher courses should be organised for women teachers from time to time.

The state government should initiate programmes of compulsory education to both male and female, which in turn will improve their socio-economic conditions and status. Social evils flourish because of illiteracy and ignorance. Education develops the minds of the people and helps in rooting out all the social evils. It brings out consciousness among the people. Concerted efforts should be made for expansion of education. The curriculum should be diversified and flexible in order to cater the different abilities and capabilities of the learners. It should be closely related to the social needs of the community. The curriculum as such, should be modified and reformed as per needs and aspirations of the people.

Bibliography

I. Reports and Public Documents

Committees and Commissions in India, 1947-1973, Vol. V, VI (Kumar, V. Ed.), Concept Publishing Company, Delhi, 1977.

District Gazetteer of Assam, Naga Hills and Manipur. (Allen, B.C. Ed.) Vol. IX, Part II, Gian Pub., Delhi, 1890.

Encyclopaedia Britannica, Vol. IV, Enclopaedia Britannica Inc., London, 1971.

Encyclopaedia of Educational Research, Vol. III, IV, V, The Free Press, Macmillan Publishing Co., New York, 1982.

Gazatteer of India, Manipur (Bhattacharjee, M.Ed.), Calcutta, 1963.

Gazetteer of Manipur, (Dun E.W. Ed.), Vivek Publishing House, Delhi, 1981.

Government of India : *Annual Administrative Reports of the Manipur Political Agency,* 1872-1941.

Government o. India : *National Policy of Education,* Ministry of Human Resource Development, Department of Education, New Delhi, 1986.

Government of India : *Report of the Radhakrishnan Commission,* Ministry of Education, New Delhi, 1948.

Government of India : *Report of the Secondary Education Commission 1952-53,* Ministry of Education, Manager Publication, New Delhi, 1955.

Government of India : *Report of the Education Commission 1964-66,*

Ministry of Education, Manag-r Publication, New Delhi, 1966.

Government of Manipur : *Economic Review 1984-85*, Directorate of Economics and Statistics, Imphal, 1986.

Government of Manipur : *Manipur at a glance, 1984*, Directorate of Economics and Statistics, Imphal, 1984.

Government of Manipur : *Pre-Budget Economic Review of Manipur 1987-88*, Imphal, 1988.

Government of Manipur : *Seventh Five Year Plan (Annual Plan) 1985.* State Planning Department, Imphal.

Government of Manipur : *Statistical Handbook of Manipur, 1975, 1982, 1983.* Department of Economics and Statistics, Imphal.

Government of Manipur : *Techno-Economic Survey of Manipur.* National Council of Applied Economic Research, Imphal, 1965.

Imperial Gazetteer of India, Vol. XVII, New Delhi, 1908.

International Encyclopaedia of Social Sciences, Vol. III, IV, IX and X. The Free Press and the Macmillan Company, New York, 1972.

Manipur University : *Manipur University Act*, Imphal 1980.

Manipur University : *First Annual Report, Manipur University (1980-82)*, Imphal, 1982.

Manipur University : *Statistical Accounts of Colleges under Manipur University*, Imphal, 1987, 1995-96, 1996-97.

N.C.E.R.T. : *Education in India*, New Delhi, 1962.

N.C.E.R.T. : *First Year book of Education*, New Delhi, 1961.

N.C.E.R.T. : *N.C.E.R.T. Survey Report*, New Delhi, 1972-73.

Roy Burman, B.K., *Demographic and Socio-Economic Profiles of the Hill Areas of North Eastern India*, Manager of Pub., Delhi, 1970.

University Grants Commission, Final report of the Visiting Committee to Colleges affiliated to the Gauhati University in Manipur, 1973.

II. Books

Ahluwalia, B.K. and Ahluwalia, S. : *Social Change in Manipur*, Cultural Publishing House, Delhi, 1984.

Brown, R. : *Statistical Account of Manipur*, Sanskaran Prakashak, Delhi, 1974.

Chatterjee, K.K. : *English Education in India*, Macmillan, New Delhi, 1977.

Chaube, S.P. : *History and Problems of Indian Education*, Vinod Pustak Mandir, Agra.

Chib, S.S. : *This Beautiful India, Nagaland*, Light and Life Publishers, New Delhi, 1980.

Chirol, V. : *India, A Historical, Economic and Intellectual Development*, Deep and Deep Publications, New Delhi, 1983.

Chodak, S. : *Societal Development*, Oxford University, New York, 1973.

Chopra Puri Das : *Social, Cultural and Economic History of India*, Macmillan, Bombay, 1974.

Constantine, R. : *Manipur Maid of Mountains*, Lancers Publishers, New Delhi, 1981.

Cormack, L.M. : *Indian Students and Social Change*, Asian Publishing House, Bombay, 1916.

Das, L. : *A Text Book of Education*, Sangam Prakash, Gauhati, 1993.

Devi, Jamini : *Education in Manipur*, Rai Pravina Brothers, Imphal, 1989.

Desai, A.R. : *Social background of Indian Nationalism*, Popular Prakashan Pvt. Ltd., Bombay, 1976.

Farquhar, J.N. : *Modern Religious Movements in India*, Munshiram Manoharlal, New Delhi, 1977.

Firth, Raymond : *Social change in Tikopia*, George Allen and Unwin Ltd., 1956.

Footlight, L. : *Dance Rituals of Manipur, India*. The Standard Press, New Delhi, 1958.

Foster, M. : *Traditional Cultures and the Impact of Technological Change*, Harper and Row, New York, 1962.

Grierson, G.A. : *Linguistic Survey of India*, Vol. III, Part III. Motilal Banarsidass, Delhi, 1967.

Grimwood, E.S.C. : *My Three Years in Manipur*, Cultural Publishing House, Delhi, 1984.

Hagen, E.E. : *On the theory of Social change*, Illinois, Dorsey, Homewood, 1962.

Hodson, T.C. : *The Meitheis*, Davis Nutt 57, 59, Long Acre, London, 1908.

Horam, M. : *Social and Cultural Life of Nagas*, BR Pub. Corp. New Delhi, 1977.

James, H.R. : *Education and Statesmanship in India*, 1911.

Johnstone, J. : *My Experience in Manipur and Naga Hills*, Sampson Low, Martson and Co., London, 1896.

Kabir, H. : *Education in New India*, George Allen and Unwin Ltd., London, 1959.

Karunakaran, K.P. : *Religion and Political Awakening in India*, Meenakshi Prakashan, Meerut, 1969.

Khoker, M. : Myths, Legends and History of Manipuri Dance in *Classical and Folk Dances of India*, Marg Publications, Bombay, 1963.

Kuppuswamy, B. : *Social Change in India*, Vani Educational Books, New Delhi, 1986.

Lerner, D. : *The Passing of Traditional Society*, Free Press of Glenco, 1962.

Majumdar, R.C. (Ed.) : *British Paramouncy and Indian Renaissance*, Vol. X, Part II, Bombay, 1969.

Manipuri Sahitya Parishad : *Glimpses of Manipuri Language*, Literature and Culture, Imphal, 1970.

Mills, J.P. : *Rongma Nagas*, United Writers, Gauhati, 1987.

Mukherjee, K.K. : *New Education and its aspects*. The Educational Publishers, Calcutta, 1953.

Mullick, B.R. : *Literary Essays*, Vol. I, S. Chand and Co., Calcutta, 1957.

Narain, V.H. : *Social History of Modern India*, Meenakshi Prakashan, Delhi, 1973.

Nunn, P. : *Education - Its data and first principles*, Edward Arnold Publishers Ltd., London, 1960.

Nurrullah, S. and Naik, J.P. : *A students history of Education in India*, Macmillan and Co. Ltd., Calcutta, 1964.

Pandey, S.N. : *Education and Social Change in Bihar*, Motilal Banarsidas, Patna, 1975.

Panikkar, K.M. : *Hindu Society at cross-roads*, Bombay, 1968.

Parrat, S.N. : *Religion of Manipur*, Firma KLM Pvt. Ltd., Calcutta, 1980.

Robert, R. : *History of Frontier Areas Bordering Assam*, Shillong, 1942.

Roy, J. : *History of Manipur*, Eastlight Book House, 20 Strand Road, Calcutta, 1973.

Saikia, S. : *History of Education in India*, Mani Manik Prakash, Gauhati, 1973.

Saini, S.K. : *Development of Education in India*, New Delhi, 1980.

Sarda, H.B. : *Life of Dayananda Saraswati*, Ajmer, 1946.

Saxena, J.S. : *Modern Essays*, Chaitanya Publishing House, Allahabad, 1956.

Sen, S.P. (ed.) : *Social and Religious Reform Movement in the 19th and 2oth Centuries*, Institute of Historical Studies, Calcutta, 1979.

Shakespeare, J. : *The Religion of Manipur*, London, 1913.

Sharma, A. and Singh, A. : *The brief description of Manipuri Dance*, Imphal, 1975.

Sharma, D.D. : *My Reminiscences*, Imphal, 1986.

Shastri, K. : *Asamba Manipuri Sahityagi Itihas*, Imphal, 1976.

Singh, K. : *A new approach to the history and problems of Indian education*. Students Store, Imphal, 1982.

Singh, L.I. : *Introduction to Manipur*, Students Store, Imphal, 1963.

Singh, M.K. : *Manipuri Samaj Hougatlakpa Amasung Chaokhatlakpa*, Imphal, 1977.

Singh, M.K. : *History of Journalism in Manipur*, Imphal, 1980.

Singh, M.K. : *Religious Developments in Manipur in the 18th and 19th Centuries*, State Kala Academy, Imphal, 1982.

Singh, M.K.P. : *Administrative Report of Manipur State Durbar 1916-1947*, Imphal, 1947.

Singh, N.I. : *The Manipur Administration 1709-1907*, Friends and Co., Imphal, 1968.

Singh, L.I. and Singh, N.K. : *Cheitharol Kumbaba*, Manipur Sahitya Parishad, Imphal, 1967.

Singh, N.I. : *Theirel Layat*, Imphal, 1981.

Sharma, N.K. : *Coronation of Naothingkhong*, Imphal, 1967.

Singh, N.K. : *Chainarol*, Imphal, 1968.

Singh, N.K. : *Ariba Manipuri Sahityagi Itihas*, Imphal, 1970.

Singh, N.K. : *Thangmeiron* (Unpublished)

Singh, N.T. : *Manipur - A Study*, Imphal, 1973.

Singh, N.T. : *Manipur the Mainstream*, Imphal, 1974.

Singh, R.K.J. : *A short history of Manipur*, O.K. Store, Imphal, 1967.

Singh, R.K.J. : *History of Manipuri Literature*, Imphal, 1976.

Singh, S.Ch. : *Manipuri Itihasta Irabot*, Imphal. 1972.

Singh and Singh : *Current Problems of Indian Education*, Krishna Brothers, Amritsar, 1966.

Singh, Th.B. : *Comrade Irabot*, Imphal, 1983.

Singh, Th.M. : *Western Education in Manipur*, Vol. I. Students Store, Imphal, 1967.

Singh, Th.M. : *Western Education in Manipur*, Vol. II. Imphal, 1970.

Singh, Th.M. : *Western Education in Manipur*, Vol. III. Imphal, 1987.

Singh, Y. and Singh, M. : *Nikhil Hindu Manipuri Mahasabha*, Imphal, 1983.

Singh, Y.B. (Ed.) : *The Economic History of India (1857-1956)*, 1956.

Sircar, M.C. : *Feminism in a traditional society : Women of Manipur Valley* : Shakti Books, New Delhi, 1984.

Solesaemardjan : *Social change in Jodjakarta*, Cornel University Press, Ithaca, 1962.

Srinivas, M.N. : *Social change in Modern India*, Orient Longman, New Delhi, 1966.

Srivastava, S.L. : *Folk Culture and Oral Tradition*, New Delhi, 1974.

Tarachand : *History of Freedom Movement in India*. Published by the Publication Division, Ministry of Information and Broadcasting, Government of India, New Delhi, 1972.

Tiwari R.P. : *Developement and Problems of Education in North-East India*, Shillong, 1995.

Thomas, F.W. : *History and Prospect of British Education in India*, Cambridge, 1981.

III. Journals and Articles

Arunodoi : Vol. II, No. 12, 1947.

Burney, S.M.H. : *Education and Social Changes*, J.N.U. News, New Delhi, 1987.

Devi, K.B. : A study of Meitheis, Socio-Cultural study, *North Eastern Region Research Bulletin*, Vol. VII, Dibrugarh University, 1979.

Devi, N.P. : Progress of Female Education in Manipur, *P.G.T. College Magazine*, Vol. IX, 1987.

Devi, M.S. : Role of Education in National Integration, *Proc. ICSSR Seminar*, Manipur University, 1986.

Devi, M.S. : Women's Education and Social changes in Manipur. *Proc. 4th Annual Conference National Environmental Science Academy*, New Delhi, 1988.

Devi, M.S. and Pandey, S.N. : Univeralisation of Primary Education in Manipur. *Proc. 75th Session, Indian, Sc. Cong.* Pune, 1988.

Ganguly, B.N. : *India, A Colonial Economy 1757-1949* (Published in Enquiry) Delhi, 1958.

Government Polytechnic : *Souvenir*, Silver Jubilee, Imphal, 1982.

Gore, M.S. : Universities and Government, *University News*, New Delhi, 1986.

Jayaram, N. : Education and the process of change, *Journal of Higher Education*, Vol. XIII, Nos. 1-3, 1987-88.

Kabui, G. : Education in North East India; Problems of democratisation. *Proc. Seminar on Democratisation of Education in North East India*, Manipur University, 1988.

Kabui, G. : Leftiest Movement in Manipur "A Case History of Comrade Irabot Singh", *Proc. 35th Session of the Indian History Congress*, Jadavpur, 1977.

Kabui, G. : Modernisation in Tribal Manipur, *Souvenir*, North East Indian History Association, Manipur University, 1982.

Pandey, S.N. and Devi, M.S. : Status of Women in Manipur, Education and changes, *Proc. 76th Session, Indian Sc. Cong. Madurai*, 1989.

Saroj, P. : The changing Scenario of Education, *University News*, New Delhi, 1989.

Singh, A. : Manipuri Ras, *Souvenir*, Jawaharlal Nehru Manipuri Dance Academy, Imphal, 1964.

Singh, Ch. M. : Post War II. Manipuri Literature, *Souvenir*, Seminar on Post War Poetry in North East India, 1987.

Singh, L. : Role of family welfare programme in achieving health for all by 2000 A.D., *Souvenir, Regional Medical College*, Imphal, 1987.

Singh, L.N. : Ethnographic history of Brahmins in Manipur, *Regional Integration*, Vol. VIII, No. 15, Imphal, 1983.

IV. Unpublished Thesis

Nagar, S.N. : *Development of Education in Manipur from 1891-1971*, Gauhati University, 1978.

Singh, L.K. : *Economic changes in Manipur*, Manipur University, 1987.

Singh, N.B. : *Socio-Religious Life of the Meiteis in the 18th Century A.D.*, Manipur University, 1987.

Singh, N.J. : *Social Movements in Manipur*, Manipur University, 1987.

Singh, S.G. : *Impact of Modern Education in Manipur : A Case Study of Two Meitei Villages*, Gauhati University, 1979.

Index